B. MODO

GRAPHIC DESIGN BASICS

GRAPHIC DESIGN BASICS

Amy E. Arntson
University of Wisconsin–Whitewater

Holt, Rinehart and Winston, Inc.

New York   Chicago   San Francisco   Philadelphia
Montreal   Toronto   London   Sydney   Tokyo

To those special students, friends, and teachers
who make living and learning
a lively, often loving process.

Acquisitions Editor: Karen Dubno
Senior Project Editor: Lester A. Sheinis
Production Managers: Pat Sarcuni, Stefania Taflinska
Design Supervisor: Gloria Gentile
Designer: Art Ritter, Inc.
Art Layout: Connie Szcwciuk
Cover Design: Gloria Gentile, Amy E. Arntson, Kirby Bock

Library of Congress Cataloging-in-Publication Data

Arntson, Amy E.
    Graphic design basics / Amy E. Arntson.
        p.   cm.
    Bibliography: p.
    Includes index.
    1. Design.   I. Title.
    NK1530.A65   1988   87–23281
    741.6—dc19   CIP

ISBN 0-03-003257-1

Printed in the United States of America

8 9 0 1   032   9 8 7 6 5 4 3 2 1

Holt, Rinehart and Winston, Inc.
The Dryden Press
Saunders College Publishing

PREFACE

Graphic Design Basics will introduce you to an exciting and demanding new field. To enter it you will need not only specific information and hands-on practice, but also an understanding of time-honored principles. Therefore this book interweaves a concern for design basics with more specialized information. Abundant illustrations let you learn by seeing, while projects and exercises challenge you to learn by doing.

Graphic Design Basics offers a broad overview of the field of graphic design. It works equally well for courses in visual communication and advertising. Chapters 1 and 2 will give you a grasp of the design process as a whole and of its importance throughout history. Chapters 3 to 5 will show you the vital principles of perception, dynamic balance, and Gestalt in action. From then on you will focus on principles and skills in special areas: using text type well (Chapter 6), designing fine layouts (Chapter 7), preparing perfect camera-ready copy (Chapter 8), and handling color (Chapter 9). You will learn about producing effective advertisements (Chapter 10), striking photographs (Chapter 11), fine illustrations (Chapter 12), and sophisticated computer graphics (Chapter 13).

To feel more at home, draw upon the extra features at the end of the book. The Appendix tells you how to use tools and equipment, the Glossary explains technical terms, and the Bibliography by topic opens the door to further discoveries.

I know you will find exploring this field exciting.

I wish to thank the following reviewers for their help in preparing this book: Mark Arends, University of Illinois, Urbana-Champaign; David Blow, North Texas State University; Richard Brough, University of Alabama; David Grimsrud, St. Olaf College; Lynda Halley, Oklahoma State University; Max Hein, Santa Rose Junior College; Rob Roy Kelly, Arizona State University; Bill Kinser, Penn State University; Newton LeVine, Ramapo College; Onyile B. Onyile, University of South Carolina; R. Roger Rennington, Rochester Institute of Technology; Glenn Ricci, Lake Sumter Community College; Roderick Robertson, St. Mary's College; and John West, Ohio Northern University.

AEA

CONTENTS

5
"GOOD" GESTALT

6
USING TEXT TYPE

7
LAYOUT

8
PREPARING CAMERA-READY ART

GRAPHIC DESIGN BASICS

The Louisville Orchestra

Lawrence Leighton Smith,
Music Director

APPLYING THE ART OF DESIGN

PRINCIPLES AND PRACTICES

These chapters are about applying the *principles* of visual perception to the *practice* of visual communication. The premise for this book is that a course of study in graphic design should begin by applying the principles and theory of basic design. Interwoven with information about how we perceive and shape a two-dimensional surface will be the application of this information to graphic design problems.

Teachers often fail to make the point that information from one class is still pertinent in the next. Students leaving a basic design class might find little carry-over in later classes. Although you will be learning special information and terminology in this text, you will discover how closely it ties in with the basic theory of design you already know.

Problems in graphic design almost always relate to communication. There are methods of making a design hold together as a unit to communicate information. This text will discuss them in simple and straightforward language. You will discover how applying basic design principles enhances visual communication. You will explore the nature of visual perception, the role of visual illusion, and the contrast between visual and verbal communication as well as the full range of basic design skills.

A graphic designer is an artist, a newcomer to a professional group that includes painters, photographers, sculptors, metal workers, ceramists, architects, and others. Visual arts in general and two-dimensional disciplines in particular share a common language. The study of shapes on a flat ground has yielded a great deal of information about how we see and interact with the image on the page. You will learn to apply this universal information to solve graphic design problems.

A designer is not in search of one solution, but of several. There is no one correct answer in graphic design, but a rich set of possibilities. This book presents principles like Gestalt unit-forming, balance, emphasis, and eye direction as tools, not as rules. Use them to increase your options and widen your vision. These methods may become intuitive after a while, but in the beginning you will need to study and consciously apply them.

WHAT IS GRAPHIC DESIGN?

Design is problem solving. Graphic design is problem solving on a flat two-dimensional surface. The designer conceives, plans, and executes designs that communicate a specific message to a specific audience within given limitations —financial, physical, or psychological.

A poster design, for example, may be restricted to two colors for financial reasons. It may be physically restricted in size because of the press it will be run on or because of the mailing method. It may be restricted psychologically by the standard viewing distance for a poster in a hall or store window, or by the age and interests of the group for which it is intended. Nevertheless the designer must say something specific to a given audience about a given product or piece of information. Commu-

nication is the vital element in graphic design.

It is this element of communication that makes graphic design such an interesting and contemporary area. Designers must present current information to modern taste with up-to-date tools. They must stay informed about trends, issues, inventions, and developments. What will be the impact of computer-aided design? How will film, television, holograms, and computers integrate? Will printed designs be delivered by computer direct to their destination? Will print become obsolete?

Design education is a lifetime activity. Constant change will require constant renewal. It is not a career for a slow-paced, nostalgic person. To keep up with this fast-changing field you must approach the basic principles and practices with a flexible, curious mind.

Values

Our current society is based on processing information rather than producing goods. The product a designer helps to sell, the information disseminated, the point of view illustrated, all contribute to shaping the world. It is a good idea to ask early in your career (now would not be too soon) where you stand on certain issues. You will be making career decisions that shape your life, and the character of our society (Fig. 1). Figure 1 is an example of design work that helps to advertise and support a not-for-profit arts organization.

A successful designer vividly described one of his early career decisions. His first job out of college was as a junior designer at a small advertising firm, where he was put to work designing a hot dog package. After preparing several roughs, he presented them to the client, only to be sent back to the drawing board. Rejected time after time, the designer grew more familiar than he ever wanted to become with hot dogs. Finally deciding he wanted to spend his life with something more meaningful, he resigned. He now has his own firm specializing in educational and ser-

1. *Julius Friedman.* The Louisville Orchestra. *Photograph from PW, Inc.*

vice-oriented accounts, which allow him a great deal of creative freedom. This work is consistent with his personal values.

The Japanese artist Kazumasa Nagai created the design in Figure 2 for the Takeo Paper Company. Such a client gives the designer an unusual degree of creative freedom. How much freedom do you need?

Each of us must satisfy our own values in the work environment. Are there products or points of view you would not want to promote? Is there something you do want to promote? How important is salary? What will make this career successful for you? What do you most enjoy doing?

Design Fields

The field of applied design includes industrial design, environmental design, and graphic design. *Industrial design* is the design and development of three-dimensional objects (Fig. 3). Machines, tools, kitchen implements, and other products are shaped by the industrial designer. Package design for these objects is

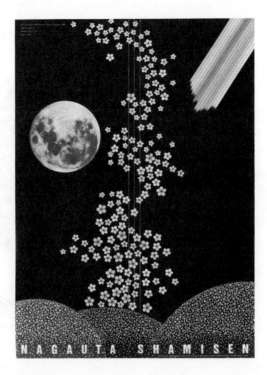

2. *Kasumasa Nagai (President, Nippon Design Center Inc). Design for Takeo Paper Co.*

often placed in the category of graphic design because it must be designed and printed flat before assembling. The indus-

3. *Marianne Brandt. Teapot. 1934. Brass, 7" (17.5 cm). Staatliche Kunstsammlunger, Weimar.*

4a.

4a, 4b. *David Saylor. Interior and floor plan of the Cohen apartment, Milwaukee. Photo by Jim Threadgill. 1983.*

4b.

boards, and brochures are some of the things graphic designers create. They attempt to maximize both communication and aesthetic quality.

Buildings, environments, products, and written communications will affect us whether they have been deliberately designed or not. Design cannot be eliminated. The printed piece will always communicate more than its words. It may, however, communicate exactly the opposite message (Fig. 5). It can damage the

trial designer attempts to simplify the use and manufacture of objects as well as increase their safety and efficiency.

Environmental design is a large general category that includes the design of buildings, landscapes, and interiors. Again, the designer attempts to fashion designs that are safe, efficient, and aesthetic. In the unified, flowing floor plan shown in Figures 4a and 4b, curves and angles and varying levels are used as unifying elements.

Graphic design is the design of things people read. Posters, books, signs, bill-

5. *This plaque could be commemorating a grandson who is not forgotten or a grandson who is "not ours," and definitely forgotten.*

image of a company or cause. Learning to apply the *theory* of design and information processing to the *practice* of graphic design will help you achieve the intended communication.

Designers must interface with fields other than their own. Learn to address the basic marketing concerns of the client, the problems of special workers such as illustrators or photographers, and the difficulties of the printer.

Some graphic designers do a whole range of work—typography, illustration, photography, corporate identity, logo design, and advertising. Others specialize in one area. Problems in any area can best be solved by following the design process.

THE DESIGN PROCESS

Research

The first step in preparing a design solution is determining the parameters of the problem. Who is the audience? What constraints are there in format, budget, and time? What is the goal of the project?

Now you must gather and study all the related materials you can find. Selling this design to a client (or an instructor) will be easier if you can back it with research and justify it from a perspective the client will understand. In the future, you may work in a large firm or agency where most of the research and information gathering is done by marketing professionals. Visual research, however, both then and now, is your area. Know what has been done before and what is being created locally and nationally for this type of design situation. Develop a feeling for contemporary work by studying design annuals and periodicals.

Keep a file of anything you find interesting or well done. A personal file of such samples can be useful to thumb through when you are stuck for ideas. Never simply lift another designer's solution; that is unethical. (Anyhow, it seldom works. Lifting isolated parts from someone else will not give you a unified design. Lifting the entire solution will be immediately recognizable as plagiarism.) Looking at how someone else solved a particular problem, however, is part of your education. As a designer you are expected to build upon the work of others. You do not create in a vacuum. You cannot help but be influenced by the hundreds of samples of good and bad design we are all exposed to every day. Channel that influence so that it is constructive.

Thumbnails

A designer needs to explore many alternative solutions. Thumbnails are the second step in the design process (Fig. 6). Thumbnails are idea sketches; they are visual evidence of the thinking, searching, sorting process that brings out solutions.

Exercising the mind with thumbnail sketches is like exercising any muscle. The

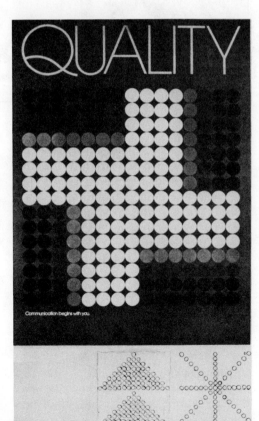

6. *Karen Gourley Lehman. Quality. 1981. Silkscreen poster and preliminary sketches. Reproduced with permission of Hewlett-Packard Company.*

7. *Amy E. Arntson. Thumbnail designs for October calendar.*

more you exercise, the more powerful it gets. The more you work to develop ideas through small preliminary sketches, the richer the range of solutions you will have to choose from for your final design. Never shortcut this stage, because it determines the strength of your final solution. For a student, the thumbnails are more important than the final project, because they demonstrate thinking, experimentation, and growth. Keep these thumbnails. The ideas in them may be of use to you later. Prospective employers may wish to see evidence of the flexibility and tenacity of your thinking (Fig. 7).

Thumbnails are usually small because they are meant to be fast and undetailed. They are around 2″ x 3″ (5 x 8 cm), and

drawn in proportion to the dimensions of the finished piece. Fill a sheet of paper with evenly spaced small rectangles and then fill them with ideas. Never reject an idea; just sketch it in and go on. Work through the idea with your pencil from every perspective you can imagine. Then try taking one good idea and doing several variations on it. Tracing paper or lightweight bond is excellent for this purpose. You may also want to cut and paste and recombine existing images for new effects. You may find it is faster to work at a size determined by existing elements, so your thumbnails may become larger or smaller. The principle of "sketching" through ideas holds true no matter what the size or format of your preliminary investigation. Be as neat and

Applying the Art of Design

precise as is necessary to show the relationship between elements and their general shapes (Fig. 7).

Roughs

Once the range of ideas has been fully explored, select the best two or three for refinement. You may want to talk this choice over with other designers and with your instructor. Later, as a professional designer, you will be presenting roughs to an art director or a client for review. Often considerable redefining and rethinking occurs at this stage. The thumbnail process may begin all over again.

Roughs are usually enlarged to half the size of the finished piece. The purpose is to test whether the idea still works on a larger scale. Take this opportunity to work out small problem areas that could not be dealt with or foreseen at the thumbnail stage. The type style, the other shapes, the exact proportional relationship of these elements to the edge of the format, and the color and value distribution can all be refined at this stage (Fig. 8).

Comprehensives

The "comp," the fourth step in the design process, is the piece of art that you will present to the client. Based on the rough, it is much more carefully done. Once again consult with art directors and editors before choosing the rough idea to refine.

The client is able to judge the design solution from the "comp" because it looks much like the finished printed piece. There is no need to explain "what would go there" or how "this would be smoother." A comp might include photographs shot to size, machine-set type, silkscreen printing, tight illustrations, pen and ink rendering, and so on. Polish to sell your idea.

In most of your projects from this text, the comp will be the final step. Executing clean comps is a good way of developing

8. *Amy Sprague (UW–Whitewater student designer). Rough sketches for wildlife advertisement.*

9. *Amy Sprague (UW– Whitewater student designer). Finished comprehensive for wildlife advertisement. 1986.*

familiarity with tools as well as precision (Fig. 9).

Comps take different forms depending upon the media for which they are intended. Television and film ideas are presented as storyboards with key scenes drawn in simplified and stylized fashion. The three-dimensional comp for a package design may be presented in multiples in order to demonstrate the stacking and display possibilities of the package. A publication such as an annual report or a newletter will usually be represented by the cover and certain "key" pages in the layout design. Sometimes, when the client and designer have a long-standing successful relationship, the labor-intensive and expensive comprehensive is eliminated.

Presentation

Practice "selling" your comprehensive verbally before you present it. Demonstrate that you understand the client's perspective and goals. Discuss your design enthusiastically in terms the client can understand. Be prepared, however, to listen and to compromise. If revisions are called for, note them carefully.

Keyline/Pasteup

The job is now ready for actual production. The comprehensive you have shown to the client may look exactly like the finished piece, but it cannot be used to produce the final printed design. Everything must be sent to the printer "camera ready," which means it must be converted into black and white art. All headline and text type must be set and pasted precisely into position. All illustrations and photographs must be indicated precisely for positioning and resizing. Printer's inks must be indicated. A separate flat or overlay must be prepared for each ink color (unless you are working with four-color reproduction).

Understanding the keyline/pasteup process is important. Many students find entry level jobs doing pasteup in combination with simple design work. Even if you begin your career as a designer, with no pasteup duties, the designs you create must be based upon a sound knowledge of the reproduction and printing process. Chapter 8 will present this information. Now would be a good time to refer to the Appendix on "How to Use Tools and Equipment." Develop a respect for these tools. No design is successful if it is flawed in execution. It is vital that you begin your first project with a respect for precision, accuracy, and cleanliness. There can be no compromise with perfection in this line of work.

Many designers are responsible for selecting and dealing with a printer. Often the work must be "bid" to two or three printers, giving each an opportunity to estimate costs. Selecting printing firms to bid for the work is often based upon prior experience. A designer unfamiliar with a printing firm should ask to see samples of its work, especially samples with production problems similar to those of the new job. Quality in printers, like quality in designers, will vary. Finding a good printer and establishing an easy working relationship is important. A good printer can be an excellent reference for answering tricky production questions and suggesting alternate solutions to an expensive design.

THE CHALLENGE

The challenge of being a designer involves working through the restrictions and demands of this design process. It involves visualizing the job although the actual finished product will not be done by your hand, but on a press, with printer's paper and inks, with elements that may have been photographed or drawn by other artists, with copy written by others. It involves meeting personal design standards as well as the needs of the client and the audience. It calls for organization and self-discipline to meet the constant deadline pressure. In the classroom, you get one project at a time and a couple of weeks to complete it. Learning is stressed. On the job, you will work on several projects at once. You will be upholding design standards while others stress time and money. A good education in design fundamentals that stresses theory and creative development as well as production technique will enable you to hold to high standards.

Your final challenge is to take a responsible stance in the world. Knowledge of current events and attitudes will help you to create designs that reflect and affect society. Traditionally it has been the fine artist who has set new visual trends and opened fresh creative ways to see ourselves. The designer now also plays this role.

GRAPHIC DESIGN HISTORY

For a graphic designer the movement of ideas is as important as changes in style. Design is affected not only by artists in other fields but by scientists, psychologists, and technologists. The study of design history is a new discipline. It can give you inspiration and insight into the future of design. This overview will help you see how design developed both as an art form and an idea.

THE BEGINNING

The birth of graphic design could be traced back 30,000 years to cave painting, or about 550 years to Gutenberg's invention of the printing press. Whatever the origin, the explosive development during the last decade of the nineteenth century is a good beginning point for study.

The Industrial Revolution brought about new attitudes and inventions, both of which contributed to the sudden growth of graphic design. A spirit of innovation and progress gave rise to a new interest in providing information to an entire culture rather than only an affluent elite. The growth of population centers, industry, and a money-based economy all increased the need for the dissemination of information. Advertising flourished during this exciting time, and great strides were made in printing. The first photographic metal engraving was invented in 1824; the first halftone screen was made in 1852. Color process work was first successfully printed in 1893. The first automated steam press for lithography was designed around 1868, and the first offset press in 1906.

Advancement in stone lithography work in color in the 1880s encouraged artists to work directly on the stone for multiple reproductions of large-scale posters. They were freed from the stiff, geometric confines of the standard printing press. The resulting burst of sensual and decorative images looks like a high-spirited visual

10. *Jules Cheret.* Pastilles Poncelet. *1895. Color lithograph, 21 3/8″ × 14 9/16″ (54 × 36.8 cm). Milwaukee Art Museum Collection, Gift of Mr. and Mrs. Richard E. Vogt.*

11. *Henri de Toulouse-Lautrec.* Divan Japonais. *1892. Color lithograph, 31 1/2″ × 23 1/2″ (80 × 59.7 cm). Milwaukee Art Museum Collection, Gift of Mrs. Harry Linde Bradley.*

celebration. These advertising posters of the 1880s are classified as *art nouveau.* The movement began in France, and the names most closely associated with its development are the Frenchmen Jules Cheret (Fig. 10) and Henri de Toulouse-Lautrec (Fig. 11), and the Czech Alphonse Mucha. Cheret himself produced over a thousand posters. These posters brought art out of the galleries and into the streets and homes of the working class. The illustrations in Figures 12 and 13 show early

12. *Trade card. Nineteenth century. Wisconsin Historical Society Iconographic Collection.*

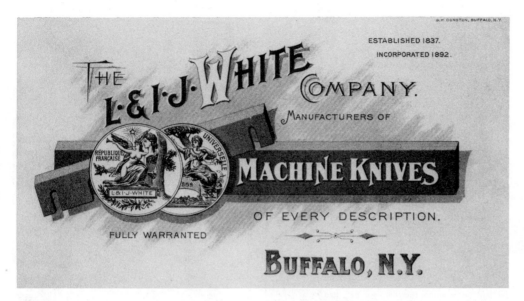

13. *Trade card. Nineteenth century. Wisconsin Historical Society Iconographic Collection.*

United States design flourishing in the form of trade cards.

All of the functional arts grew during this period. In the United States Lewis Tiffany created stained glass windows, lamps, and glassware. Scottish architect, designer, and watercolorist Charles Rennie Mackintosh, his wife, Margaret Macdonald, and her sister Frances Macdonald developed furniture and cutlery designs as well as interior and graphic design (Fig. 14).

Not all reactions to the Industrial Revolution embraced progress. William Morris founded the Kelmscott Press in 1890 against what he regarded as the mass-produced, inferior, inhuman product of the machine. Styles of past eras were being copied in art schools and factories with an emphasis on quantity over quality. He and the writer/philosopher John Ruskin wished to renew an appreciation for hand-crafted, unique, labor-intensive products. Morris worked with every kind of design, including fabric, rugs, wallpaper, furniture, and typography. His highly stylized hand-printed books and tapestries are examples of English art nouveau. Morris was a key figure in the English Arts and Crafts movement. An intensely romantic idealist, he was deeply concerned with the ethics of art. He is credited, along with the

14. *C. R. Mackintosh, Margaret Macdonald, and Frances Macdonald. Chair. 1905. Private Collection, Berlin. Photo Marburg/Art Resource.*

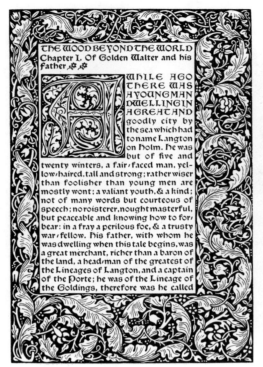

Bauhaus, for bringing about a renewal of the standards of craftsmanship (Fig. 15).

Another Englishman whose work is an important example of art nouveau style is Aubrey Beardsley. His illustrations for Oscar Wilde's *Salome* and other books are characterized by a curving, sensual line and a compelling tension between the figure and background (Fig. 16).

Among the many United States art nouveau artists is Maxfield Parrish, an illustrator for *Harper's* and *Life* as well as many other clients (Fig. 17).

THE TURN OF THE CENTURY

The turn of the century brought fundamental changes in our understanding of the world. In 1905 Albert Einstein made public his theory of relativity and altered our ideas of space and time. They became interrelated variables instead of isolated absolutes. After Sigmund Freud published *The Interpretation of Dreams* in 1909, dreams were no longer considered simply fantastic, clearly divided from reality. Sexuality also was no longer safely reserved

17. *Maxfield Parrish. Cover illustration for* Success *Magazine. December 1901.*

for the bedroom, but appeared in various symbols in everyday life. The accepted boundaries of reality began to shift.

Existentialism further undermined faith in absolutes by suggesting that there is no single correct answer or moral action. Instead we are individually responsible for shaping meaning.

Meanwhile travel and the growth of a communications network made it possible for us to hear of cultures with different lifestyles, beliefs, and perceptions. This communications explosion continues to be one of the most important influences on society today. As designers we are an important part of its development.

In 1907 Pablo Picasso completed his painting *Les Demoiselles d'Avignon* (Fig. 18). Pointing the way to cubism, it emphasized the flat surface of the canvas and resembled the symbolic, patterned figures of African art. The relationship between the figures and the picture plane itself was ambiguous. As cubism developed, shapes became increasingly abstracted, showing objects from multiple points of view, with transparent overlapping that denied an absolute, inviolate place in space for any single object. In these respects cubism influenced the subsequent development of twentieth-century design. Nature was no longer the only form of reality to depict. The human mind itself played a part in structuring reality.

In Germany, Friedrich Nietzsche and the nihilist rebellion contributed to the

18. *Pablo Picasso.* Les Demoiselles d'Avignon. *1907. Oil on canvas, 8′ × 7′8″ (2.4 × 2.3 m). Collection, The Museum of Modern Art, New York. Acquired through the Lillie P. Bliss Bequest.*

expressionist movement, which appeared around 1905. The idea that art is primarily self-expression led to a dramatic non-naturalistic art that is typified by Oskar Kokoschka and Ernst Kirchner (Fig. 19). In Paris in 1905 the first exhibition of a group of artists who would be called "les Fauves" ("the wild beasts") was held. Similar in look to expressionism, with its open disregard of the forms of nature, fauvism favored wild expressive colors. Neoexpressionism, influenced by the expressionists and the fauves, shows up in contemporary illustration.

In 1890 the German psychologist Christian von Ehrenfels published an essay called "On Gestalt Qualities." Within this paper was the suggestion that the "Gestalt" (total entity) is larger than the sum of its parts. Ehrenfels suggested that the parts interact to form a new whole. Our perception of an object is influenced by the arrangement of objects around it. This work pointed the way to another new idea. Reality could be seen as dependent on context rather than as absolute.

In 1910 at the Frankfurt Institute of Psychology, Max Wertheimer, an admirer of Ehrenfels, began research on apparent movement, which is the basis for the motion picture. He asked why we perceive some images as belonging together and others not. He arrived at the Gestalt principle of unit forming, which describes how we organize and interpret patterns from our environment: Simply put, things that are similar will be perceptually grouped together. (A more detailed description of unit-forming factors is in Chapter 5.) Wertheimer's investigations were carried on by Wolfgang Köhler and Kurt Koffka and later by Rudolf Arnheim.

Germany also gave birth to Peter Behrens, a pictorial and graphic artist who moved into architecture. He was an artist of the Deutscher Werkbund, founded in 1907. Inspired by William Morris and the English Arts and Crafts movement, the Werkbund artists believed in examining the moral questions inherent in art and in preventing commercial and industrial abuse. Behrens was given the first corporate identity job in the history of design. He was asked to design for AEG a large German corporation: the architecture, advertising, products, and everything else (Fig. 20). He taught Walter Gropius, who would later become famous as a leader of the Bauhaus.

19. *Ernst Kirchner. Cover for catalog of K. G. Brucke exhibition. 1905/07. 32.7″ × 31.9″ (83 × 81 cm). Collection Kaiser Wilhelm Museum.*

WORLD WAR I

The years before World War I brought new movements that continued to expand our notion of reality. The futurist movement showed time itself on canvas by capturing motion through multiple images. The movement was established around 1909 by the Italian poet Emilio Marinetti and developed by artists such as Giacomo Balla and Gino Severini (Fig. 21). The futurist artists were so named for their optimistic belief that the machines of the industrial age would lead to a better future. Ironically, most of the leaders of the movement were killed in the war.

Futurism's influence continued. Motion pictures were popular by 1910. They widened our visual reality, creating art that

moved through time, as music had always done.

Around that same time, a movement surfaced that would strongly influence graphic design. Dada was founded in 1916 by a group of poets, the chief of whom was the Rumanian Tristan Tzara. Its name, like the movement itself, had no meaning, according to the Dadaists. The following poem is by Tzara:

Colonial syllogism
No one can escape from destiny
No one can escape from DADA
Only DADA can enable you to escape from
*   destiny.*
*   You own me: 943–50 francs.*
No more drunkards!
No more aeroplanes!
No more vigor!
No more urinary passages!
No more enigmas!

The Dadaists have been extremely important in twentieth-century art and philosophy because they questioned meaning itself with an assault on all accepted values and conventional behavior. Marcel Duchamp exhibited such things as bicycle wheels, urinals, and bot-

tle racks, challenging the criteria by which we define something as art (Fig. 22). He stated, "I was interested in ideas—not

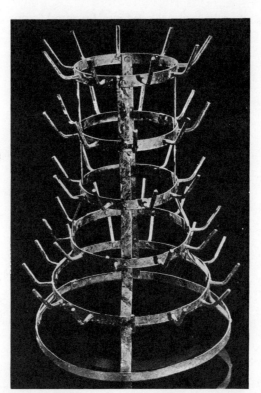

merely in visual products. I wanted to put painting again at the service of the mind."

The Dadaist poet Guillaume Apollinaire created a series of "Calligrammes" around 1918 that seemed to break every known rule of typography. One of the many Dada publications, *Der Dada,* introduced photomontage. It was characterized by an intentional disorder. Letters of all types and sizes, Hebrew characters, sentences in French, and dictionary illustrations mingled with the statement, "He who eats of Dada dies if he is not Dada." Figurative photographic images were treated with the same freedom from conventions (Figs. 23, 24). With "rayographs" or photograms and techniques such as solarization, Man Ray made an important contribution to graphic design (Fig. 25). Kurt Schwitters, another Dada artist, combined cubism with Dada for a series of collages that remain a rich visual resource for artists today (Fig. 26). Francis Picabia created

a strong series of designs that integrated image with typography. Figures 27 and 28 are good examples of two of his object-portraits.

ABSTRACT MOVEMENTS

The first totally abstract poster is attributed to Henry van de Velde in 1897 (Fig. 29). A Belgian art nouveau artist, he moved to Germany in 1906 to teach and became interested in architecture and a more structural approach to art. His ideas contributed to the later development of the Bauhaus movement. The first abstract painting is attributed to Russian Wassily Kandinsky. He, František Kupka, and others were working in an abstract fashion by 1911 (Fig. 30). Such paintings, in Kandinsky's words, issue from "inner necessity." For Kandinsky, painting was above all "spiritual," an attempt to render insights and awareness transcending obviously descriptive realism. Author of *On the Spiritual in Art*, he later joined the Weimar Bauhaus around 1920, where

his shapes became more geometric in his search for a formal harmony.

26. *Kurt Schwitters.* Merz 83: Drawing F. *1920. Collage of cut paper wrappers, announcements, tickets, 5 3/4" × 4 1/2" (14.6 × 11.4 cm). Collection, The Museum of Modern Art, New York. Katherine S. Dreier Bequest.*

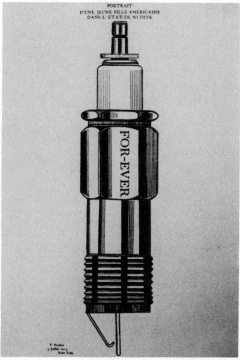

left: 27. *Francis Picabia.* Portrait of Steiglitz from 291, *1915. Line blocks, 17" × 34" (43.5 × 86 cm). Collection, The Chicago Art Institute. Frank B. Hubacheck Restricted Gift, 1974.27 (cover page).*

right: 28. *Francis Picabia.* Portrait of a Young American Women in a State of Nudity *for 291, 1915. Line blocks, 17" × 34" (43.5 × 86 cm). Collection, The Chicago Art Institute. Frank B. Hubacheck Restricted Gift, 1974.27 (inner page).*

29. *Henry van de Velde. Tropon. 1897. Poster, 13 3/4" × 10 5/8" (35 × 27 cm). Collection Kaiser Wilhelm Museum. Photo courtesy UW–Whitewater Slide Library.*

In 1913 the Russian Kazimir Malevich began painting abstract geometric compositions. Malevich formulated a theoretical basis for his paintings, which he called suprematism. He saw them as the last chapter in easel painting that would point to a universal system of art headed by architecture. The architectonic approach led the way to constructivism, which is the idea that painting is construction, like architecture.

The Russian revolution of 1917 saw many Russian artists eagerly contributing to the social and cultural aspect of revolutionary change. Malevich continued to create paintings based on simple geometric forms of the square, circle, and triangle. Often they made a symbolic propaganda statement. The movement is thought to have made an important contribution to modern advertising, because visual images were used in an attempt to inform and per-

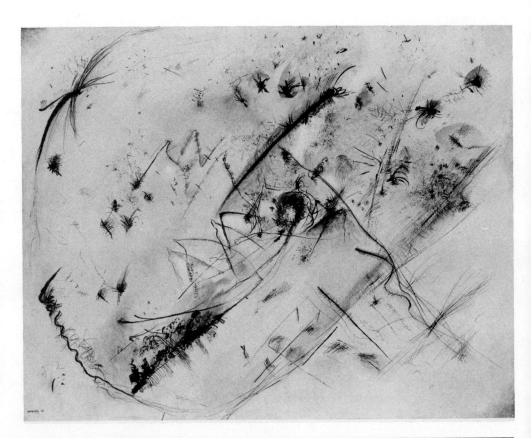

30. *Wassily Kandinsky. Light Picture. December 1913. Oil on canvas, 30 5/8" × 39 1/2" (77.7 × 100.3 cm). Collection, Solomon R. Guggenheim Museum, New York. Photo by Robert E. Mates.*

31. *Kazimir Malevich. Suprematist Composition. (n.d.) Oil on canvas, 31 5/8″ × 31 5/8″ (80 × 80 cm). Collection, The Museum of Modern Art, New York.*

suade. Information and persuasion is the basis of contemporary advertising design (Fig. 31).

El Lissitzky is a Russian constructivist and designer who devoted a great deal of effort to propaganda work. He also developed rules of typography and design that laid the groundwork for the development of grids. Designing a book of Vladimir Mayakovski's poetry, he wrote: "My pages relate to the poetry in a way similar to a piano accompanying a violin. As thought and sound form a united imagination for the poet, namely poetry, so I have wanted to create a unity equivalent to poetry and typographical elements" (Figs. 32 and 33). Lissitzky experimented with the photogram and foresaw the impor-

32. *El Lissitzky. Table of Contents from* Plastic Figures of the Electro-Mechanical Show: Victory over the Sun. *1923. Collection, The Chicago Art Institute. Gift of the Print and Drawing Club, Gaylord Donnelley and Wm McCallin Mckee Fund 1966.*

tance photography would come to have in graphic design. His beautifully constructed series of paintings, "Proun," emphasizing an architectural, ambiguous feeling of space and form, remain of interest to any serious student of design (Fig. 34). The contemporary designer Paula Scher uses the strong constructive approach of Lissitzky's layouts to create a modern design (Fig. 35).

Closely related to constructivism, de Stijl was created in Holland, where artists avoided a direct involvement in World War I It flourished during the 1920s in Europe and strongly influenced the later Bauhaus work. The most widely known painter of the period is Piet Mondrian. His style is the epitome of de Stijl, with straight black lines set at right angles to one another and a careful asymmetrical balancing of primary colors. Van Doesburg is a de Stijl artist who influenced graphic design (Fig. 36).

The School of Applied Arts and Crafts, founded by Henry van de Velde in 1906 and closed at the outbreak of war, was reopened as the Bauhaus at Weimar in 1919. Walter Gropius, who had worked with Peter Behrens at the German Werkbund, became the Bauhaus director. In 1922 the constructivist El Lissitzky met with Theo van Doesburg and Laszlo Moholy-Nagy in a congress of constructivists and dadaists in Germany. Their exchange of ideas formed a core for the Bauhaus after 1923. The school moved to Dessau in 1925.

The Bauhaus trained artists in all areas. It attempted to bridge the gap between pure and applied art, to place equal importance on all areas of arts and crafts. It stressed clean functional forms. The weavers, metalsmiths, and carpenters did not attempt to produce works of art, but rather good and useful designs. The industrial designer was born from this movement.

The important contributions by artists of the Bauhaus are too numerous to mention in this brief overview. Here are a

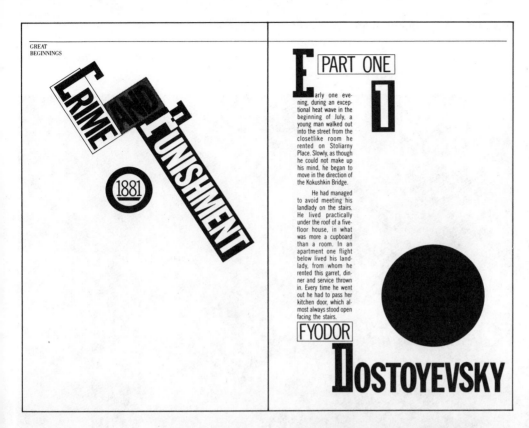

E arly one eve-
ning, during an excep-
tional heat wave in the
beginning of July, a
young man walked out
into the street from the
closetlike room he
rented on Stoliarny
Place. Slowly, as though
he could not make up
his mind, he began to
move in the direction of
the Kokushkin Bridge.

He had managed
to avoid meeting his
landlady on the stairs.
He lived practically
under the roof of a five-
floor house, in what
was more a cupboard
than a room. In an
apartment one flight
below lived his land-
lady, from whom he
rented this garret, din-
ner and service thrown
in. Every time he went
out he had to pass her
kitchen door, which al-
most always stood open
facing the stairs.

PART ONE

1

FYODOR
DOSTOYEVSKY

left: **35.** *Paula Scher.*
Two-page layout from
Great Beginnings. *1980.*

below: **36.** *Theo van*
Doesburg. Kontra-
Komposition mit
Dissonanzen XVI. *1925.*
Oil on canvas, 39 1/2"
× 71" (100 × 180 cm).
Haags Gemeentemuseum,
Den Haag.

few who are influential in the development of graphic design. Josef Albers is known for his research into color and structural relationships (Figs. 37, 38). Laszlo Moholy-Nagy developed photography as illustration. Seek out his work for

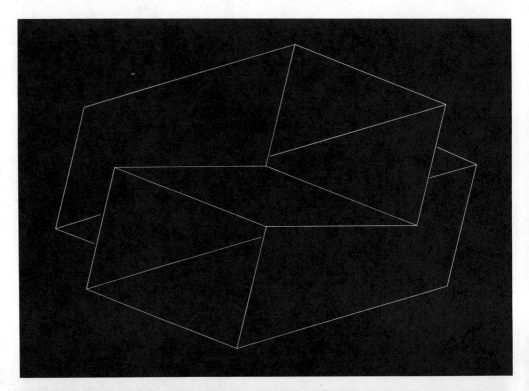

37. *Josef Albers.* Structural Constellation NN–1. *1962. Machine-engraved vinylite, 20″ × 26 1/2″ (50.8 × 67.3 cm). Anni Albers and the Josef Albers Foundation, Inc. Photo by Joseph Szaszfai.*

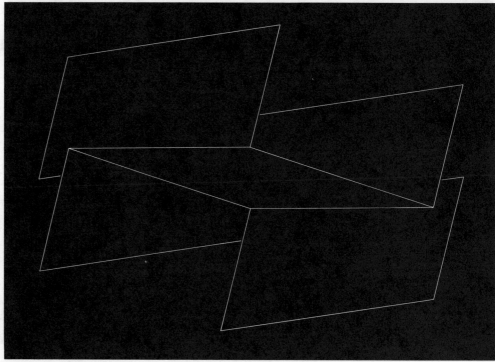

38. *Josef Albers.* Structural Constellation NN–2. *1962. Machine-engraved vinylite, 20″ × 26 1/2″ (50.8 × 67.3 cm). Anni Albers and the Josef Albers Foundation, Inc. Photo by Joseph Szaszfai.*

39. *Herbert Bayer.* Studie zum Universalalphabet. *1925. Bauhaus-Archive.*

futher study; you will not be disappointed. Herbert Bayer created several typeface designs, among them Futura and the "Universal" style (Fig. 39). In keeping with the Bauhaus philosophy, he believed in removing personal values from the printed page, leaving it purely logical. Figure 40 is a looser design by Lyonel Feininger, the title page for a portfolio, featuring the work of many famous Bauhaus artists.

Many of the Bauhaus artists emigrated to the United States after the Nazis forced the closing of the Bauhaus in 1933. There they had a great influence on architecture and graphic design. The Swiss also continued to develop the ideas of the Bauhaus in typography and layout design from the 1950s onward. Among those artists are Josef Müller-Brockmann and Jan Tschichold.

FIGURATIVE MOVEMENTS

Art deco appeared as a definite style in Paris around 1925. It was especially influenced by art nouveau and also by African sculpture and cubism. Although developing at the same time as the Bauhaus, Art deco emphasized the figurative image with decorative appeal. Artists associated with this movement include the Russian Erté, who contributed to *Vogue* magazine and designed theatrical costumes and sets, and Georges Lepape, illustrator for *Vogue* magazine (Fig. 41). The best known and respected art deco artist, who continues to exert a strong influence today, is A M Cassandra. His posters and advertisements show the influence of cubism, but the forms retain a recognizable physical identity balanced with an intricate Gestalt unity. (See Figure 76.) Art deco was out of favor for a time in the eyes of architects and designers because it followed none of the Bauhaus tenets of functional, nonornamental design. Now the style is enjoying a renaissance, inspiring many designers.

Surrealism also surfaced in the 1920s. Owing a philosophical debt to Dada for its questioning attitude, it was joined by several Dada artists. It was formally

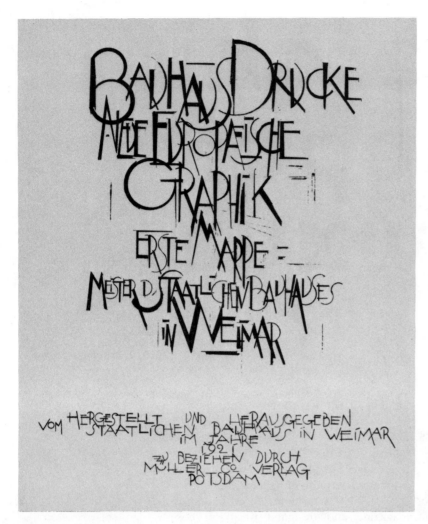

scious motivation continues to interest today's advertiser.

LOOKING AHEAD

Many styles influence the contemporary graphic design field. You can find examples of pop art, trompe l'oeil, and neoexpressionism on most magazine racks. Figure 42 combines many of these influences. You will learn more about them in Chapter 12.

New media such as film, video, and computers are also shaping design today. Possibly the strongest new influence on design during the current decade is computer graphics. Even in such a high-tech area, the eye and mind of the designer remain as important as ever.

Graphic designers and illustrators today draw ideas from many movements. Familiarity with successful work from the past will make you a better designer. It will also keep you alert to "history in the making." Reality was being redefined on every front

40. *Lyonel Feininger. Title page from* Nelle Europaeische Graphik I, *First Bauhaus Portfolio. 1921. Gift of Mrs. Henry C. Woods, Steuben Memorial Fund, Emil Eitel Fund and Harold Joachine Purchase Fund. Collection, The Chicago Art Institute.*

established in 1924 by André Breton, yet another poet and writer starting a philosophical movement that would find visual expression. The surrealists drew inspiration from Freud's *Interpretation of Dreams.* Like the author James Joyce, who was using a stream-of-consciousness technique rather than rational, linear development of characters, surrealists sought to reveal the subconscious.

Surrealism has exerted a strong influence on illustration. René Magritte is much imitated today, and in fact did quite a lot of advertising illustration (see Figure 176). Other surrealists, like Max Ernst and Man Ray, show the influence of Dada in the unorthodox and compelling arrangement of elements. Surrealism's search for uncon-

41. *Georges Lepape. Cover for* Vogue *Magazine. 1930. Gouache. Courtesy Vogue. Copyright 1930 (renewed 1958, 1986) by The Conde Nast Publications Inc. Photo courtesy UW–Whitewater Slide Library.*

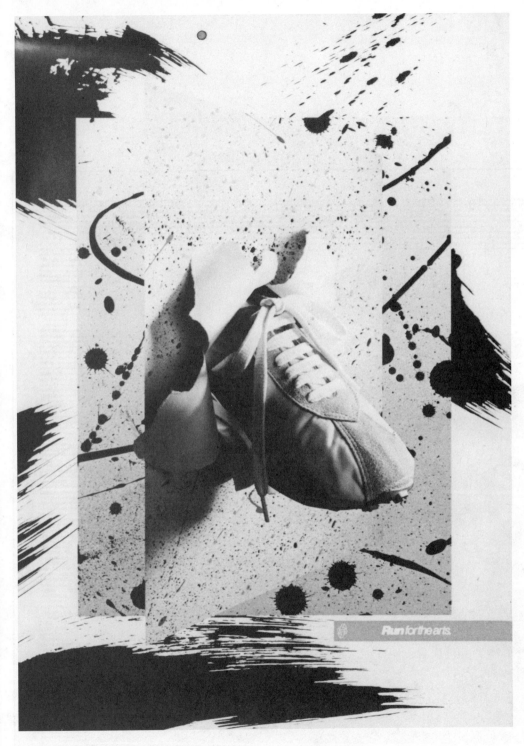

42. *Julius Friedman and Walter McCord.* Run for the Arts. *Photo by Joe Boone.*

at the turn of the last century. The turn of the next century will bring newer perceptions. The Industrial Revolution spurred on important philosophical, scientific, and artistic discoveries. In our time, it is information and communication that are revolutionizing society. It will be an exciting future for designers.

PERCEPTION

SEEING AND BELIEVING

Graphic designers do more than decorate a surface. They work with the fundamental principles of perception. When we look at a printed page, whether it is covered with type, an illustration, or a photograph, there is more than meets the eye. The brain is sifting and cataloging the images. We carry a load of experiences, innate responses, and physiological considerations that interact with those images. Designs that effectively use that process have the creative strength of sight itself on their side (Figs. 43, 44).

As soon as the first mark is made on a blank sheet of paper, it is altered by the eye. We cannot see only a flat mark on a flat piece of paper. Our past experience, our expectations, and the structure of the brain itself filter the information. The visual illusions created through this process are a real part of perception. Realism in art and design is not an absolute but a convention that our culture and personal background create from visual data.

Search for Simplicity

The Gestalt psychologists have investigated the way humans process information from a two-dimensional surface. There is an interplay of tensions among shapes on a flat surface because the appearance of any one element or shape depends upon its surroundings. These elements and surroundings are interpreted by an active eye that seeks the simplest satisfactory explanation for what it sees. Any mark drawn

43. *Josef Albers.*
Structural Constellation
NN–3. *1962. Machine-engraved vinylite, 20″ ×
26 1/2″ (50.8 × 67.3 cm).
Anni Albers and the
Josef Albers Foundation,
Inc. Photo by Joseph
Szaszfai.*

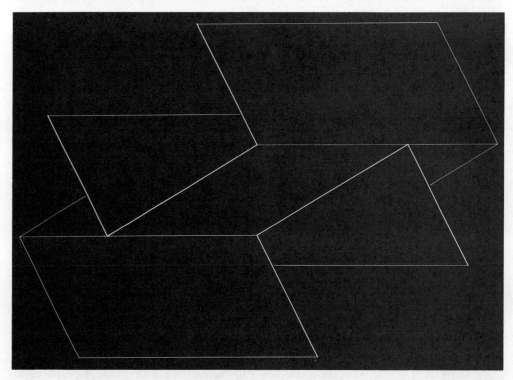

44. *Josef Albers.*
Structural Constellation
NN–4. *1962. Machine-engraved vinylite, 20″ ×
26 1/2″ (50.8 × 67.3 cm).
Anni Albers and the
Josef Albers Foundation,
Inc. Photo by Joseph
Szaszfai.*

on paper stimulates this active, interpretive response from eye and brain: We finish uncompleted shapes, group similar shapes, and see foreground and background on a flat surface. Their experiments have led Gestalt psychologists to describe the basic law of visual perception: Any stimulus pattern tends to be seen as a structure as simple as conditions permit. This law is similar to the principle of parsimony known to scientists, which states that when several hypotheses fit the facts, the simplest one should be accepted.

Elegance and success result from explaining a phenomenon with the minimum number of steps. A similar elegance can be achieved on the printed page. There can be a great deal happening on a page although there are few marks. In fact, adding *more* marks without understanding their effect can often make *less* happen. That is poor design.

The manner in which the Gestalt psychologists believe our brain interprets and groups the images on a flat surface will be discussed in following chapters. It is generally recognized as a useful prescription for designing pictures so they will be comprehended as we want. No single theory, however, explains all there is to visual perception. Most of what there is to know has yet to be discovered.

Interpretations

The lines in Figures 45 to 49 demonstrate our busy interaction with simple marks drawn on a page. These interpretations are influenced by the culture in which we live. We accept the black mark in Figure 45 as nearer than the white field it occupies although they both exist on the same physical plane on the surface of the page. Adding a second mark of a larger size (Fig. 46) causes another interpreta-

tion. The larger mark seems closer in space than the smaller one. A line placed vertically that divides the space (Fig. 47) will not disturb the two-dimensional quality. However, a line set at an angle surrounded by a white field (Fig. 48) will seem to recede in space. Add a second line (Fig. 49) and suddenly the eye sees the perspective of a road or railroad tracks running into the distance.

FIGURE/GROUND

If we are aware of how the eye and brain organize marks on a flat surface to give them meaning, we will be much more successful in showing what we mean. The most fundamental organizational principle of sight for an artist working on a flat, two-dimensional surface is figure/ground. It is sometimes called positive/negative space. An ability to see and structure both areas is crucial to the designer.

Whenever we look at a mark on a page we see it as an object distinct from its background. This distinction is the fundamental, first step in perception. A thing (figure) is only visible to the extent that it is seen as separate from its background (ground). This theory has application in every area of perception. A tree, for example, can only be seen in relation to the space around it, the "not-treeness."

We are able to look at the shapes and lines of a photograph and recognize a "picture" because of figure/ground grouping. We are able to recognize and read words because we organize the letters into a figure lying against a ground. In

45.

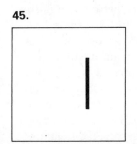

46.

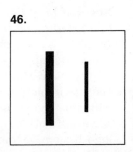

47.

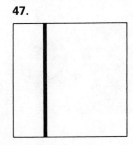

48.

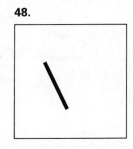

49.

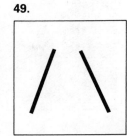

Figure 50, designer Herb Lubalin uses a switch in figure/ground in letterforms to make a point. The figure of the letterform becomes background for cockroaches in the final word "left." This figure/ground interplay becomes a vital part of the message. At its best, design becomes inseparable from communication.

Categories

Every figure seems to lie at some location in front of the ground. Designing well depends upon handling both areas. Many beginning artists concentrate only on the mark they make and are not aware of the white space surrounding it. Remember

that this space or "ground" is as integral a part of the page as the "figure" placed upon it. The three main categories in figure/ground shaping are stable, reversible, and ambiguous.

Stable figure-ground *All two-dimensional marks or shapes are perceived in an unchanging relationship of object against background.* Aubrey Beardsley played deliberately with the tension of a stable figure/ground relationship on the verge of breaking down. Move your eye around Beardsley's work and figure/ground will reverse or become unclear, only to establish itself again. (See Figure 16.)

Reversible figure/ground *Figure and ground can be focused on equally.* What was initially ground becomes figure. Because we cannot simultaneously perceive both images as figure, we keep switching. M. C. Escher worked with this switch in a systematic manner using a grid (Fig. 51). A great many logo designs also use reversible figure/

Visual texture makes for figure perception. The eye will be drawn to a textured area before it is to a nontextured area (Fig. 54).

Convex shapes are more easily seen as figure than concave (Fig. 55).

Simplicity (especially symmetry) predisposes area to be seen as figure (Fig. 56).

Familiarity causes a shape to pull out from its surroundings. As we focus on it, it becomes figure, while the surroundings become ground (Fig. 57).

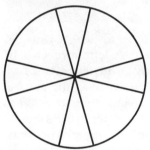

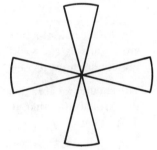

54.

53.

ground, as you will discover in Chapter 5.

Ambiguous figure/ground *In some puzzle pictures one figure may turn out to be made up of another, or of several different pictures* (Fig. 52).

Conditions

Once mastered, figure/ground grouping is an invaluable tool. Here are some conditions under which one area appears as figure and another as ground. Use these principles when completing Exercise 1.

The enclosed or surrounded area tends to be seen as figure; the surrounding, unbounded one as ground (Fig. 53).

55.

56.

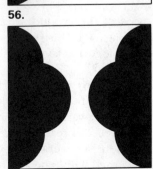

57.

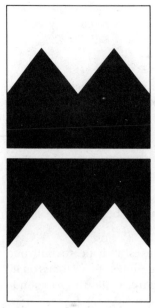

58.

59.

The lower half of a horizontally divided area reads as the solid figure to which gravity anchors us (Fig. 58).

The smaller an area of space, the greater the probability that it will be seen as figure (Fig. 59).

Letterforms

How does this figure/ground phenomenon affect letterforms, the basic ingredient of the printed page? Stop now and do Exercise 1. As you do the exercise you will realize that figure/ground affects letterforms the same as any mark on the page. Using type effectively depends on seeing both the black shapes of the letters and the white shapes between, within, and around them. You must pay close attention to the shape of the ground areas, called *counters* (Fig. 60). This rule has direct application in logo and layout design (Chapters 5 and 7).

Because we tend to read for verbal information and not for visual information, we are rarely aware of the appearance of the type itself. We read it, but do not "see" it. For the first several projects, we will be concerned with type as a pure design ele-

ment while you learn to "see" it. Only display or "headline" size letterforms will be used. Look closely at the letter *As* shown in this chapter and study all the parts of their structure, paying close attention to the counters. Renaissance artist Albrecht Dürer constructed his own type style. His structural diagrams demonstrate the careful shaping and measurements necessary when hand-constructing letterforms (Fig. 61).

SHAPE

Design is the arrangement of shapes. They underlie every drawing, painting, or

60.

and

graphic design. It is possible for an artist to become enamored with the subject matter and forget its basic shapes. Develop the ability to see and think in terms of shapes even though those shapes look like apples or oranges or letterforms. Shape occurs in figure and in ground.

Shape Versus Volume

A shape is an area created by an enclosing boundary that defines the outer edges. The boundary can be a line, a color, or a value change. "Shape" describes two-dimensional artwork, "volume" a three-dimensional work such as a ceramic piece or a sculpture. A rectangle and a circle are shapes, whereas a box and a sphere are volumes. As pictorial shapes, the former might be made to resemble a camera and an orange or a book and a ball (Fig. 62).

Grouping Shapes

Every visual experience is seen in the context of space and time. As every shape is affected by surrounding shapes, so it is influenced by preceding sights.

The normal sense of sight grasps shape immediately by seizing on an overall pattern. Research has demonstrated that grouping letters into words makes it possible to recall the letters more accurately than when they are presented alone. If it is possible to group marks into a recognizable or repeating shape, the eye will do so, because it is the simplest way to perceive and remember them.

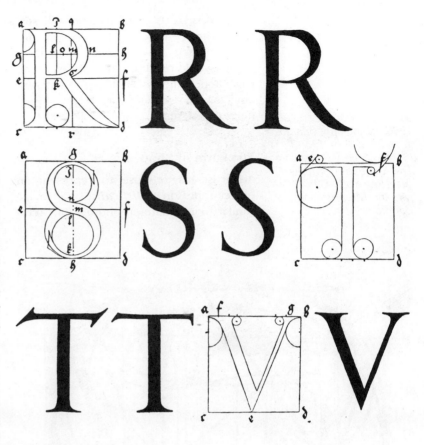

Shape Versus Subject

For the graphic designer, the shape of a circle may represent the letter *O* a diagram of a courtyard, a drawing of a wheel, or a photograph of a muscial instrument. These objects are not linked by subject matter to any common theme. They are linked by shape. Through basic shape you can bring unity to a group of seem-

61. *Albrecht Dürer.* On the Just Shaping of Letters. *1525.*

62. *This rectangle can be made to resemble a camera, but it is still only made up of two-dimensional shapes.*

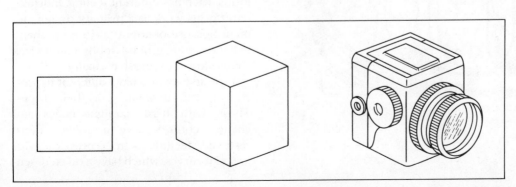

ingly disparate objects. As you will see, the designer works with so many disparate objects that to be blind to their shapes would result in utter chaos on the page. Repeating similar shapes in different objects is an excellent way to bring visual unity to a design.

The Form of Shapes

An artist may choose to represent an object or person *realistically,* by an image similar to an unaltered photograph. Actually, reality is a little more difficult to define than that. Philosophers have been working on it for centuries. As artists we know that visual reality is a combination of the shapes on the page and the viewer's interaction with them.

An artist may also represent the subject in a purposeful *distortion* or *stylization* that can bring extra emphasis to an emotional quality.

Abstraction is another approach. It implies a simplification of existing shapes. Details are ignored, but the subject is still recognizable. Often the pure design shapes of the subject are emphasized.

Purely *nonobjective* shapes such as the constructivists worked with give structure and character to a layout. They are the basis of the invisible, underlying structure of layout design.

Letterform Shapes

The ability to see shapes is especially important with letterforms. True, they are a symbol of something, but first and foremost they are pure shape, a fundamental design element. Successful layout and logo design depend upon creating unity through variations on letterform shape.

The distinction is often made between geometric shapes and curvilinear, organic shapes. Jasper Johns utilizes a free, expressive, curvilinear line. Our eye alternates among numerals as we recognize the multiple overlap in Figure 63. The straight clean edge and more geometric quality of the design by Robert Indiana (Fig. 64) still emphasizes the basic shape of the letterforms. Each has different feeling. Indiana's letterforms work as a primary design element because of attention to basic shape in figure and in ground. Johns' emphasizes a curvilinear, expressive quality.

Type styles often have different expressive qualities depending on their shapes. Those with hard, straight edges and angular corners have a colder, more reserved feeling than typestyles with graceful curves, which have a relaxed, sen-

63. *Jasper Johns. 0–9. 1960. Lithograph, printed in black, 24″ × 18 7/8″ (61 × 48 cm). Collection, The Museum of Modern Art, New York. Gift of Mr. and Mrs. Armand P. Bartos.*

64. *Robert Indiana. Art. 1972. Oil on canvas, 72″ × 72″ (182.8 × 182.8 cm). Collection of Robert L. B. Tobin. Photo by Michael Smith.*

sual feeling. What feel does the typeface used in this book convey?

To become sensitive to the shapes in a letterform, look carefully at its anatomy (Fig. 65). Then learn the differences among type styles. Chapter 6 goes into the history and classification of type styles. Right now, however, concentrate on making comparisons among a few classic type styles (Figs. 66–70).

Terminology

The following list of definitions will help you know what to look for when comparing shapes in letterforms.

65. *Parts of a letterform.*

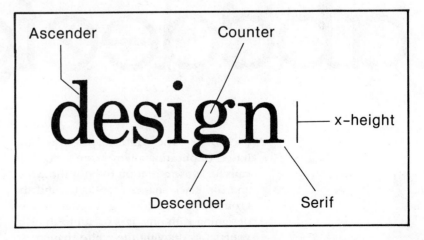

abcdefghijklmn

66. *Garamond.*

abcdefghijklmnop

67. *Baskerville.*

abcdefghijklmnopq

68. *Bodoni.*

abcdefghijklmnop

69. *Univers.*

abcdeefghijkl

70. *ITC Lubalin Graph Book.*

Counter The white shapes inside the letter. Duplicating a letterform accurately calls for close attention to both the white and the black shapes (the figure and the ground). When drawing a letterform or designing with one, it is useful to think of yourself as drawing the white shapes.

Serif The stroke that projects off the main stroke of the letter at the bottom or the top. Letters without serifs are called sans serif.

x-height The height of the body of a lowercase letter like the letter *x* or *a.* It does not include ascender or descender. The x-height will vary in typefaces of the same size. Size is measured from the top of the ascender to the bottom of the descender. Thus 10 point Garamond has a small x-height and long ascenders and descenders; 10 point Univers has a larger x-height and smaller ascenders and descenders.

Ascender The part of the lowercase letter that rises above the body of the letter. The letter *a* has no ascender, but the letter *b* does.

Descender The part of the lowercase letter that falls below the body of the letter. The letters *a b c d e* have no descenders, but the letters *f* and *g* do.

Typeface Style of lettering. Most typefaces vary a great deal, when you develop an eye for the differences. Each "family" of typefaces may contain variations like "italic" and "bold" in addition to regular or "roman."

Font A font is a complete set of type of one size and one variation on a typeface. (Bold Century is a different font than italic Century.)

Stress The distribution of weight through the thinnest part of a letterform. It can be easily seen by drawing a line through the thinnest part of an *o* and observing the slant of the line (Fig. 71).

71.

Using this terminology, look at each style and ask yourself the following questions:

How much variation is there between thick and thin strokes?

Which style has a short x-height?

Which style has a tall x-height?

Which has the longest ascenders and descenders?

What are the differences in the serifs?

Which type has the most vertical stress?

What are the similarities among letters that belong to one style?

EXERCISE 1

Refer to the information on figure/ground perception demonstrated in Figures 53 through 59 for this exercise.

a. Group several copies of the arrow in Figure 72 to form an interesting and symmetrical pattern. Stress the creation of shapes in figure and in ground.

72.

b. Figure 73 is drawn so that it is equally possible to see the white or the black area as figure. How can you change this diagram to make one area appear to be figure?

73.

c. Place the letter **H** inside a rectangular format. Use a Helvetica type style (see Fig. 149). Place the letter and its values so that the **H** becomes ground instead of figure. Familiarity makes this exercise difficult.

d. Repeat the Helvetica letter **A** in a symmetrical pattern. What do you see as figure? Why?

EXERCISE 2

The letter *A* has been shown to you in five different typefaces. To help you recognize the shapes of different faces and learn to handle your tools, trace each of these letters and transfer them to illustration board. Reproduce them in ink or pencil so that they are "letter perfect."

When you have finished and your work has been critiqued, you will be ready to proceed with the first main project.

PROJECT
Figure/Ground and Letterforms

Choose two letterforms from the type styles shown in this chapter. Create a design that uses one letter as the figure and another as the ground. This relationship can be stable, reversible, or ambiguous as long as it remains possible to "read" both letterforms. Remember the importance of thumbnails. Explore a minimum of fifteen possibilities.

Fit your design within an 8″ × 10″ (20 × 25 cm) format. Leave a 2″ (5

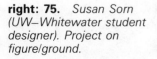

above: 74. *Seng Xiong (UW–Whitewater student designer). Project on figure/ground.*

right: 75. *Susan Sorn (UW–Whitewater student designer). Project on figure/ground.*

cm) white "matte" area around the design. Use black India ink on cold press illustration board. Keep your letters "true to form" and "letter perfect." Use solid black or white shapes without outlining, cross-hatching, or stippling. You can (1) extend the edge of a shape, (2) overlap a form, or (3) hide an edge by painting a black letter against a black background or white against white. Do not, however, distort their basic shapes. Bring out the beauty, variety, and personality of those shapes. Figures 74 and 75 are student designs based on this project.

Objectives

Learn to see and duplicate standard letterforms.

Use thumbnails to explore and evaluate alternative solutions.

Learn to control the application of India ink and inking tools.

Experiment with creating figure/ground relationships.

For Extra Credit Try an expressive painting based on letterforms.

"Let's go girl, low. "But phone mumm stepped into a booth and true and well

said the first I must She · public dialed, using her finger"

Death in The Afterno AFTERNO ON
CHAPTER ONE

4

TOWARD A DYNAMIC BALANCE

VISUAL AND INTELLECTUAL UNITY

There are two kinds of unified communication in graphic design. Intellectual unity is idea-generated and word-dominated. The mind, not the eye, makes the grouping. Visual unity, on the other hand, is created by placement of design elements visible to the eye.

The poster in Figure 76 by the famous early twentieth-century designer A M Cassandra is unified both intellectually and visually. It is a poster for an eyeglass company, so it is intellectually unified by the slogan, the emphasis on the eyeglasses, and the bright, clear area of vision through which the eyes peer at us. It is visually unified through a complex series of events as the small type leads our eye down and into the O of "Leroy." The size of this small type echoes the serif on the larger word. The squareness of the typography in "Leroy" is echoed by the bright square surrounding the face.

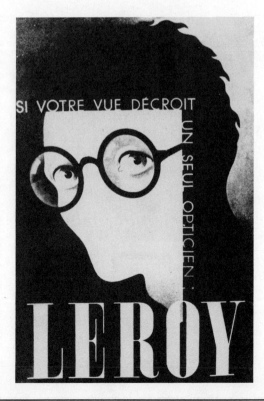

76. *A. M. Cassandra. Poster for an optician.*

Imagine that a designer and a writer are hanging a gallery show of a photojournalist's work. The designer is hanging photographs together that have similar value and shapes. The writer is following behind, rehanging the photos together according to subject matter: a picture of a burning building next to one of firemen. One is *thinking* of subject matter (intellectual unity); the other is *looking* at design (visual unity).

As a design student you are learning to see the visual unity in a composition, and to create with an eye for it. Few people have this skill. Study the form of your design. Once you have mastered the visual "language," you will be able to use it to strengthen both visual and intellectual communication. Both are important.

Design as Abstraction

Abstract art drew attention to pure visual design. It was "about" color, value, shape, texture, and direction. In a painting by Mondrian (Fig. 77) we are intrigued by the break-up of space and the distribution of value and color. There is no "picture" to distract us from the visual information. Theo van Doesburg, Mondrian, and the de Stijl movement had a tremendous influence on graphic design, as layout artists began arranging their shapes and blocks of type into asymmetrically balanced compositions.

A good graphic artist must be a good abstract artist. Figure 78 shows a layout by Swiss designer J. Müller-Brockmann that demonstrates a strong eye for abstract design shapes reminiscent of Mondrian's surface divisions and strong horizontal/vertical orientation.

Graphic design is essentially an abstract art. A work should be balanced and compelling in its own right as well as supportive of an idea.

Working Together

In a design firm the visual design of a project is given full consideration. The ad agency, however, is often dominated

above: 77. *Piet Mondrian.* Composition Gray-Red, *1935, oil on canvas, 57.5 × 55.6 cm. Gift of Mrs. Gilbert W. Chapman, 1949.518. © 1987 the Art Institute of Chicago. All Rights Reserved.*

right: 78. *J. Müller-Brockmann.* Poster for Kunstgewerbemuseum, Zurich. *1960.*

by copywriters. Many other places that employ designers also have word people in key positions. These people tend to be sensitive primarily to words and ideas (intellectual unity). They are not trained in visual comunication. For this angle they will rely on you. Together you can assure, as the Bauhaus would say, that the *form* of a design matches its *function*.

To quote El Lissitzky, "The words on the printed page are meant to be looked at, not listened to." How do we *look* at designs, and how do we give them visual unity? The answer has to do largely with balance.

VISUAL DYNAMICS

A ladder leaning precariously against a wall will make us tense with a sense of impending collapse. A diver poised at the top of the high dive fills us with suspense. We are not passive viewers. We project our experience into all that we see, including the printed page.

How do we project our physical experience into that flat rectangular surface? *Kinesthetic projection* (sensory experience stimulated by bodily movements and tensions) is operating, whether we deal with pictures of people or the abstract shapes of type design. Figure 79 by Don Egensteiner demonstrates the attraction of gravity on type. Our culture also reads a page from top to bottom, a movement that matches our experience with gravity. It is harder to read a design of words or images that asks the eye to go from bottom to top.

We project emotional as well as physical experience onto the page. An illustration of a man stabbed (Fig. 80) causes discom-

left: 79. *Don Egensteiner (Young & Rubicam Inc.). Ad in* Fortune *magazine. 1960.*

below: 80. *Michael David Brown.* Creativity Illustrated. *1983.*

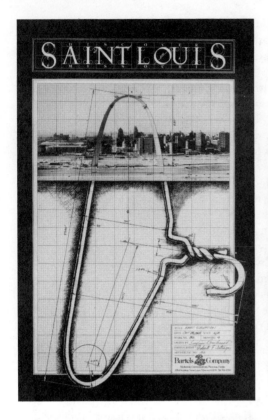

above left: 81. *Self-Promotional Ad. Bartels and Company, St. Louis.*

above right: 82. *Milton Glaser.* Portrait of Nijinsky & Diaghilev *designed and illustrated for* Audience *magazine.*

fort due to such projection. Visual form stirs up memories and expectations. That is why visual perception is so dynamic.

Loose strokes that allow the process of construction to show through also arouse this dynamic tension. The visible brush stroke or mark of the maker pulls viewers into the process of creation. Many interesting and appealing printed pieces are created by allowing the tension of the creative process to show through (Fig. 81).

As you saw in the preceding chapter, any mark made on a sheet of paper upsets the surface and organizes the space around the mark. This dynamic tension is not contained in the paper itself, nor in the graphite, markers, or ink we use. It is created by our interaction with the image. Let us examine this dynamic interplay.

Top to Bottom

We are uncomfortable with shapes clustered at the top of a page with open space beneath them. We have observed in the

world around us that there are many more things at rest on the ground than in the sky. There is a sense of suspense as we wait for the fall if they are not "standing" on anything. We experience a design as "top-heavy" much more quickly than as "bottom-heavy."

Milton Glaser, a contemporary designer, illustrator, and author, deliberately plays with this tension in his double portrait of dancer Nijinsky (Fig. 82). All that anchors the dancing gravity-defying feet is the line of the wall under the right foot and the vertical line at the corner.

Type designers have long believed in the importance of putting extra weight at the bottom of a letterform to make it look firm and stable. The 3 and 8 in Figure 83 look top-heavy when viewed upside down, as here. Book designers customarily leave more space at the bottom than at the top of a page. They understand that a sense of balance cannot be achieved by placing identical objects or identical margins at the top and bottom of a composition.

Vertical and Horizontal

We find horizontal and vertical lines stable, probably because they remind us of our vertical bodies on the horizontal earth. Milton Glaser again deliberately violates this sense of stability in Figure 84. As he comments, "The diagonal of this figure gives the illustration its surreal perversity."

We find diagonal lines dynamic because they seem in a state of flux, poised for movement toward the more stable horizontal or vertical. The de Stijl artist Theo van Doesburg deviated from Mondrian's horizontal and vertical compositions, stating that the modern human spirit felt a need to express a sharp contrast to those right angles found in architecture and landscape. An oblique angle is one of the quickest, most effective means of showing tension. This tension can be created by placing a single shape at an oblique angle or by placing the entire composition at an angle.

Left to Right

In Western cultures we read from the left to the right side of the page, and this experience may influence the way we look for balance between those two sides of a design. The left side is the more important, emphasized by the fact that our attention goes there first. Pictorial movement from the left toward the right seems to require less effort than movement in the opposite direction. An animal speeding from the right to the left, for example, seems to be overcoming more resistance than one shown moving from left to right. You can explore this left-to-right balance by holding your designs up to a mirror. They may now appear unbalanced.

Overall

Every two-dimensional shape, line, figure/-ground relationship, value, color, and so on possesses visual dynamics. We have seen the dynamic value of a kinesthetic reaction, or empathy with the image. There is more to the dynamics of perception, however. We have all seen images of a supposedly moving figure that appears in awkward, static immobility. The objects of dancer or automobile can lead us to expect movement, but only skillful control

83. *Type turned upside-down looks top-heavy.*

left: 84. *Milton Glaser. A drawing created to illustrate a story in* Audience *magazine about a man with a crooked head.*

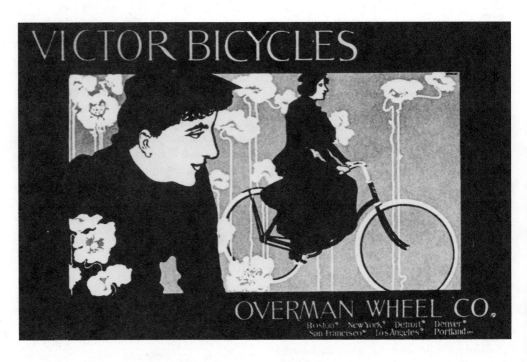

VICTOR BICYCLES

OVERMAN WHEEL CO.
Boston° New York° Detroit° Denver°
San Francisco° Los Angeles° Portland—

85. *Will Bradley. Poster for Victor Bicycles. 1899. Courtesy UW–Whitewater Slide Library.*

86. *Elements in balance.*

of visual language can evoke it. Successful communication requires balance, the directing and conducting of visual tensions.

BALANCE

Every healthy person has a sense of balance. It allows us to remain upright and walk or ride a bicycle. Our eye is pleased with a balanced composition, just as we are pleased with our ability to ride a bicycle and not wobble (Fig. 85). Lack of balance in a design will irritate viewers and impair the communication. In isomorphic terms, they feel in danger of "falling off the bicycle." How do we create a unified, "ridable" design?

When the dynamic tension between elements is balanced, we are most likely to communicate our intended message. Otherwise, the eye is confused. It shifts from element to element, wanting to move things so that they "sit" right on the page, as we want to straighten a picture hanging crooked on a wall. The viewer so bothered will pay little attention to the quality or content of the picture.

Balance is achieved by two forces of equal strength that pull in opposite directions, or by multiple forces pulling in different directions whose strengths offset one another. Think of visual balance as a multiple rope pull where, for the moment, all teams are exerting the same strength on the rope. It is not a state of rest, but a state of equal tension (Fig. 86).

If the simplist and quietest form of balance were always desirable, we would see dull art. However, too much predictability and unity disturbs us just as too much chaos. We are animals of change and tension. We strive for growth and life. A simple decrease in visual tension resulting in a quiet balance will not satisfy us for long. An interplay between tension-heightening and tension-reducing visual devices seems to satisfy us and match our kinesthetic and emotional experience. We yearn for diversity as well as unity.

Symmetry

There are two basic types of balance: symmetry and asymmetry. In symmetrical balance identical shapes are repeated from left to right in mirrored positions on either side of a central vertical axis. Figure 87 is a symmetrical poster design for the Glas-

Toward a Dynamic Balance

gow Institute of Fine Arts. Some symmetrical designs also repeat from top to bottom. They are often radial designs. Symmetrical balance dominated painting and architecture until after the Renaissance. It dominated graphic design throughout the first centuries of the printing trade, when type was carefully set in centered, formally ordered pages. The traditional book form is a classic example of symmetry (Fig. 88). The white areas are symmetrical, as are the areas of gray type.

Symmetrical design with its quiet sense of order is useful whenever stability and tradition are important. It uses contrasts of value, shape, and so on to relieve boredom and introduce variety.

Asymmetry

Asymmetrical design has a greater sense of movement and change, of possible instability and relative weights. It is like taking your bike through an obstacle course. You may fall off, but the effort is worth it and the audience is thrilled. It is a contemporary balance that reflects the changing times. There is a logical certainty in

below left: 87. *Herbert McNair, Margaret Macdonald. and Frances Macdonald. Notice the symmetry. (Courtesy Glasgrow Institute of Fine Art). GIFA poster.*

below right: 88. *Scott Walker and Tim Girvin. Page design for* Fine Print. *1979.*

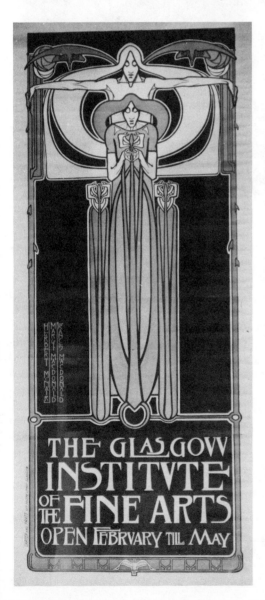

The Five Books of J.G. Lubbock

BY COLIN FRANKLIN

Mr. J.G. Lubbock, book artist, printmaker and author, lives in an obscure corner of Suffolk well protected by a confusing maze of lanes; thus there need be no fear of mass intrusion if I suggest that to know his books one should visit him. Since 1966 his surprising productions have grown among us, bearing his varied and splendid prints and his own struggling cosmic prose printed with the Cambridge taste of Will and Sebastian Carter of The Rampant Lions Press, and nobody has known quite what to make of it all. "Prints are okay," people say, "so long as you don't have to read the books." The sea comes into his writing, and he lives near an estuary. Thinking of another member of his family, Basil Lubbock, whose book *The Last of the Windjammers* I desired as a boy, I had imagined a blustery bearded sailor, talented as seamen often are with their hobbies but greatly out of depth in prose. Mostly it was rather high-flying stuff, like this from his first book:

> The process of production of the work of art is of more interest than the results even to the spectator, because the work must always, by virtue of the artist's imperfection as a transmitter, be inferior to the transcendent reality sensed by him.

He seemed to range rather casually over the universe, taking in science or the sea as a car needs to pause at the garage. Was it all rather peculiar and pretentious?

It was not. Mr. Lubbock looks a little like portraits of James Joyce, and keeps the Cambridge diffidence of his youth. Few men preserve themselves without worldly corruption through a full span of professional life and return to complete their proper artistic purpose, but he appears to be achieving just that. "Art in books" had appealed to him since undergraduate years at Trinity, where varied Books of Hours and the Trinity College Apocalypse had

provided an enduring wish. As an engineer and living at the edge of London, there had simply been no time for all that; the vanity and indulgence of art waited, and at his retirement burst with energy upon a sudden summer.

He works in mixed method – etching, aquatint, engraving – but always like Graham Sutherland, Paul Nash, and Ivon Hitchens; but most of all in such works as some little known, but extremely beautiful engravings by J.G. Lubbock, and Morris Cox." The link with Morris Cox and the Gogmagog Press, with comparable and complex examples of color printing, is apt, of course, and I find it entirely sympathetic, though deep differences suggest themselves if one thinks of the two together. Morris Cox has spent his life as an artist, humbly and with a single mind; Lubbock's religious art has survived a conventional career in one of the professions, showing its strength in release. The Gogmagog Press of Morris Cox makes everything, prints, binds, adapts to a table-press and by laborious improvisation produces "form in Nature," as Mr. Lister phrases it.

89. *Michael David Brown. Death in the Afternoon from Creativity Illustrated. 1983. An example of asymmetrical balance.*

symmetrical design that is lacking in asymmetrical. In symmetrical design a two-inch square in the upper left dictates another such square in the upper right. In asymmetrical design that square could be balanced by a vast number of shapes, values, colors, or textures. It is difficult, challenging, and visually exciting.

Asymmetrical designs are balanced through contrast to achieve equal visual weight among elements. To be effective, contrast must be definitive. Shapes that are almost, but not definitely different are irritating to the eye. Figure 89 is an asymmetrical design that uses several forms of contrast in both figures and letterforms to achieve a balanced, intriguing design.

Balance Through Contrast

Symmetry is balance through likeness; asymmetry is balance through contrast.

The easiest way to achieve visual unity would be to make one shape into an overall symmetrical pattern on the page. A full book page with nothing on it but a solid block of type is visually unified, no matter what the words say. It is also visually dull. In the case of novels, this visual dullness is deliberate. The reader is directed to the content of the words without distraction. In most publications and advertising design, however, this unity must be tempered with contrast if it is to attract and hold the viewer. The designer is usually working with many different elements. Most successful designs rely on a carefully juggled balance of similarities and contrasts.

There are two considerations in setting up balance through contrast: weight and direction. *Weight* is the strength or dominance of the visual object. *Direction* is the way the eye is drawn between elements

Toward a Dynamic Balance

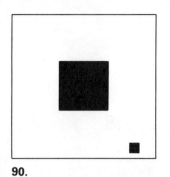

90.

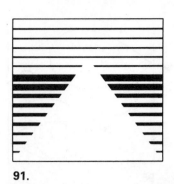

91.

92.

over the flat surface. Balance is determined by the natural weight of an element and by the directional forces in the composition. Weight and direction are influenced by several forces.

Location

The center of a composition will support more weight than the edges. Although a shape is most stable when in the center, it also is visually "light." Small shapes at the edges of a composition can balance large ones in the middle (Fig. 90).

Spatial Depth

Vistas that lead the eye into the page have great visual strength. We project ourselves into the spatial illusion, so it seems to have greater presence or size (Fig. 91).

Size

Visual weight also depends upon size (Fig. 92)—the larger the heavier. Size is the most basic and often used form of contrast in graphic design. The contrast between large and small should be sharp and definite without overpowering the smaller elements so that they cannot contribute their share. In Figure 93, three posters from a series for Mobil Oil rely on contrast of size between elements. There are few successful designs that do not benefit from size contrast in type or in image. In layout design the contrast

93. *Diana Graham (Gips & Balkind & Assoc., Inc.). Posters for Mobil Oil. Copyright 1982 Mobil Corporation.*

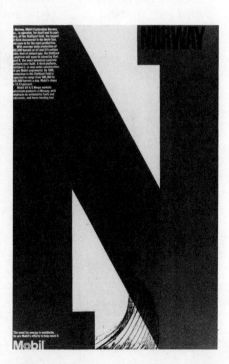

94.

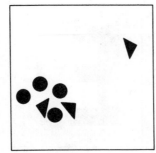

95.

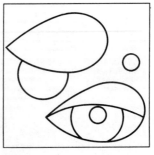

96.

97.

is often between large and small photographs and between headline and text type.

An interesting sort of size contrast is contrast in expected size. The large element is played small and vice versa, resulting in a visual double take. This surprise happens in the Mobil ad where the woman rests on a letterform.

Texture

A small, highly textured area will contrast with and balance a larger area of simple texture (Fig. 94). This rule refers to visual, not tactile texture. Contrast of texture is especially useful with text type (type smaller than 14 point, used to set the body of copy). The Mobil Oil posters (Fig. 93) provide a good example of balance between the small, busily textured block of text type and the simple texture of the larger shapes.

Isolation

A shape that appears isolated from its surroundings, will draw attention to itself more quickly and have greater visual weight than one that is surrounded by other shapes (Fig. 95).

Subject Matter

The natural interest of a subject matter will draw the viewer's eye and increase visual weight. It also can create directional movement as we move our eyes between lovers or follow the eye direction of a figure. Our eyes are drawn to the realistic representation of something that interests us (Fig. 96).

Value

Areas of high contrast have strong visual weight. A small area of deep black will contrast with and balance a larger area of gray when both are placed against a white background (Fig. 97). The creation of light and dark areas in a drawing, painting, photograph, or illustration produces a dramatic play of values that delights the eye. Figure 98 by Toulouse-Lautrec uses both value and textural contrast to this end.

Typography also uses value contrast. The contrast of a black, heavy type against a light one helps relieve boredom and makes the page more readable. Contrasts

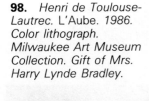

98. *Henri de Toulouse-Lautrec. L'Aube. 1986. Color lithograph. Milwaukee Art Museum Collection. Gift of Mrs. Harry Lynde Bradley.*

NOTES   from   A F A R

a friend

soon IN THE MORNING   **behind** THE   *mountains*

THE SOUND OF

h o r n s   horns   E M E R A L D S

emeralds

between headings and text matter and the white areas of paper can create three distinct weights: the black bar of the heading is played against the gray, textured rectangle of the text type, both of which contrast with the white areas of the background page. Designers will sometimes alternate boldface and regular weight type for a visual pattern. Figure 99 is an illustration based on a poem by Paul Klee; it uses many kinds of contrast to emphasize the meaning of the words.

Shape

The shape of objects generates a directional pull along the main structural lines. Complicated contours also have a greater visual weight than simple ones. Therefore a small complex shape will contrast with and balance a larger simple shape (Fig. 100). One block of type might be set in a

99. *Amy E. Arntson. Illustration based on a poem by Paul Klee.*

long, thin ragged rectangle while another is set in a large square block form. Contrast in shape also works with single letterforms. You might play the round openness of an *O* against the pointed complexities of a *W* or the shape of an uppercase *A* against a lowercase *c* (Fig. 101).

Structure

In type design structure refers to the contrasting characteristics of type families. It is a kind of contrast of shape. Compare the *G* in Helvetica with the *G* in Baskerville (Fig. 102). They are the same basic shape, but their differences are important in typography. Their structures—thick/thin, serif/sans serif—are dif-

100.

101.

102.

ferent. Fig. 103 contrasts serif and sans serif structure as well as different sizes in the word "women."

Color

The brighter and more intense the color, the heavier. A large dark blue shape will be balanced by a small bright red shape. A small, bright, intense green will contrast with and balance a large, toned-down, low intensity green. In graphic design each additional color costs money, so it must be used wisely. A second color can be used to enliven a magazine from cover to cover, or only on those pages that are cut from the same printed signature. Remember that in one-color design, that color need not be black. It can be a rich gray, a deep green, or any color you can envision.

EXERCISE 1

Do some sketches on full-sized separate sheets of paper to experiment with the statements listed below. It is a good idea to use letterforms for these sketches in order to become better acquainted with them. What design dynamics are influencing each of these situations?

A shape placed in a corner is protected by the two sides of the rectangle. Place the same shape further out into the space around it, and it seems more vulnerable.

Two shapes placed side by side will look less lonely than one.

Two shapes (an *e* or an *a* works well) placed back to back will appear uncommunicative, unfriendly.

A point placed against a soft curve will cause a sensation of discomfort. (An *A* and an *e* again work well.)

EXERCISE 2

Go through several magazines locating printed samples of the various methods of achieving balance through contrast. Save them for discussion and for your files.

PROJECT
Word Illustration

This project asks you to concentrate on placement, contrast, and isomorphic projection to create a balanced and interest-

103. *Allen Wong. (Brown Design Group, Brown University).* Women in Transition. *1984. 20 1/2″ × 9 1/2″ (52 × 24 cm).*

ing design. Figures 104 and 105 are student designs based on this project.

Choose a word to illustrate. Practice on those listed below. Then find your own word from class discussion or your own research. A dictionary can be useful. Do a minimum of 15 thumbnails. Base these thumbnails and your project upon existing type styles. Search for an appropriate one. Do not use pictures or distort your letterforms into pictures to tell your story. Let the letterforms communicate their message *visually* through size, color, value, shape, structure, texture, placement, and isomorphic projection. Tell visually what the word says intellectually. Be able to describe the tensions and balancing forces.

Execute your design on cold press illustration board so that it fits with an 11″ 14″ (28 36 cm) format. Leave 2″ (5 cm) matte around the sides. Use black ink or paint. You may also use one shade of gray if it will strengthen your design.

Objectives

Learn to make a design balance.

Explore the personalities of varying type styles.

Increase your control of media and tools and your respect for precision.

Practice Words

Black and White
Elephant
Headache
Divide
Direction
Invisible
Allover
Black and Blue
Wrong Font
Alone
Repeat

5

"GOOD" GESTALT

THE WHOLE AND THE PARTS

The Gestalt school of psychology, which began in Germany around 1912, investigated how we see and organize visual information into a meaningful whole. The conviction developed that the whole is more than the sum of its parts. This whole cannot be perceived by a simple addition of isolated parts. Each part is influenced by those around it.

WHOLE

As you read the word above, you are perceiving the whole word, not the individual letterforms that make it up. Each letter can still be examined individually, but however you add it up, the *word* is more than the sum of those separate letterforms (Fig. 106).

When you sew a shirt, you begin with pieces of fabric that are cut into parts. When the parts have been assembled, a

new thing has been created. The collar, the facing, and the sleeve still exist, but they have a new "whole" identity called a shirt.

The sixteenth-century painter Giuseppe Arcimboldo demonstrates the principle clearly in this portrait. A close examina-

106.

tion reveals the separate parts that make up this head (Fig. 107). A similar example is this contemporary alphabet made up of objects (Fig. 108).

The early Gestalt psychologists and many other researchers into visual perception have discovered that the eye seeks a unified whole or gestalt. Knowing how the eye seeks a gestalt can help you analyze and create successful designs. Knowing what connections the eye will draw for itself will help you eliminate clutter and produce a clean, clearly articulated design.

GESTALT PRINCIPLES

A designer works not simply with lines on paper, but with perceptual structure. Learn these gestalt perceptual principles so you can take advantage of the way object, eye, and graphic creation interweave.

Similarity

When we see things that are similar, we naturally group them. Grouping by similarity occurs when we see similar shape, size, color, spatial location (proximity), angle, or value. All things are similar in some respects and different in others. In a group of similar shapes and angles, we will notice a dissimilar shape or angle (Fig. 109).

Similarity is necessary before we can notice differences. In the photograph by Gordon Baer (Fig. 110), we are amused by

107. *Giuseppe Arcimboldo. Portrait. 1586. Collection Kunsthistorisches Museum, Vienna.*

108. *Julius Friedman. Logo for "Images."*

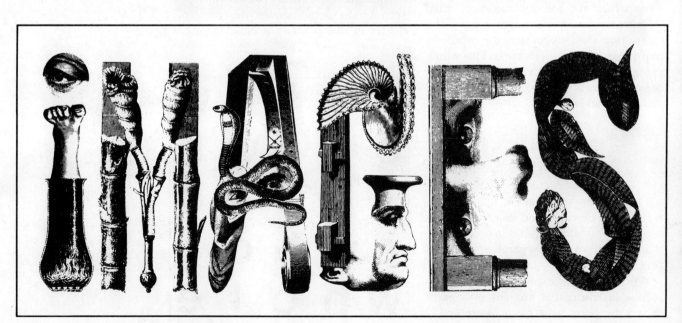

similarity

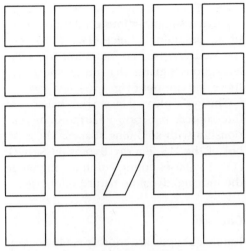

109.

110.

a similarity of sleeping forms. It is useful for the designer to know that the eye will notice and group similarities while separating differences. The symbol and logotype created for Alcoa by Saul Bass, a renowned United States designer, relies on similarity of shape (Fig. 111). How many triangles can you see? In Figure 112 the symbol for a photographer relies on

several kinds of similarity: similarity of shape, similarity of placement, and the final gestalt similarity to the diaphram of a camera shutter.

Proximity

Grouping by similarity in spatial location is called proximity, or nearness. The closer

above right: 110. *Gordon Baer, Lousville, KY. Two Old Men.*

below left: 111. *Saul Bass. Trademark for Alcoa. Courtesy, Aluminum Company of America.*

below right: 112. *Gerald Gallo (Graphics by Gallo). Personal symbol for photographer Karen Keeney.*

111.

112.

proxi mity

113.

larity of the individual parts (resembling syringes) and their close placement.

Continuation

The viewer's eye will follow a line or curve. Continuation occurs when the eye is carried smoothly into the line or curve of an adjoining object (Fig. 115). Victor Vasarely uses continuation to create ambiguous squares that mysteriously are there, yet are not (Fig. 116).

The eye is pleased by shapes that are not interrupted, but form a harmonious relationship with adjoining shapes. The symbol of the U.S. Energy Extension Service (Fig. 117) uses continuation to emphasize the moving, dynamic nature of energy.

Closure

Familiar shapes are more readily seen as complete than incomplete. When the eye completes a line or curve in order to form a familiar shape, closure has occurred (Fig. 118). This step is sometimes accompanied by a gasp, "Oh, now I see!" Figure 119 is a symbol created by the 1 + 1 Design Firm. Do you see the plus sign? Part of the closure in this example includes a sudden

114. *Robert Shelley (Partner, R.S. Jensen, Inc., Baltimore). Symbol for Industrial Medical Consultants, Inc.*

two visual elements are, the more likely it is that we will see them as a group (Fig. 113). The proximity of lines or edges makes it easier for the eye to group them to form a figure. In Figure 114, symbol for Industrial Medical Consultants, the gestalt of the cross is caused by both the simi-

115.

continuation

116.

117.

connection with the name of the firm. This sort of connection is especially useful in trademark design.

When closure happens too soon, without participation from the eye and mind of the viewer, the design can be boring.

Figure/Ground

The fundamental law of perception that makes it possible to discern objects is

118.

CLOSURE

119.

above left: 116. *Victor Vasarely. Sir Ris. 1952–62. Oil on canvas, 6′6″ × 3′3″ (1.98 × 0.99 m). Courtesy Sidney Janis Gallery, New York.*

above right: 117. *George Jadowski (Designer), Danny C. Jones (Art Director). Symbol for the U.S. Energy Extension Service.*

below right: 119. *Pat Hughes and Steve Quinn. Symbol for 1 + 1 Design Firm.*

FIGURE GROUND

120.

the figure/ground relationship. The eye and mind separate an object from its surroundings. As you read this page, your eye is separating out words (figure) from ground (paper). Many times the relationship between figure and ground is dynamic and ambiguous, offering more than one solution to the searching eye (Fig. 120).

Sometimes referred to as positive and negative space relationship, this principle is crucial to shaping a strong design. The designer must be aware of creating shapes in the "left-over" ground every time a figure is created. Figure 121 uses this fact in an entertaining way, similar to the work of M. C. Escher. Figure 122 is a poster design with two doors. Each door shapes and becomes the ground for the other.

In Figure 123, the logo for Case Equipment Company, the figure/ground relationship is so strong, one cannot be shaped without the other.

TRADEMARKS

The interplay of gestalt principles is clearest in the creation of logo and symbol trademarks. Here form and function are closely related.

Functions

Symbols and trademarks have served many functions in history. The early Christians relied on the symbol of the fish to identify themselves to one another secretly. The Dark Ages used family trademarks. No nobleman in the same region could wear the same coat of arms. These "arms" came to mark the owner's possessions, while peasants used simpler "housemarks." They were especially useful because few people could read (Figs. 124 and 125). Also, each medieval craftsman inscribed a personal mark on his products, and hung out a sign showing his calling. During the Renaissance the three golden balls of the Medici family symbolized moneylending. The Medici mark can still be seen today, pirated by modern pawnbrokers. More recently, in the western United States, each cattle rancher had a brand or mark.

Today, trademarks are most commonly used by corporations. The trademark is any unique name or symbol used to iden-

121. *Whitney Sherman (Illustrator), Martin Bennett and Mary Pat Andrea (Designers). North Charles Street Design Organization poster.*

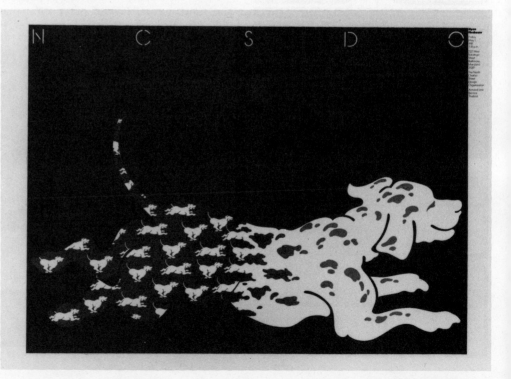

"Good" Gestalt

122. *Amy Cyra (UW–Whitewater student designer). Theater poster for University of Wisconsin-Whitewater production of Stage Door.*

tify a product and to distinguish it from others. These unique marks can be registered and protected by law. Their primary use is to increase brand recognition and advertise products.

Making "Marks"

Unlike other forms of advertising, the modern trademark is a long-term design. It may appear on letterhead, company trucks, packaging, employee uniforms, newsletters, and so on. Designers often spend months developing and testing one trademark. Only a strong design with a simple, unified gestalt will stand the test of repeated exposure.

Keep several other points in mind when developing a "mark":

1. You are not just "making your mark on the world"; you are making a mark to symbolize your client and your client's product. It must reflect the nature and quality of that product to an audience. Research the company, product, and audience. As designer Paul Rand said, "A trademark is created by a designer, but *made* by a corporation. A trademark is a picture, an image . . . of a corporation."
2. The mark is often reproduced in many different sizes, from the company vehicle to a business card. Your design must remain legible and strong in all circumstances.
3. Because this mark may be reproduced in newspaper advertising, or with severely limited in-house duplicating facilities, it must reproduce well in one color.
4. Many trademarks are seen in adverse viewing conditions, such as short exposure, poor lighting, competitive surroundings, and lack of viewer interest. Under such conditions, simplicity is a virtue. A simple, interesting shape with a good gestalt is easier to remember than a more complex design.

Some designers refer to all trademarks as "logos," whereas others have a complex system of subtle categories. The two most common categories of trademarks, however, are symbol and logo.

124.

123. *Lippincott and Margulies, Inc. Trademark for Case Equipment Company.*

Symbols

Webster's Seventh New Collegiate Dictionary says a symbol is "something that represents something else by association, resemblance, or convention, especially a material object used to represent something invisible. A printed or written sign used to represent an operation, element, quantity, quality, or relation." Historically

125.

126. *Stephan Kantscheff. Symbol for the Staatliches Operettentheater in Sofia, Bulgaria.*

below left: 127. *Michael Vanderbyl. Symbol proposed but not adopted for the California Conservation Corps.*

below right: 128. *Roger Cook and Don Shanosky (Cook and Shanosky Associates). Department of Transportation pictograms prepared by the American Institute of Graphic Arts (AIGA).*

important symbols include national flags, the cross, and the swastika.

The symbol for a company or product can be abstract or pictorial, but it does not usually include letterforms. It represents invisible qualities of a product, such as reliability, durability, strength, or warmth. Figure 126, the symbol for an opera company, appropriately juxtaposes music and the heart, using gestalt principles to make the point that they are different and yet the same.

The advantages of a symbol include:

1. Original construction.
2. Simple gestalt resulting in quick recognition.
3. A wealth of associations.

Figure 127, a symbol proposed for the California Conservation Corps, demonstrates all three qualities.

A pictogram is a symbol that is used to cross language barriers for international signage. It is found in bilingual cities such as Montreal for traffic signs. It is also found in airports and in safety instructions inside airplanes. It is pictorial rather than abstract (Fig. 128).

Logos

The second category of trademark is called logo or logotype. The logo is a unique type or lettering that spells out the name of the company or product. It may be handlettered but is usually constructed out of variations on an existing typeface. Historically, it developed after the symbol, because it requires a literate audience.

It is extremely important to choose type that suits the nature of your client and audience. A successful, unique logo is often more difficult to design than a symbol, because it entails both visual and verbal communication. Figure 129 was created for *Reader's Digest* by one of the most respected and influential logo designers, Herb Lubalin. The clean, bold type style makes it easy to see the play on similar shapes that creates the "family connection" hidden in the word. Figure 130 was created by Lubalin for *Eros* Magazine. In Greek mythology, Eros was the god of love. This type style, with the round *O* and sensual, reaching serifs, is appropriate for such a god. Figure 131 was created for Ditto Company, a duplication products manufacturer. Compare this type style with the one before. Each is distinctively suited to its use.

The advantages of a logotype include original construction and easy identification with company or product.

A combination mark is a symbol and logo used together. These marks are difficult to construct with a good gestalt because of their complexity. They are often used, however, because they combine the advantages of symbol and logo (Fig. 132).

In all these marks, gestalt principles help to create a unified and striking design. With "good" gestalt, form and function interweave in a powerful whole.

EXERCISES

1. Most designs use more than one gestalt principle. Look through this chapter and identify all the gestalt principles operating in each example.
2. Combine five copies of the triangle in Figure 133 into a star shape. Then use them to create a star in the negative area.
3. Combine four of the shapes shown in Figure 134 into a square, creating shapes in both figure and ground.
4. Combine the shapes in Figure 135 into the initials *FE,* using continuation.
5. Begin a clipbook of trademark designs that interest you. Analyze them to discover the gestalt principles operating and the appropriateness of the design to its purpose.

129. *Herb Lubalin. Trademark created for Reader's Digest. Assigned to Military Family Communication, Publisher of* Family *magazine.*

130. *Herb Lubalin. Logo for* Eros *magazine. A magazine with a graphically beautiful approach to love and sex, there were only four issues published.*

131. *Logotype for Ditto Corporation.*

MORE EXERCISES

Figures 136 and 137 are student designs based on the following series of exercises. This assignment is best done with graph paper. This process is often used to develop logo designs.

132. *Lance Wyman, Linda Iskander, and Stephen Schlott. Logotype and applications for the Minnesota Zoological Gardens.*

133.

134.

135.

1. Select a circle $1\frac{1}{2}''$ (4 cm) in diameter (or slightly more) and practice overlapping it to create new and varied shapes. Then try two and three circles. Do not use line, only shape and black and white values.
2. Place a circle in various positions within a square. Do not use line. Use black and white shapes.
3. Set up a series of vertical lines so that the white lines gradually grow small while the black lines expand. (Start by making a series of vertical lines $\frac{1}{4}''$ (5 mm) apart. Each line can then be thickened.
4. Create a break or anomaly in a series of vertical lines.
5. Combine any of these effects for a new creation.

PROJECT
Combination Mark

Design a combination mark for a company described below. You may combine logo and symbol into one image, or present them as two images, carefully placed together. Experiment with many alternatives in your thumbnail sketches. Incorporate each of the gestalt principles discussed in this chapter into your thumbnail investigation.

Begin with an existing type style and make careful alterations. Spend time looking through typebooks. Experiment with fonts, finding which are appropriate for the company you have selected. List the name of the font and the page it can be found on next to your pencil sketch.

After consultation with the instructor, select two thumbnails to enlarge to full-size roughs for final review. Execute the strongest on illustration board within an $8'' \times 10''$ (19 × 25 cm) format, leaving a 2" (5 cm) white matte around it. Use only one color. Execute in either paint, ink, or cut paper.

Keep your design visually strong and uncluttered. Be prepared to discuss the gestalt principles involved during the cri-

left: 136. *Tom Yasitis (UW–Whitewater student designer). Grid and circle variations.*

below right: 137. *Tom Yasitis (UW–Whitewater student designer). Grid variations.*

RIVE GAUCHE

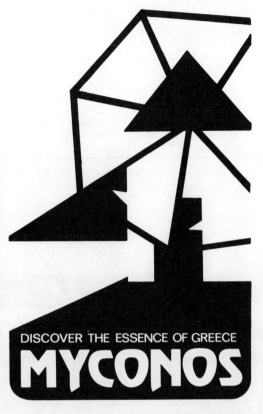

DISCOVER THE ESSENCE OF GREECE
MYCONOS

far left: 138. *Lynette Schwartz (UW–Whitewater student designer). Combination mark for a "Yuppie" men's clothing store.*

near left: 139. *Sophia Asimomitis (UW–Whitewater student designer). Combination mark for a Greek vacation spot.*

tique. Use at least two of them in your final trademark. Also consider the audience your trademark will be reaching. What will appeal to them? Consider the company. What will be an accurate and positive image? Be prepared to discuss the function of your trademark and why the design suits it.

Figures 138 and 139 are student designs created for a similar project.

Companies

Manard
A national heavy equipment manufacturer, specializing in tractors, end loaders, and so on.

Antique Oak
A trendy eatery located on Chicago's North Side, catering to young professionals.

Aurora
Manufacturer for retail sales of hiking clothing, tents, and camping equipment.

Quadrata
An interior design firm specializing in corporate accounts.

Objectives

Communicate the nature of a company with a design that appeals to a particular audience.
Apply gestalt principles to develop a trademark that is more than the sum of its parts.

Variations. Let your instructor invent new corporations, or assign existing ones that need a new trademark design.

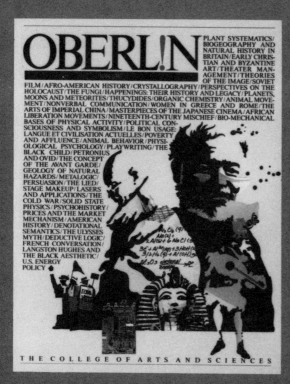

OBERL!N

PLANT SYSTEMATICS/ BIOGEOGRAPHY AND NATURAL HISTORY IN BRITAIN/EARLY CHRISTIAN AND BYZANTINE ART/THEATER MANAGEMENT/THEORIES OF THE IMAGE/SOVIET FILM/AFRO-AMERICAN HISTORY/CRYSTALLOGRAPHY/PERSPECTIVES ON THE HOLOCAUST/THE FUNGI/HAPPENINGS: THEIR HISTORY AND LEGACY/PLANETS, MOONS AND METEORITES/THUCYDIDES/ORGANIC CHEMISTRY/ANIMAL MOVEMENT/NONVERBAL COMMUNICATION/WOMEN IN GREECE AND ROME/THE ARTS OF IMPERIAL CHINA/MASTERPIECES OF THE JAPANESE CINEMA/AFRICAN LIBERATION MOVEMENTS/NINETEENTH-CENTURY MISCHIEF/BIO-MECHANICAL BASES OF PHYSICAL ACTIVITY/POLITICAL CONSCIOUSNESS AND SYMBOLISM/LE BON USAGE: LANGUE ET CIVILISATION ACTUELLES/POVERTY AND AFFLUENCE/ANIMAL BEHAVIOR/PHYSIOLOGICAL PSYCHOLOGY/PLAYWRITING/THE BLACK CHILD/PETRONIUS AND OVID/THE CONCEPT OF THE AVANT GARDE/GEOLOGY OF NATURAL HAZARDS/METALOGIC/PERSUASION/THE LIED/STAGE MAKEUP/LASERS AND APPLICATIONS/THE COLD WAR/SOLID STATE PHYSICS/PSYCHOHISTORY/PRICES AND THE MARKET MECHANISM/AMERICAN HISTORY/DENOTATIONAL SEMANTICS/THE ULYSSES MYTH/DEDUCTIVE LOGIC/FRENCH CONVERSATION/LANGSTON HUGHES AND THE BLACK AESTHETIC/U.S. ENERGY POLICY

THE COLLEGE OF ARTS AND SCIENCES

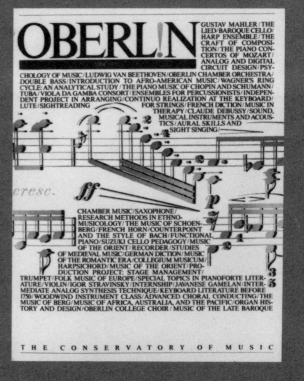

OBERL!N

GUSTAV MAHLER/THE LIED/BAROQUE CELLO/HARP ENSEMBLE/THE CRAFT OF COMPOSITION/THE PIANO CONCERTOS OF MOZART/ANALOG AND DIGITAL CIRCUIT DESIGN/PSYCHOLOGY OF MUSIC/LUDWIG VAN BEETHOVEN/OBERLIN CHAMBER ORCHESTRA/DOUBLE BASS/INTRODUCTION TO AFRO-AMERICAN MUSIC/WAGNER'S RING CYCLE: AN ANALYTICAL STUDY/THE PIANO MUSIC OF CHOPIN AND SCHUMANN/TUBA/VIOLA DA GAMBA CONSORT/ENSEMBLES FOR PERCUSSIONISTS/INDEPENDENT PROJECT IN ARRANGING/CONTINUO REALIZATION AT THE KEYBOARD/LUTE/SIGHTREADING FOR STRINGS/FRENCH DICTION/MUSIC IN THERAPY/CLAUDE DEBUSSY/SOUND, MUSICAL INSTRUMENTS AND ACOUSTICS/AURAL SKILLS AND SIGHT SINGING/CHAMBER MUSIC/SAXOPHONE/RESEARCH METHODS IN ETHNOMUSICOLOGY/THE MUSIC OF SCHOENBERG/FRENCH HORN/COUNTERPOINT AND THE STYLE OF BACH/FUNCTIONAL PIANO/SUZUKI CELLO PEDAGOGY/MUSIC OF THE ORIENT/RECORDER/STUDIES OF MEDIEVAL MUSIC/GERMAN DICTION/MUSIC OF THE ROMANTIC ERA/COLLEGIUM MUSICUM/HARPSICHORD/MUSIC OF THE ORIENT/PRODUCTION PROJECT: STAGE MANAGEMENT/TRUMPET/FOLK MUSIC OF EUROPE/SPECIAL TOPICS IN PIANOFORTE LITERATURE/VIOLIN/IGOR STRAVINSKY/INTERNSHIP/JAVANESE GAMELAN/INTERMEDIATE ANALOG SYNTHESIS TECHNIQUE/KEYBOARD LITERATURE BEFORE 1750/WOODWIND INSTRUMENT CLASS/ADVANCED CHORAL CONDUCTING/THE MUSIC OF BERG/MUSIC OF AFRICA, AUSTRALIA, AND THE PACIFIC/ORGAN HISTORY AND DESIGN/OBERLIN COLLEGE CHOIR/MUSIC OF THE LATE BAROQUE

THE CONSERVATORY OF MUSIC

6

USING TEXT TYPE

THE DEVELOPMENT OF WRITTEN COMMUNICATION

Since the first person made a mark in the sand for another to find, we have been communicating with a visual language. The earliest forms of visual communication were pictorial drawings of everyday objects, such as weapons and animals. As the desire to communicate grew, these pictures were combined to convey thoughts and ideas.

With visual language, it became possible to "conquer" time. An individual's mark could be seen and understood after the maker had moved on or even died. Civilization developed along with our visual record of the spoken language. So did the importance of the individual.

Alphabets

The first systematized alphabet was created by the Egyptians. It was partly abstract symbols and partly pictures. The Phoenicians added consonants around 1600 B.C. A nation of merchants, they needed an efficient, condensed language for business transactions. This need led to a significant breakthrough: Symbols were used to represent not objects, but the sounds of speech. A different symbol stood for each recognizable spoken sound. It was a much shorter and more efficient system of written language.

The Greeks adapted the Phoenician system, and around 1000 B.C. the Romans modified the Greek alphabet. Our alphabet is derived from the Roman. They devised a total of 23 letters. The letter *J* was added to our alphabet only 500 years ago (Fig. 140).

As designers working with the letters of the alphabet, we have thousands of years of history behind us. The shape of letters has been largely determined by the tools used to create them. The Egyptians used reeds for writing on papyrus. This method created a pattern of thick and thin strokes. The Greeks used a stylus on tablets, whereas important Roman inscriptions were chiseled into stone. These forms developed with few curved lines, because curves were difficult to carve. The Greek and Egyptian alphabets had no serifs. They evolved with the Roman alphabet, perhaps to make inscriptions seem to sit better optically when chiseled in stone. Medieval handwritten scrolls kept the alphabet alive during the Middle Ages. These scrolls gradually evolved into folded manuscript books, produced by religious orders. Our most common typefaces are imitations of early handwriting or modifications of early typefaces modeled after the lettering in manuscript books. From the invention of the first printing press in 1440 until the eighteenth century, type designs were based on handwriting. The rounded style favored by Renaissance artists is the inspiration for our modern roman style. Computers now make it possible to develop variations on existing styles quickly. Specialized software makes the creation of new styles simpler and more accessible than ever before. Whatever tools are used, the eye of the designer remains the most important factor.

Type Styles

Like the alphabet, type has undergone a long development. A brief look at its history will help you assemble types with similar attributes. History provides a key to proper use.

The type category we refer to as *old style* was created in 1470 by Nicholas Jenson, a Venetian printer. The French typographer Claude Garamond built his type style "Garamond" on Jenson's design. It remains a classic, in use today. A modern revival of fifteenth-century Italian types occurred in Europe and the United States around 1890. Englishman William Morris produced a type called "Golden" that recalled the spirit of the fifteenth century. (See Fig. 15.)

Most roman types have a variation available called italics. They are a slanted form that relates to the original type style but does not duplicate it. Venetian printer Aldus Manutius is credited with developing italics in 1501 as a method of fitting more characters on a line to save space. For about 40 years italic was simply another style of type, until an italic was consciously developed from an upright roman mold. Today most roman types have "matching" italics as well as several other variations.

Today's roman faces, with strong contrast between thick and thin strokes and with thin serifs, were developed in the eighteenth century. These faces are generally classified as *transitional.* They were more precise because they were designed for the printing industry. A widespread

140. *The Phoenician, Greek, and Roman alphabets.*

1. Phoenician alphabet

2. Greek alphabet

3. Roman alphabet

Using Text Type

**THE MAGIC
MOUNTAIN
1 9 2 4**

CHAPTER 1

ARRIVAL.

THOMAS

An unassuming young man was travelling, in mid-summer, from his native city of Hamburg to Davos-Platz in the Canton of the Grisons, on a three weeks' visit.

From Hamburg to Davos is a long journey—too long, indeed, for so brief a stay. It crosses all sorts of country; goes up hill and down dale, descends from the plateau of Southern Germany to the shore of Lake Constance, over its bounding waves and on across marshes once thought to be bottomless.

MANN

141. *Paula Scher. Layout design for* The Magic Mountain *in "Great Beginnings" brochure.*

interest in copperplate engraving at that time helped the development of types with a very fine line. Bodoni and Didot imitated the engraver's tool with precise hairline strokes. The term "Modern" is used to describe eighteenth-century type, confusing many a student.

In the nineteenth century, many new faces were developed, with a wide variety of looks. The sans serifs and the Egyptians are among them. A revival of the old classic typefaces such as Jenson occurred at this time. Printers such as Ben Franklin and William Morris contributed to the history of typography during this time, creating some handsome typefaces.

Since the early nineteenth century, serif and sans serif types have alternated in popularity. There was a great interest in sans serif in the mid-twentieth century. Bauhaus designers in Germany during the 1920s began designing sans serif faces such as Futura. In the 1950s Helvetica became the dominant typeface used by design professionals. Its dominance lasted over a decade, due to a clean precision and understated elegance of line. The horizontals are cut along a common line. Univers and Folio are sans serif type styles developed during this period. Figure 141 is a layout design by Paula Scher that uses sans serif type creatively.

TYPE CATEGORIES

Old Style

Characteristics of old style faces (Fig. 142) include thick and thin stroke serifs that seem to merge into the main strokes. This feature is called bracketing. Garamond and Caslon are examples. Garamond was originally credited to Claude Garamond who died in 1561. It was recently discovered that Jean Jannon, a French printer, designed this face based on Claude Garamond's work. Created in 1617, it was the first typeface designed to appear uni-

142a. *Garamond Book, a revised old style face. (See p. 73 for Fig. 142b., Garamond in different point settings.)*

ITC Garamond Book

abcdefghijklmn
opqrstuvwxyz
ABCDEFGHIJK
LMNOPQRSTU
VWXYZ$12344
567890(.,""''-;:!)?&

143a. *Baskerville, a transitional face. (See p. 74 for Fig. 143b., Baskerville in different point settings.)*

Baskerville

abcdefghijklmnop
qrstuvwxyzAB
CDEFGHIJKLM
NOPQRSTUV
WXYZ$1234567
890(.,""''-;:!)?&

Garamond Book

Since the first person made a mark in the sand for another to find, we have been communicating with a visual language. The earliest forms of visual communication were pictorial drawings of everyday objects such as weapons and animals. As the desire to communicate grew, these pictures were combined to convey thoughts and ideas. With visual language, it became possible to "conquer" time. An individual's mark could be seen and understood after the maker had moved or even died. Civilization developed along with our visual record of the spoken language. So did the importance of the individual.

8/9

Since the first person made a mark in the sand for another to find, we have been communicating with a visual language. The earliest forms of visual communication were pictorial drawings of everyday objects such as weapons and animals. As the desire to communicate grew, these pictures were combined to convey thoughts and ideas. With visual language, it became possible to "conquer" time. An individual's mark could be seen and understood after the maker had moved or even died. Civilization developed along with our visual record of the spoken language. So

8/10

Since the first person made a mark in the sand for another to find, we have been communicating with a visual language. The earliest forms of visual communication were pictorial drawings of everyday objects such as weapons and animals. As the desire to communicate grew, these pictures were combined to convey thoughts and ideas. With visual language, it became possible to "conquer" time. An individual's mark could be seen and understood after the maker had moved or even died. Civilization de-

8/11

Since the first person made a mark in the sand for another to find, we have been communicating with a visual language. The earliest forms of visual communication were pictorial drawings of everyday objects such as weapons and animals. As the desire to communicate grew, these pictures were combined to convey thoughts and ideas. With visual language, it became possible to "conquer" time. An individual's mark could be seen and understood after the maker had moved or even died. Civilization de-

9/10

Since the first person made a mark in the sand for another to find, we have been communicating with a visual language. The earliest forms of visual communication were pictorial drawings of everyday objects such as weapons and animals. As the desire to communicate grew, these pictures were combined to convey thoughts and ideas. With visual language, it became possible to "conquer" time. An individual's mark could be seen and understood

9/11

Since the first person made a mark in the sand for another to find, we have been communicating with a visual language. The earliest forms of visual communication were pictorial drawings of everyday objects such as weapons and animals. As the desire to communicate grew, these pictures were combined to convey thoughts and ideas. With visual language, it became possible to "conquer"

9/12

Since the first person made a mark in the sand for another to find, we have been communicating with a visual language. The earliest forms of visual communication were pictorial drawings of everyday objects such as weapons and animals. As the desire to communicate grew, these pictures were combined to convey thoughts and ideas. With visual language, it became possible to "conquer" time. An individu-

10/11

Since the first person made a mark in the sand for another to find, we have been communicating with a visual language. The earliest forms of visual communication were pictorial drawings of everyday objects such as weapons and animals. As the desire to communicate grew, these pictures were combined to convey thoughts and ideas. With visual language,

10/12

Since the first person made a mark in the sand for another to find, we have been communicating with a visual language. The earliest forms of visual communication were pictorial drawings of everyday objects such as weapons and animals. As the desire to communicate grew, these pictures were combined to convey thoughts and ideas. With visual language,

10/13

Since the first person made a mark in the sand for another to find, we have been communicating with a visual language. The earliest forms of visual communication were pictorial drawings of everyday objects such as weapons and animals. As the desire to communicate grew, these pictures were

12/13

142b.

Baskerville

Since the first person made a mark in the sand for another to find, we have been communicating with a visual language. The earliest forms of visual communication were pictorial drawings of everyday objects such as weapons and animals. As the desire to communicate grew, these pictures were combined to convey thoughts and ideas. With visual language, it became possible to "conquer" time. An individual's mark could be seen and understood after the maker had moved or even died. Civilization developed along with our visual record of the spoken language. So did the importance of the individual.

8/9

Since the first person made a mark in the sand for another to find, we have been communicating with a visual language. The earliest forms of visual communication were pictorial drawings of everyday objects such as weapons and animals. As the desire to communicate grew, these pictures were combined to convey thoughts and ideas. With visual language, it became possible to "conquer" time. An individual's mark could be seen and understood after the maker had moved or even died. Civilization developed along with our visual record of the spoken

8/10

Since the first person made a mark in the sand for another to find, we have been communicating with a visual language. The earliest forms of visual communication were pictorial drawings of everyday objects such as weapons and animals. As the desire to communicate grew, these pictures were combined to convey thoughts and ideas. With visual language, it became possible to "conquer" time. An individual's mark could be seen and understood after the maker had moved or even died. Civili-

8/11

Since the first person made a mark in the sand for another to find, we have been communicating with a visual language. The earliest forms of visual communication were pictorial drawings of everyday objects such as weapons and animals. As the desire to communicate grew, these pictures were combined to convey thoughts and ideas. With visual language, it became possible to "conquer" time. An individual's mark could be seen and understood after the maker had moved or even died.

9/10

Since the first person made a mark in the sand for another to find, we have been communicating with a visual language. The earliest forms of visual communication were pictorial drawings of everyday objects such as weapons and animals. As the desire to communicate grew, these pictures were combined to convey thoughts and ideas. With visual language, it became possible to "conquer" time. An individual's mark could be seen and

9/11

Since the first person made a mark in the sand for another to find, we have been communicating with a visual language. The earliest forms of visual communication were pictorial drawings of everyday objects such as weapons and animals. As the desire to communicate grew, these pictures were combined to convey thoughts and ideas. With visual language, it became possible to

9/12

Since the first person made a mark in the sand for another to find, we have been communicating with a visual language. The earliest forms of visual communication were pictorial drawings of everyday objects such as weapons and animals. As the desire to communicate grew, these pictures were combined to convey thoughts and ideas. With visual language, it became possible to "con-

10/11

Since the first person made a mark in the sand for another to find, we have been communicating with a visual language. The earliest forms of visual communication were pictorial drawings of everyday objects such as weapons and animals. As the desire to communicate grew, these pictures were combined to convey thoughts and ideas.

10/12

Since the first person made a mark in the sand for another to find, we have been communicating with a visual language. The earliest forms of visual communication were pictorial drawings of everyday objects such as weapons and animals. As the desire to communicate grew, these pictures were combined to convey thoughts and ideas.

10/13

Since the first person made a mark in the sand for another to find, we have been communicating with a visual language. The earliest forms of visual communication were pictorial drawings of everyday objects such as weapons and animals. As the desire to communicate grew,

12/13

143b.

abcdefghijklmnopq
rstuvwxyzABCDEFG
HIJKLMNOPQRST
UVWXYZ$12345678
90(.,"""''-;:!)?&

144a. *Bodoni, a modern face. (See p. 76 for Fig. 144b., Bodoni in different point settings.)*

abcdeefghijkl
mnopqrstuvwx
yzABCDEFGHI
JKLMNOPQRST
UVWXYZ$123
4567890(.,""-,;!)?&

145a. *Lubalin Graph, an "Egyptian" slab-serif face. (See p. 77 for Fig. 145b., Lubalin Graph in different point settings.)*

Bodoni

Since the first person made a mark in the sand for another to find, we have been communicating with a visual language. The earliest forms of visual communication were pictorial drawings of everyday objects such as weapons and animals. As the desire to communicate grew, these pictures were combined to convey thoughts and ideas. With visual language, it became possible to "conquer" time. An individual's mark could be seen and understood after the maker had moved or even died. Civilization developed along with our visual record of the spoken language. So did the importance of the individual.

8/9

Since the first person made a mark in the sand for another to find, we have been communicating with a visual language. The earliest forms of visual communication were pictorial drawings of everyday objects such as weapons and animals. As the desire to communicate grew, these pictures were combined to convey thoughts and ideas. With visual language, it became possible to "conquer" time. An individual's mark could be seen and understood after the maker had moved or even died. Civilization developed along with our visual record of the spoken language. So did the impor-

8/10

Since the first person made a mark in the sand for another to find, we have been communicating with a visual language. The earliest forms of visual communication were pictorial drawings of everyday objects such as weapons and animals. As the desire to communicate grew, these pictures were combined to convey thoughts and ideas. With visual language, it became possible to "conquer" time. An individual's mark could be seen and understood after the maker had moved or even died. Civilization developed along

8/11

Since the first person made a mark in the sand for another to find, we have been communicating with a visual language. The earliest forms of visual communication were pictorial drawings of everyday objects such as weapons and animals. As the desire to communicate grew, these pictures were combined to convey thoughts and ideas. With visual language, it became possible to "conquer" time. An individual's mark could be seen and understood after the maker had moved or even died. Civilization developed

9/10

Since the first person made a mark in the sand for another to find, we have been communicating with a visual language. The earliest forms of visual communication were pictorial drawings of everyday objects such as weapons and animals. As the desire to communicate grew, these pictures were combined to convey thoughts and ideas. With visual language, it became possible to "conquer" time. An individual's mark could be seen and understood after the

9/11

Since the first person made a mark in the sand for another to find, we have been communicating with a visual language. The earliest forms of visual communication were pictorial drawings of everyday objects such as weapons and animals. As the desire to communicate grew, these pictures were combined to convey thoughts and ideas. With visual language, it became possible to "conquer" time. An

9/12

Since the first person made a mark in the sand for another to find, we have been communicating with a visual language. The earliest forms of visual communication were pictorial drawings of everyday objects such as weapons and animals. As the desire to communicate grew, these pictures were combined to convey thoughts and ideas. With visual language, it became possible to "conquer" time. An individual's

10/11

Since the first person made a mark in the sand for another to find, we have been communicating with a visual language. The earliest forms of visual communication were pictorial drawings of everyday objects such as weapons and animals. As the desire to communicate grew, these pictures were combined to convey thoughts and ideas. With visual language, it

10/12

Since the first person made a mark in the sand for another to find, we have been communicating with a visual language. The earliest forms of visual communication were pictorial drawings of everyday objects such as weapons and animals. As the desire to communicate grew, these pictures were combined to convey thoughts and ideas. With visual language, it

10/13

Since the first person made a mark in the sand for another to find, we have been communicating with a visual language. The earliest forms of visual communication were pictorial drawings of everyday objects such as weapons and animals. As the desire to communicate grew, these pictures were

12/13

144b.

ITC Lubalin Graph Book

Since the first person made a mark in the sand for another to find, we have been communicating with a visual language. The earliest forms of visual communication were pictorial drawings of everyday objects such as weapons and animals. As the desire to communicate grew, these pictures were combined to convey thoughts and ideas. With visual language, it became possible to "conquer" time. An individual's mark could be seen and understood after the maker had moved or even died. Civilization developed along with our visual record of the spoken language. So did the importance of the individual.

8/9

Since the first person made a mark in the sand for another to find, we have been communicating with a visual language. The earliest forms of visual communication were pictorial drawings of everyday objects such as weapons and animals. As the desire to communicate grew, these pictures were combined to convey thoughts and ideas. With visual language, it became possible to "conquer" time. An individual's mark could be seen and understood after the maker had moved or even died. Civilization de-

8/10

Since the first person made a mark in the sand for another to find, we have been communicating with a visual language. The earliest forms of visual communication were pictorial drawings of everyday objects such as weapons and animals. As the desire to communicate grew, these pictures were combined to convey thoughts and ideas. With visual language, it became possible to "conquer" time. An individual's mark could be seen and understood

8/11

Since the first person made a mark in the sand for another to find, we have been communicating with a visual language. The earliest forms of visual communication were pictorial drawings of everyday objects such as weapons and animals. As the desire to communicate grew, these pictures were combined to convey thoughts and ideas. With visual language, it became possible to "conquer" time. An individual's mark could be seen and understood after the

9/10

Since the first person made a mark in the sand for another to find, we have been communicating with a visual language. The earliest forms of visual communication were pictorial drawings of everyday objects such as weapons and animals. As the desire to communicate grew, these pictures were combined to convey thoughts and ideas. With visual language, it became possible to "conquer" time. An individu-

9/11

Since the first person made a mark in the sand for another to find, we have been communicating with a visual language. The earliest forms of visual communication were pictorial drawings of everyday objects such as weapons and animals. As the desire to communicate grew, these pictures were combined to convey thoughts and ideas. With visual language, it became possible to "conquer" time. An individu-

9/12

Since the first person made a mark in the sand for another to find, we have been communicating with a visual language. The earliest forms of visual communication were pictorial drawings of everyday objects such as weapons and animals. As the desire to communicate grew, these pictures were combined to convey

10/11

Since the first person made a mark in the sand for another to find, we have been communicating with a visual language. The earliest forms of visual communication were pictorial drawings of everyday objects such as weapons and animals. As the desire to communicate grew, these pictures were combined to convey

10/12

Since the first person made a mark in the sand for another to find, we have been communicating with a visual language. The earliest forms of visual communication were pictorial drawings of everyday objects such as weapons and animals. As the desire to communicate grew, these pictures were combined to convey

10/13

Since the first person made a mark in the sand for another to find, we have been communicating with a visual language. The earliest forms of visual communication were pictorial drawings of everyday objects such as weapons and animals. As the desire to com-

12/13

145b.

ABCDEFGHIJKL MNOPQRSTUV WXYZ&abcdefg hijklmnopqrstuvw xyz1234567890 $.,"-:;!?

146a. *Helvetica, a sans serif face. (See p. 79 for Fig. 146b., Helvetica in different point settings.)*

Helvetica

Since the first person made a mark in the sand for another to find, we have been communicating with a visual language. The earliest forms of visual communication were pictorial drawings of everyday objects such as weapons and animals. As the desire to communicate grew, these pictures were combined to convey thoughts and ideas. With visual language, it became possible to "conquer" time. An individual's mark could be seen and understood after the maker had moved or even died. Civilization developed along with our visual record of the spoken language. So did the importance of the individual.

8/9

Since the first person made a mark in the sand for another to find, we have been communicating with a visual language. The earliest forms of visual communication were pictorial drawings of everyday objects such as weapons and animals. As the desire to communicate grew, these pictures were combined to convey thoughts and ideas. With visual language, it became possible to "conquer" time. An individual's mark could be seen and understood after the maker had moved or even died. Civilization developed along with our visual record of the spoken

8/10

Since the first person made a mark in the sand for another to find, we have been communicating with a visual language. The earliest forms of visual communication were pictorial drawings of everyday objects such as weapons and animals. As the desire to communicate grew, these pictures were combined to convey thoughts and ideas. With visual language, it became possible to "conquer" time. An individual's mark could be seen and understood after the maker had moved or even died. Civi-

8/11

Since the first person made a mark in the sand for another to find, we have been communicating with a visual language. The earliest forms of visual communication were pictorial drawings of everyday objects such as weapons and animals. As the desire to communicate grew, these pictures were combined to convey thoughts and ideas. With visual language, it became possible to "conquer" time. An individual's mark could be seen and understood after the maker had moved or even died.

9/10

Since the first person made a mark in the sand for another to find, we have been communicating with a visual language. The earliest forms of visual communication were pictorial drawings of everyday objects such as weapons and animals. As the desire to communicate grew, these pictures were combined to convey thoughts and ideas. With visual language, it became possible to "conquer" time. An individual's mark could be seen and

9/11

Since the first person made a mark in the sand for another to find, we have been communicating with a visual language. The earliest forms of visual communication were pictorial drawings of everyday objects such as weapons and animals. As the desire to communicate grew, these pictures were combined to convey thoughts and ideas. With visual language, it became possible to

9/12

Since the first person made a mark in the sand for another to find, we have been communicating with a visual language. The earliest forms of visual communication were pictorial drawings of everyday objects such as weapons and animals. As the desire to communicate grew, these pictures were combined to convey thoughts and ideas. With visual

10/11

Since the first person made a mark in the sand for another to find, we have been communicating with a visual language. The earliest forms of visual communication were pictorial drawings of everyday objects such as weapons and animals. As the desire to communicate grew, these pictures were combined to convey thoughts and ideas. With visual

10/12

Since the first person made a mark in the sand for another to find, we have been communicating with a visual language. The earliest forms of visual communication were pictorial drawings of everyday objects such as weapons and animals. As the desire to communicate grew, these pictures were combined to convey thoughts and ideas. With visual

10/13

Since the first person made a mark in the sand for another to find, we have been communicating with a visual language. The earliest forms of visual communication were pictorial drawings of everyday objects such as weapons and animals. As the desire to communicate grew, these

12/13

146b.

formly "printed" rather than hand-lettered. It remained the principal type for over 200 years, with many derivatives.

Transitional

A blending of old style and modern, the transitional has emphasis on thicks and thins and gracefully bracketed serifs (Fig. 143). It is lighter than old style and has a more precise, controlled character. It is less mechanical and upright, however, than the modern faces.

Baskerville was designed in 1757 by John Baskerville, an amateur printer. The transitional Baskerville has straighter and more mechanical lines than the old style typefaces, with flatter serifs that come to a fine tip. Increased contrast between the thick and thin strokes of the letterforms and the rounded brackets give it more delicacy than old style faces such as Caslon.

John Baskerville introduced several technical innovations that affected the appearance of his type. He began passing printed sheets through heated copper cylinders to smooth out the rough texture of the paper then in use. This smooth surface made it possible to reproduce delicate serifs clearly.

Modern

The modern styles evolved from transitional types. They have still greater variation between thicks and thins. Modern typefaces are characterized by thin serifs that join the body with a stiff unbracketed corner. There is strong vertical stress to the letters. The serifs are hairline thin.

Bodoni (Fig. 144) is the best known of this category. It was created in the late 1700s by Firmin Didot, a Frenchman who also gave Europe a fully developed type measurement system. It is sometimes attributed to Giambattista Bodoni, an Italian typographer.

Egyptian

The first slab-serif type style was introduced in 1815. The category was dubbed

"Egyptian" because Egyptian artifacts and Egyptian travel were in vogue. Napoleon's conquest of Egypt aroused great enthusiasm for that country. During this period type design became less predictable and more eclectic. The characteristics were mixed and recombined, producing many variations. The heavy square serifs in this category often match the strokes in thickness. There is less difference between thicks and thins than in the modern and transitional periods. Clarendon and Century are examples of this group.

The popularity of square slab-serif type decreased greatly in this early twentieth century. There was a revival of interest around 1955. Lubalin Graph (Fig. 145), designed in 1974 by Herb Lubalin, Tony Di Spigna, and Joe Sundwall, has the characteristics of Egyptian type styles.

Sans Serif

In the fifties the available type styles were analyzed and found wanting. Weight changes were not subtle enough, and the various weights and widths in a type family often lacked coherency. This disorder was natural, because they were often designed by different people. A young Swiss type designer named Adrian Frutiger developed a sans serif style called Univers. He created a complete family of types in all possible weights and widths.

Several classic sans serif typefaces were designed at the German Bauhaus (see Chapter 2). Influenced by the Bauhaus, the Swiss firm "Haas" worked with the German "Stempel" foundry to produce Helvetica (Fig. 146). It is still considered by many designers to be the perfect type—versatile, legible, and elegant.

Miscellaneous Faces

Many type styles do not seem to belong to any category. They are often experimental, ornamental styles of limited application. These eccentric types are almost never suitable for text type, but do sometimes find appropriate usage in display headings (Fig. 147).

147. "Abramesque," an ornate, experimental type style.

American typewriter light	Benguiat medium cond	Beton light	ITC Bookman light italic
ABCDEFGHIJ KLMNOPQRR STUVWXYZØ abcdeefghijkl mnopqrstuv?! wxyzæœø12 34567890£¢$	ABCDEFGHIJKL" MNOPQRSTUVW XYZÆŒÇØabcd efghijklmnopqrs tuvwxyzæœçø1 234567890ß£$¢ ?!&%§()/«--~~⌐•''/*:;	ABCDEFGHIJKL MNOPQRSTUV WXYZabcdefghi jklmnopqrstuvwx yz1234567890 Æ ŒÇØæœçøß £$ ¢&%?!()«»/*;~⌐•~	ABCDEFGHIJKLMNO PQRSTUVWXYZ AB ABCDEFGHIJJK LMNOPQRR STU VVWWWXYZÇTh ÆŒØabcdefghijklm nopqrstuvwxyze-fific fihK mno·pqr·ræœø ß12345678901234567 890£$¢&%?!§@#![(⁖⁖;⁖/)]
American typewriter med	Benguiat medium cond	Beton bold	Bookman
ABCDEFGHIJ! KLMNOPQRŒ STUVWXYZ Ø ÆÇabcdefghij klmnopqrstu? vwxyzæœçøß 1234567890£ $¢&%§(«»:;-⁖*/)	ABCDEFGHIJKL MNOPQRSTUV*;; WXYZ ÆŒÇØ ab cdefghijklmnop» qrstuvwxyz æœ çø1234567890ß £$¢?!&%§()/«--~~	ABCDEFGHIJK LMNOPQRST() UVWXYZabcd efghijklmnopq, rstuvwxyz1234! 567890ÆŒÇØ? æœçøß£$¢&%.	AA ABBCDDEF EFGHIIJJKK L LMM NNOPQR PRSTU UVV WX WXYYZÆabcde fghijklmnopqrr˘stu vwxyy˘zæœøç1234 567890ÆŒØÇB&! ?@ᴤ$(⁖/⁖.⁖)
American typewriter bold	Benguiat bold cond	Beton extra bold	Bookman italic
ABCDEFGHI JKLMNOPQ RSTUVWX? YZ!abcdeefg hijklmnopq rstuvwxyzl 234567890˘⁖*	ABCDEFGHIJKL" MNOPQRSTUVW XYZÆŒÇØ abcd efghijklmnopqr stuvwxyzæœçø* 1234567890 ß£$ ¢?!&%§()/«--~~⌐•''/	ABCDEFGHIJ KLMNOPQR STUVWXYZ? abcdefghijkm lnopqrstuvwx yzæœçø:1234 567890ÆŒØ! £$¢%&ß(ᾱᾶ⁚÷;)	AAA ABBCCD DEEFFGGHII HJJKKKLLMM MNNNOPQR PRRR SSTTU! UVVWWXYZa bcdefghhijkklmnn opqrr˘ß Stuvww˘xy˘z 1234567890&ThCB⁚⁖

148a.

It is possible to use specialized, ornate styles in display headlines and not hamper readability much. In large amounts of body copy, however, every subtle variation has a cumulative effect that can seriously hinder readability. A classic, all-purpose type style will remain legible and unobtrusive as body type. Selecting an appropriate, legible text type calls for a sensitive, educated eye. Figure 148 shows a few of the all-purpose styles.

TYPE FAMILIES

The five categories of type we have discussed are filled with type families, such as Bodoni and Baskerville. Each family comes in a variety of weights and sizes. A family is all the variations of a particular typeface. Helvetica, for example, now comes in a series of variations described as light condensed, medium condensed, bold condensed, ultra light, ultra light condensed,

148. *Some good type styles for body copy as well as display type (continues on pp. 82–83).*

Caslon antiqua medium	Cheltenham book	Futura light	Futura extra bold
ABCDEFGHI JKLMNOPQ RSTUVWX YZabcdefghijk lmnopqrstuvw xyz123456789 0&ß?!%$£(ⁿ⁰«÷+)	ABCDEFGHIJ KLMNOPQRS TUVWXYZ a bcdefghijklmn opqrstuvwxy zæl234567890 ŒØ&ß$£¢%‿	ABCDEFGHIJKL! MNOPQRSTUV WXYZÆŒÇØ abcdefghijklmno pqrstuvwxyzæ? œçø 12345678 90ß£$¢&%()«»;;	ABCDEFGHIJK LMNOPQRST¢ UVWXYZ ÆŒ ÇØabcdefghij! klmnopqrstuv wxyzæœçøß1 234567890£ $&%?(«».;; -*)
Caslon italic	Cheltenham book italic	Futura medium	Futura extra bold italic
ABCDEFGHI JKLMNOPQR STUVWXYZ Œabcdefghijkln mopqrstuvwxyz 1234567890Æ? &%ß$£¢!O(*⁑*)	ABCDEFGHIJ KLMNOPQRS TUVWXYZŒ abcdefghijklm nopqrstuvwxy zæl234567890 ØÆ&ß$£¢%?!	ABCDEFGHIJK LMNOPQRSTU VWXYZ abcde fghijklmnopqrst uvwxyzø12345 67890ŒÆØ& %ß?!£$(ⁿⁿⁿ/:«»)	ABCDEFGHIJK LMNOPQRSÆ TUVWXYZŒÇ Øabcdefghijk lmnopqrstuv? wxyzæœçøß1 234567890$ £&%!(«».,; -*)
Caslon modern	Cheltenham ultra	Futura demi bold	Futura extra
ABCDEFGH IJKLMNOPQ RSTUVWXZ Yabcdefghijkl mnopqrstuvw xyzœæøçl234 567890ÆŒß &%$£?!O(*⁑*)	ABCDEFGHI JKLMNOPQ RSTUVWXY Zabcdefghij klmnopqrst uvwxyz1234 567890ŒØ&	ABCDEFGHIJK LMNOPQRSTU VWXYZabcde fghijklmnopqrs tuvwxyz-1234 567890ŒÆ£ $Ø&%ß?!(«ⁿ/;)	ABCDEFGHIJK LMNOPQRSTU VWXYZÆŒøÇ abcdefghijkln mopqrstuvwx yzœl2345678 90!?&£$ß(«»»)

148b.

ultra light italic, light, medium, regular, medium light, bold, bold italic, and bold extended. Figure 149 illustrates the Helvetica family.

A specific variation in a specific size is called a font. For example, 18 point Helvetica italic is a font. A great variety of shapes exist in a single font. There are 26 capitals, 26 lowercase letter forms, and assorted numerals and punctuation marks. These various shapes can be successfully combined into a unified design because of the similarities in width, brackets, serifs, and x-height. A well-designed type font is an excellent example of the interplay of repetition and variety that makes for good design.

SELECTION

Now that you are familiar with the different styles of type, how do you select which to use? What factors are involved in designing with text type? Selecting the type for a

Goudy old style	Optima	Palatino	Times new roman
ABCDEFGHIJ KLMNOPQRS TUVWXYZa bcdefghijklmn! opqrstuvwxyz1 234567890ÆØ Œ&ß?$£¢%«»·*	ABCDEFGHIJKL MNOPQRSTU VWXYZabcd! efghijklmnopqr stuvwxyz1234 567890ÆŒÇ? Øæœçøß£$¢;	ABCDEFGHIJK; LMNOPQRST? UVWXYZabcd! efghijklmnopqrs tuvwxyz123456 7890ÆŒØæœø £$¢&%()/·•~··~	ABCDEFGHIJK LMNOPQRSTU VWXYZÆŒÇ? Øabcdefghijklmn opqrstuvwxyzæœ çøß1234567890 £$¢&%!(«‹›»∓·.;/*)
Goudy bold	Optima semi bold	Palatino italic	Times bold
ABCDEFGHIJ KLMNOPQR! STUVWXYZ abcdefghijklm? nopqrstuvwxy zæø1234567890 ŒÆØ&·$£¢%··	ABCDEFGHIJ! KLMNOPQR? STUVWXYZa bcdefghijklm nopqrstuvwx yz123456789; 0£$¢&%()/*	ABCDEFGHIJK LMNOPQRST» UVWXYZÆ£ ŒÇØabcdefghijkl- mnopqrstuvwxyzæ œçø1234567890ß;: $¢%&§?!()/«·~·∘	ABCDEFGHI JKLMNOPQ RSTUVWXY Zabcdefghijkl mnopqrstuvwx yz1234567890 ŒÆ$£&?!%,«»
Goudy heavyface	Optima black	Palatino black	Times bold italic
ABCDEFGHIJK LMNOPQRSTU VWXYZÆŒÇ Ø abcdefghijkl mnopqrstuvw xyzæœçø1234 567890£$¢ß&% ?!;:()/*·····∘·+«»	ABCDEFGHIJ* KLMNOPQRS TUVWXYZ ab cdefghijklmno pqrstuvwxyz1 234567890Æ& ŒØæœø£$¢? %!()/;·~···	ABCDEFGHIJ; KLMNOPQRS TUVWXYZabc defghijklmnop qrstuvwxyz123 4567890ÆŒÇ Øæœçøß$¢&/* %?!«»·~···	ABCDEFGHI JKLMNOPQ RSTUVWXY Zabcdefghijkl mnopqrstuvwx yz1234567890! Œ£$&%?ß(;&!·)

148c.

given layout means making decisions in six interrelated areas: type size, line length, type style, leading, spacing, and format.

Size

Text type is any type that is under 14 points in size. A point is a unit of measurement based on the pica. There are 12 points in a pica and approximately 6 picas in an inch, so there are 72 points in an inch (Fig. 150). The point system of measurement was introduced in the eigh-teenth century because the small sizes of text type called for a measuring system with extremely fine increments. Type size is measured in points until it reaches about 2″ (5 cm) high. It is available from 5 points to 72 points on most typesetting systems and pressure graphics sheets (Fig. 151). When measuring type size, include the ascender and descender in the measurement. The best way to measure type is by comparing it with a type specimen book and matching the size visually.

Helvetica LIGHT CONDENSED

Helvetica MEDIUM CONDENSED

Helvetica BOLD CONDENSED

Helvetica ULTRA LIGHT

Helvetica ULTRA LIGHT ITALIC

Helvetica LIGHT

Helvetica MEDIUM

Helvetica REGULAR

Helvetica MEDIUM ITALIC

Helvetica BOLD

Helvetica BOLD ITALIC

Helvetica BOLD EXTENDED

HELVETICA OUTLINE

HABERULE "10" TYPE GAUGE
POINT SIZE
AGATE 6 7 8 9 10 11 12

near right: 149. *The Helvetica family.*

far right: 150. *This pica rule gives measurements in points, picas, and inches.*

When choosing a type size, keep the audience in mind. Type that is smaller than 10 point is often difficult for older people to read.

Line Length

Line length also is measured by the pica system. It is the length in picas of a line of text type. When laying out a page and marking copy for the typesetter, use pica measurements. The dimensions of the page itself, however, are usually expressed in inches (or centimeters). An 8 point type is set in a 22 pica line length on an 8 1/2″ x 11″ (22 x 28 cm) page format.

151. *Type is measured in points until it reaches about 2″ (5 cm) high.*

The length of a line is closely related to the size of type. A small point size such as 6 point or 8 point on a line 44 picas long is difficult to read. The type seems to jump around along the midsection of the line, and the eye must search for the beginning of each new line. This trouble is worse when there is insufficient space between lines. Usually you want the reader's eye to move smoothly, never being forced to slow down or lose its place. The standard line length and point size ratio for optimal legibility is a line of 50 to 70 characters long (Fig. 152). Variations on this theme can be used purposely to slow the reader down.

| 5 points | 6 points | 8 points | 10 points | 12 points | 14 points | 18 points | 24 points | 30 points | 36 points | 45 points | 54 points | 60 points | 72 points |

The length of a line is an important factor in legibility. If you prefer that no one read the text, choose a small point size on a long line length. 8 point set 30 picas long is nearly impossible to read. As a designer and typographer however, your intent will usually be to insure that the reader's eye moves smoothly, never being forced to slow down or lose its place. The standard line length and point size ratio for optimal legibility is a line 50 to 70 characters long.

8 point GARAMOND

The length of a line is an important factor in legibility. If you prefer that no one read the text, choose a small point size on a long line length. 8 point set 30 picas long is nearly impossible to read. As a designer and typographer however, your intent will usually be to insure that the reader's eye moves smoothly, never being forced to slow down or lose its place. The standard line length and point size ratio for optimal legibility is a line 50 to 70 characters long.

9 point GARAMOND

The length of a line is an important factor in legibility. If you prefer that no one read the text, choose a small point size on a long line length. 8 point set 30 picas long is nearly impossible to read. As a designer and typographer however, your intent will usually be to insure that the reader's eye moves smoothly, never being forced to slow down or lose its place. The standard line length and point size ratio for optimal legibility is a line 50 to 70 characters long.

10 point GARAMOND

The length of a line is an important factor in legibility. If you prefer that no one read the text, choose a small point size on a long line length. 8 point set 30 picas long is nearly impossible to read. As a designer and typographer however, your intent will usually be to insure that the reader's eye moves smoothly, never being forced to slow down or lose its place. The standard line length and point size ratio for optimal legibility is a line 50 to 70 characters long.

11 point GARAMOND

The length of a line is an important factor in legibility. If you prefer that no one read the text, choose a small point size on a long line length. 8 point set 30 picas long is nearly impossible to read. As a designer and typographer however, your intent will usually be to insure that the reader's eye moves smoothly, never being forced to slow down or lose its place. The standard line length and point size ratio for optimal legibility is a line 50 to 70 characters long.

12 point GARAMOND

152.

Helvetica ultra light	Helvetica medium	Helvetica bold	Helvetica medium outline
ABCDEFGHIJ KLMNOPQRS TUVWXYZØa bcdefghijklmno pqrstuvwxyzæ 1234567890&! ?\$£%ßCEÆ	ABCDEFGHI JKLMNOPQ RSTUVWXY Zabcdefghijk lmnopqrstuv wxyz123456 7890ß&?!(	ABCDEFGHIJ KLMNOPQRS TUVWXYZab cdefghijklmn opqrstuvwxy zæœøç12345 67890ÆŒØ? !£\$¢%ß&(	ABCDEFGH IJKLMNOP QRSTUVW XYZ123456 7890ÆŒ&! %?£\$¢Ø
Helvetica ultra light italic	Helvetica bold italic	Helvetica light	Helvetica light cond
ABCDEFGHIJ KLMNOPQRS TUVWXYZabc defghijklmnopq rstuvwxyzæœ 1234567890\$ £&%?!ßÆØ	ABCDEFGHIJ KLMNOPQRS TUVWXYZab cdefghijklmn opqrstuvwxy zæœç:12345 67890ÆŒØ! ?&%£\$¢ß(	ABCDEFGHIJ KLMNOPQRS TUVWXYZab cdefghijklmno pqrstuvwxyz1 234567890?! %\$£&BØ(	ABCDEFGHIJKL MNOPQRSTUVW XYZÆŒØabcde fghijklmnopqrstu vwxyzæœç1234 567890ŒÇØÆ¢ £\$ß%?!&/(
Helvetica medium italic	Helvetica bold extended	Helvetica regular	Helvetica medium cond
ABCDEFGHIJ KLMNOPQRS TUVWXYZØa bcdefghijklmn opqrstuvwxyz 1234567890?! ß&£\$%Œ	ABCDEFGH IJKLMNOP QRSTUVXY WZÆŒÇØ abcdefghik jlmnopqrst uvwxyzç12 34567890 ß\$£&?!%(	ABCDEFGHI* JKLMNOPQ? RSTUVWXY- ZÆØabcdef! ghijklmnopqr stuvwxyzæø 1234567890 £\$&%(; /)	ABCDEFGHIJKL MNOPQRSTUVW XYZabcdefghijkl mnopqrstuvwxy zæ1234567890! ?&%£\$ßÆŒ(

153. *There is a great deal of variety in one type family.*

Style

When choosing text type, legibility is a prime consideration. There are many beautiful, elegant, and accessible styles. Stay away from styles with an excess of ornamentation.

Next, seek a type that is appropriate to the audience, the publication, and your own sense of aesthetics. Sans serif has a modern feel and is highly legible in the limited amounts of copy in most annual reports, newsletters, and so on. The serif types are generally more traditional and classical in feeling. They are easier to read in large amounts. Many of the newest styles strive to combine the virtues of serif and sans serif type.

There are trends in type, just as in music, clothes, and lifestyles. Notice how they change from year to year. Only choose the ones you consider legible, appropriate, and aesthetic.

The printing process can help to determine type selection. Delicate, hairline serifs are not appropriate when a heavy ink coverage is required, because the ink will block up the serifs and result in a blotchy look. Heavily textured paper will also make a delicate serif unadvisable. The texture of the paper will cause the finely inked serifs to break up.

Beginning designers often combine several type styles in a typographical layout. They choose each for its own beauty and interest, but forget the effect of the whole design. Diverse styles usually refuse to combine into an organized whole and have an undisciplined and chaotic look. Many experienced designers prefer to work within one type family, drawing upon its bold, italic, and roman faces (Fig. 153). They achieve a look of variety without risking going outside one family. This course is certainly the "safest" for a new designer.

The most exciting layouts, however, often do mix distinctively different typefaces. Mixing takes sensitivity to how the styles affect one another and contribute to the whole. A good rule of thumb when mixing type families is to make certain they are very different. The composition will work if there is either deliberate similarity or definite variety. It can confuse

and displease the eye if the distinctions are muddy. Figures 154 and 155 are two successful designs that combine type styles.

Leading

Leading (pronounced like the metal lead) describes the vertical spacing between lines of type. It strongly affects the look and readability of the layout. Type is considered to be set "solid" when there is no space inserted between the descender of the top line and the ascender of the bottom line. A 10 point type set on a 10 point leading is an example of solid leading. Sample leadings are shown in Figures 142 to 146. How much leading you use is important. There are several factors affecting that decision. Among those factors are type size, line length, and type style.

Type Size

Leading must be proportionate to the size of the type. Although there is no standard, correct leading for any certain type size, one often finds 10 point type set on 12 point leading. An extra 2 points of space have been inserted between lines of type. A larger or smaller type size will

below left: 154. *Paula Scher. Layout design for* The Metamorphosis *in "Great Beginnings" brochure.*

below right: 155. *Charles Skaggs. Cover design for* Fine Print. *1984.*

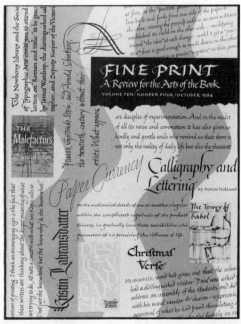

Typography
TOUCHING

Typography
VERY TIGHT

Typography
TIGHT

Typography
NORMAL

Typography
TV SPACING

156. *There is a great deal of difference between tight and loose letterspacing.*

157. *Spacing between letterforms must vary.*

Type Style

Three aspects of the type style also affect leading: x-height, vertical stress, and serif versus sans serif. The x-height, as you know, refers to the size of the body of the letter, without its ascender and descender. The x-height of Helvetica is much greater than the x-height of an older type such as Garamond. Consequently the Helvetica would probably require more leading. It does not have lots of extra white space packed around its body, so the lines of type appear closer together.

The vertical stress of a type style affects leading because the stronger the vertical emphasis, the more the eye is drawn up and down instead of along the line of type. Hence, the greater the vertical stress, the more leading required. A type style such as Baskerville has a strong vertical stress and requires more leading than Garamond.

A serif helps to draw the eye along in a horizontal direction, so serif type is generally considered to be easier to read than sans serif type. Sans serif type usually requires more leading than the serif style to keep the eye moving smoothly along.

Spacing

Letter spacing is the amount of space between the letters of a word (Fig. 156). A good figure/ground relationship between letterforms is as important with text type as with display type. If the letters are spaced too far apart, the eye must "jump" between letters, and reading becomes strained.

Whether designing with text type or display type, keep an eye out for the creation of equal volumes of white space between individual letterforms. "Kerning" is a term that describes the specific adjustment of space between individual letterforms. An "IH," for example, will require a different spacing than an "MN" (Fig. 157).

The amount of space between words is called word spacing. If it is too great, it is difficult for the eye to move quickly along the line of type. There is a tendency to pause between individual words. The

require less extra leading. A 14 point type might need only 14 or 15 point leading, for instance. It is rare to find minus leading, or a 10 point type set on a 9 point leading. Modern typesetting equipment can set one line of type on top of another, but it is seldom appropriate.

Line Length

Line length is an important factor in determining leading. The longer the line, the more leading is appropriate. With longer line lengths, the eye has a tendency to wander. If there is insufficient space between lines, you will find yourself reading the line above or beneath and having difficulty finding the beginning of each line.

> **The head of the nation's military, Gen. Fidel Ramos, warned Thursday of a possible plot by disaffected officers. His office said he had "warned any military adventurers against embarking on such a rash course of action because it could be bloody and destabilizing."**

158. *Justifying copy in a short line length will cause white holes to appear.*

reader should be unaware of the space between words, and aware instead of their content.

Word spacing usually is not a problem with text type, unless the type is being set in a justified format (flush left and flush right edges). This job is now done by computer. To make the lines come out even, the computer will insert extra space between words. If the line length is long, with many words, this addition is not noticeable. However, if the line length is short, great white holes seem to appear in the copy (Fig. 158). Look at your local newspaper, and squint. Often rivers of white will appear in the columns of text type as a result of poor word spacing.

Format

Format design refers to the arrangement of lines of type on the page (Fig. 159). There are two basic categories: justified

159. *Variations in format.*

and unjustified. In justified type the lines are all the same length, so that the left and right edges of the column of type are straight. This format is commonly used in newspaper layout and text and trade books. It is appropriate when speed and ease of reading are the primary considerations. Justified copy is considered slightly easier to read than unjustified copy. The straight, squared-off columns of type give an orderly, classical feeling to the page.

Unjustified copy can be arranged in a variety of ways: flush left, flush right, centered, and asymmetrical.

Flush Left

The flush left format calls for a straight left edge and a ragged right edge. Typewritten copy is usually flush left. This format is commonly used in annual reports, brochures, identification lines under photographs, and any time when a slightly more informal look is desired than can be achieved with justified type. One of the benefits of this format is that it is possible to avoid hyphenated words.

Flush Right

Flush right format is unusual and consequently difficult to read. It has a ragged left edge and is used for design effect in special situations. It is difficult for the eye to search out the beginning of each new line without a common starting point.

Centered

Centered copy is often found in headlines or invitations, but rarely in standard copy. It is a slow-reading, classical format that encourages the reader to pause after each line. It is important to make logical breaks at the end of each line. This format has a pronounced irregular shape and packs a lot of space around itself. The white space and irregular outline can draw the eye strongly. Consider the content of your material, how rapidly it should be read, and the overall look of the page before deciding on a centered format.

Asymmetrical

Asymmetrically arranged type can put across the point of a poem or an important statement. Asymmetry is also used in display type to achieve better balance among letterforms. Contour type is a form of asymmetry that fits the shape of an illustration, following its contour. It is often difficult and expensive to have typeset. Type that is set around the squared edge of a photo is called a runaround. Occasionally type will be set in the shape of a contour itself.

The ancient Egyptians and Greeks originally experimented with this format. It was used early this century by the poet Apollinaire and more recently yet by contemporary designers (Fig. 160).

EXECUTION

Comping Type

In order to visualize a layout before the type is set, the designer makes an actual size layout. It may be a rough or a more detailed comprehensive. The headline type on this layout must be indicated letter by letter, with careful attention to indicating type style and size, placement, and letter and word spacing. Designers often use tracings of letterforms found in type manuals.

Drawing in the tiny letters of text type would be too time-consuming. Instead the designer draws a suggestion of text type matching its line length, format, leading, height, and presumably its gray value. This procedure is called "comping" type. (In small preliminary sketches, the text areas are often indicated with simple rectangles.)

Type may be indicated by using a chisel-point pencil or a gray marker (Fig. 161). The width of a single stroke should match the width of the x-height of the type. Type may also be comped by drawing two lines, indicating the top and bottom of each line of type. In this case, the separation of the lines should correspond with the x-height. When x-height, line length, and leading

match the chosen type, the comped layout will give the same visual impression as the finished typeset publication. This method of comping works for text type that is 14 points or larger. Remember, display type must be comped by drawing each individual letterform.

Figure 162 adds three more methods of comping. Hand "greeking" involves simple letter-like nonsense shapes. You can also buy "greeking" transfer sheets, or paste in any block of type from another source with the right specifications.

Remember to pay close attention to details such as paragraph indentations, large initial caps, inserts, captions, and headings. These fine details make or break a layout design.

Copyfitting

Once the typeface has been chosen and the general layout determined, you may want to determine exactly how much copy will fit into a given space. Point size, leading, and line length can be adjusted to make the copy fit more attractively and legibly into the available space. Copyfitting

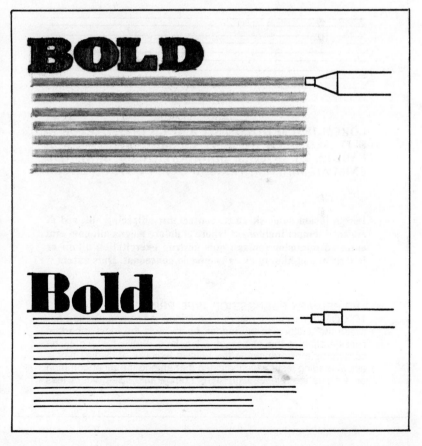

is a method of determining just how much space a typed manuscript will fill when it is converted to typeset copy.

There are several methods of copy-fitting. This method starts with the manuscript and your basic layout design.

162. *Other methods of comping type.*

```
8/10
```

```
10/12
```

```
12/14
```

LOREM IPSUM DOLOR SIT AMET, CONSECTETUR A ELIT, SED DIAM NONUMY EIUSMOD TEMPOR INCI LABORE ET DOLORE MAGNAALIQUAM ERAT VOL ENIM AD MINIMIM VENIAMI QUIS NOSTRUD EXCER

Lorem ipsum dolor sit amet, consectetur adipscing elit, sed di eiusmod tempor incidunt ut labore et dolore magna aliquam erat enim ad minimim veniami quis nostrud exercitation ullamcor laboris nisi ut aliquip ex ea commodo consequat. Duis autem v

THE PRIMARY PURPOSE OF TYPE PRINTED ON PAPER IS TO CONVEY ideas, to serve as a bridge for communication between the author and the reader. Legibility is the most important consideration in the choice of a typeface. While there may be considerable differences in the relative legibility of display types, actual reading tests have indicated that among the most common body types the relative legibility of comparable sizes differs less

1. Count the total number of lines in the manuscript.
2. Find a line of average length. Count the number of characters in it.
3. Multiply the average number of characters in step 2 by the total number of lines from step 1. The result is the total number of characters in the manuscript.
4. Find the character per pica count for the type style and point size from a type specification chart (Fig. 163).
5. Multiply the characters per pica from step 4 by the chosen line length. The answer is the number of typeset characters per line.
6. Divide the total number of typewritten characters from step 3 by the number of typeset characters per line from step 5. Now you have the number of lines that the copy will occupy when set in the chosen type style and size.
7. Finally, choose the leading. Now a tool such as "Haberule" will tell you how long the copy will be. To determine it mathematically, multiply the number of typeset lines from step 6 by the leading. Divide this number by 12 for the total length in picas, or divide by 72 for the total length in inches.

Specifying Copy

Next it is time to mark the copy for typesetting. This process is called type specifying or more commonly, "specing" copy. When you "spec" copy, you provide all the information necessary to set the type from the typewritten copy: type style, size, leading, format, line length, sometimes letter spacing, and special instructions.

The copy should be double-spaced, typed on one side only, with a wide margin on all sides for instructions. Always keep a duplicate for the files. The deadline for delivery must be established as well as the cost of the original typesetting and corrections. Most design firms, advertising agencies, and art departments have their own procedures.

The exact method of marking copy will

TYPEFACE NAME   CHARACTER PER PICA

TYPEFACE NAME	6	7	8	9	10	11	12	14	18	24	30	36	48	60	72
American Typewriter Light (ITC) T	–	–	2.92	2.59	2.33	2.12	1.94	1.66	1.29	.97	–	–	–	–	–
American Typewriter Light (ITC) D	–	–	–	–	–	–	–	1.63	1.27	.95	.76	.63	.48	.38	.32
American Typewriter Medium (ITC) T	–	–	2.92	2.59	2.33	2.12	1.94	1.66	1.29	.97	–	–	–	–	–
American Typewriter Medium (ITC) D	–	–	–	–	–	–	–	1.63	1.27	.95	.76	.63	.48	.38	.32
American Typewriter Bold (ITC) T	–	–	2.92	2.59	2.33	2.12	1.94	1.66	1.29	.97	–	–	–	–	–
American Typewriter Bold (ITC) D	–	–	–	–	–	–	–	1.79	1.39	1.04	.83	.70	.52	.42	.35
Baskerville T	4.65	3.98	3.48	3.09	2.78	2.53	2.32	1.98	1.54	1.16	–	–	–	–	–
Baskerville D	–	–	–	–	–	–	–	2.23	1.73	1.30	1.04	.86	.65	.52	.43
Baskerville Italic T	4.65	3.98	3.48	3.09	2.78	2.53	2.32	1.98	1.54	1.16	–	–	–	–	–
Baskerville Italic D	–	–	–	–	–	–	–	2.23	1.73	1.30	1.04	.86	.65	.52	.43
Baskerville Bold T	–	–	3.28	2.91	2.62	2.38	2.19	1.87	1.45	1.09	–	–	–	–	–
Baskerville Bold D	–	–	–	–	–	–	–	1.85	1.44	1.07	.86	.72	.54	.43	.36
Baskerville Bold Italic T	–	–	3.28	2.91	2.62	2.38	2.19	1.87	1.45	1.09	–	–	–	–	–
Benguiat Medium Condensed (ITC) T/D*	4.93	4.22	3.69	3.28	2.95	2.69	2.46	2.11	1.64	1.23	.99	.82	.62	.49	.41
Benguiat Medium Condensed Italic (ITC) T/D	4.89	4.19	3.67	3.26	2.93	2.67	2.44	2.09	1.63	1.22	.98	.81	.61	.49	.41
Benguiat Bold Condensed (ITC) T/D	4.60	3.94	3.45	3.07	2.76	2.51	2.30	1.97	1.53	1.15	.92	.77	.58	.46	.38
Bodoni T	4.52	3.88	3.40	3.02	2.71	2.46	2.26	1.93	1.50	1.13	–	–	–	–	–
Bodoni Italic T	4.52	3.88	3.40	3.02	2.71	2.46	2.26	1.93	1.50	1.13	–	–	–	–	–
Bodoni Bold T	4.13	3.54	3.10	2.75	2.48	2.25	2.06	1.77	1.37	1.03	–	–	–	–	–
Bodoni Bold Italic T	4.13	3.54	3.10	2.75	2.48	2.25	2.06	1.77	1.37	1.03	–	–	–	–	–
Bodoni Extrabold T	–	–	2.50	2.22	2.00	1.82	1.66	1.42	1.11	.83	–	–	–	–	–
Bodoni Extrabold Italic T	–	–	2.50	2.22	2.00	1.82	1.66	1.42	1.11	.83	–	–	–	–	–
Bookman Light Italic (ITC) T/D	3.78	3.24	2.84	2.52	2.27	2.06	1.90	1.62	1.26	.95	.76	.63	.47	.38	.32
Bookman Medium (ITC) T/D	3.65	3.13	2.74	2.43	2.19	1.99	1.82	1.56	1.22	.91	.73	.61	.46	.37	.30
Bookman Medium Italic (ITC) T/D	3.55	3.04	2.66	2.37	2.13	1.94	1.78	1.52	1.18	.89	.71	.59	.44	.35	.30
Cheltenham Book (ITC) T/D	4.50	3.85	3.37	2.99	2.70	2.45	2.25	1.93	1.50	1.12	.90	.75	.56	.45	.37
Cheltenham Book Italic (ITC) T/D	4.52	3.88	3.40	3.02	2.72	2.47	2.26	1.94	1.51	1.13	.91	.79	.57	.45	.38
Cheltenham Ultra (ITC) T/D	3.28	2.81	2.46	2.18	1.96	1.79	1.64	1.40	1.09	.82	.65	.55	.41	.33	.27
Futura Light T	5.00	4.29	3.75	3.34	3.00	2.73	2.50	2.14	1.66	1.25	–	–	–	–	–
Futura Light D	–	–	–	–	–	–	–	2.30	1.79	1.33	1.07	.89	.67	.53	.45
Futura Book T	4.45	3.82	3.34	2.97	2.67	2.43	2.23	1.90	1.48	1.11	–	–	–	–	–
Futura Book D	–	–	–	–	–	–	–	1.99	1.55	1.16	.93	.77	.58	.46	.39
Futura Medium T/D	4.36	3.74	3.27	2.90	2.61	2.38	2.18	1.87	1.45	1.09	.87	.73	.54	.44	.36
Futura Demibold Italic T/D	4.36	3.74	3.27	2.90	2.61	2.38	2.18	1.87	1.45	1.09	.87	.73	.54	.44	.36
Futura Bold T/D	3.95	3.37	2.95	2.61	2.36	2.15	1.97	1.68	1.31	.98	.79	.66	.49	.39	.33
Futura Bold Italic T/D	3.95	3.37	2.95	2.61	2.36	2.15	1.97	1.68	1.31	.98	.79	.66	.49	.39	.33
Garamond Light (ITC) T/D	4.25	3.65	3.19	2.84	2.55	2.32	2.13	1.82	1.42	1.06	.85	.71	.53	.43	.35
Garamond Light Italic (ITC) T/D	4.27	3.66	3.20	2.85	2.56	2.33	2.13	1.83	1.42	1.07	.85	.71	.53	.43	.36
Garamond Book (ITC) T/D	4.23	3.62	3.17	2.82	2.54	2.31	2.11	1.81	1.41	1.06	.85	.70	.53	.42	.35
Garamond Book Italic (ITC) T/D	4.18	3.58	3.13	2.79	2.51	2.28	2.09	1.79	1.39	1.04	.84	.70	.52	.42	.35
Garamond Bold (ITC) T/D	3.77	3.24	2.83	2.52	2.27	2.06	1.89	1.62	1.26	.94	.76	.63	.47	.38	.31
Garamond Bold Italic (ITC) T/D	3.75	3.22	2.81	2.50	2.25	2.05	1.88	1.61	1.25	.94	.75	.63	.47	.38	.31
Goudy Oldstyle T/D	4.72	4.06	3.55	3.16	2.84	2.58	2.36	2.03	1.58	1.18	.94	.78	.59	.47	.39
Goudy Bold T	4.34	3.73	3.26	2.89	2.61	2.37	2.17	–	–	–	–	–	–	–	–
Goudy Bold D	–	–	–	–	–	–	–	1.75	1.36	1.02	.82	.68	.51	.41	.34
Goudy Heavyface D	–	–	–	–	–	–	–	1.42	1.10	.83	.66	.55	.41	.33	.28
Lubalin Graph Extra Light (ITC) D	–	–	–	–	–	–	–	1.65	1.28	.96	.77	.64	.48	.38	.32
Lubalin Graph Book (ITC) D	–	–	–	–	–	–	–	1.64	1.28	.96	.77	.64	.48	.38	.32
Lubalin Graph Medium (ITC) D	–	–	–	–	–	–	–	1.55	1.21	.91	.73	.60	.45	.36	.30
Lubalin Graph Demi (ITC) D	–	–	–	–	–	–	–	1.56	1.22	.91	.73	.46	.46	.36	.30
Lubalin Graph Bold (ITC) D	–	–	–	–	–	–	–	1.60	1.25	.93	.75	.62	.47	.37	.31
Lubalin Graph Extra Light Oblique (ITC) T/D	3.87	3.31	2.90	2.58	2.32	2.11	1.93	1.66	1.29	.97	.77	.64	.48	.39	.32
Lubalin Graph Book Oblique (ITC) T/D	3.92	3.36	2.94	2.61	2.35	2.14	1.96	1.68	1.31	.98	.78	.65	.49	.39	.33
Lubalin Graph Medium Oblique (ITC) T/D	3.78	3.24	2.84	2.52	2.27	2.06	1.89	1.62	1.26	.95	.76	.63	.47	.38	.32
Lubalin Graph Demi Oblique (ITC) T/D	3.80	3.26	2.85	2.53	2.28	2.07	1.90	1.63	1.27	.95	.76	.63	.47	.38	.32
Lubalin Graph Bold Oblique (ITC) T/D	3.79	3.25	2.84	2.53	2.27	2.07	1.90	1.62	1.26	.95	.76	.63	.47	.38	.32

*Text/Display

163. *Characters per Pica Chart.*

SPECIFYING COPY

After the copy has been typed, draw a horizontal line to and above the first line of your copy. Above this line place all the information about the type style, such as size, family name, family structure, caps or caps and lowercase. Below the line indicate the information about the format of the copy, such as column width, centered, justified, ragged right, and letter spacing.

The copy will probably have several changes in this information. Each change is indicated by hooking another line above the copy with the new information.

164. *An example of "specing."*

vary depending on the conventions of the typesetting system being used. Sometimes copy is written, speced, copyfit, and set and the page layout completed entirely on computer. Still, the nature of the information that must be provided remains unchanged. Here is a standard procedure that is not specific to any system.

After the copy has been typed, draw a horizontal line to and above the first line of the copy. Above this line write all the information about the type style, such as size, family name, family structure, and caps or caps and lower case. Below the line indicate the information about the format of the copy, such as column width, centered, justified, ragged right, and letter spacing. The copy will probably have several changes in this information. Each change is indicated by hooking another line above the copy with the new information (Fig. 164).

Extra space may be inserted between areas of copy, with the symbol (#), which means an extra line space of the current leading. More subtle spacing changes are indicated with " + 6 pts," or " + 3 pts," and so on. The depth of the copy should correspond to the depth of the area allowed on the layout. If it does not, adjustments must be made to the type size, the leading, or on rare occasion, the typeface.

Often certain words or phrases must be set in a special typeface within a type family. This fact is indicated by underscoring the word and abbreviating the special face in the margin (Fig. 165).

| Italics | small capitals | Sm C |
| capitals | boldface | BF |

165. *Marking for special typefaces.*

Delete ℯ⁄	Close up ⌒
Insert here ∧	Elevate a word ⌐¬
Move to left ⌐	Move to right ⌐
Lower a letter ⌐¬	Insert an Em space ▢
Insert 2 Em spaces ⊓⊔	Broken type, please reset ✗
New paragraph ¶	No new paragraph 𝓃ℴ ¶
Open up a␣space #	Close ⌣up ⌣a⌣ space
Restore to original stet	Wrong font wf
Transpose ∩	Set in caps and lower case
Set in all caps ‗	Set in small caps
Set in boldface	Set in (roman) rom
Set in italics	Change to lower case lc
Insert period ⊙	

166. *Proofreader's marks.*

Marking Corrections

You will almost always make some corrections in the typeset copy, either last-minute revisions or printer's mistakes. A good proofreader (several are better) must read the copy carefully. You will need to know proofreader's marks for corrections from a design point of view, such as damaged copy, poor breaks in words, or incorrect font. The standard proofreader's marks are shown in Figure 166. It is a good idea to use one color for corrections. The color that you choose will come to be a visual symbol signaling your corrections (Fig. 167).

EXERCISES

1. Study various magazines, newspapers, and other publications, looking for samples of the different formats. Which are successful, and which flawed?
2. Choose two of your less effective samples for analysis. Determine their line length, leading, point size, and type style. Recommend specific changes.
3. Practice comping a page of type from this book. Then stand back, squint, and ask yourself if your comping matches the value of the actual typeset copy. How can it be improved? Are the x-height and leading accurate?

CORRECTED PROOF

This paragraph is marked for correction using the proofreader's marks shown above. if you are in doubt about which mark to use, write the instructions in the margin, or cross out the line and write in a new one.

¶ Paragraph indentations are not always necessary, but it is important to the keep layout consistent Exercises

167. *Corrected proof.*

WATER

waves On the water
a boat On the waves
On the boat deck, a woman
On the woman, a man

168. *Ann Ladich (UW–Whitewater student designer). Poem illustration.*

Practice the use of pressure graphics.

Experience designing with text type.

Learn the standard rules of good type design and the creative potential of rule breaking.

PROJECT
Layouts Using Text Type

Create three separate layout designs on 8″ x 8″ (20 x 20 cm) illustration board. Arrange the elements so that you are using similarity, eye direction, figure/ground shaping, and continuation. Figures 170 and 171 are student designs based on this project.

4. Using a section of copy from this chapter designated by your instructor, measure point size, leading, and line length. Copyfit it into a justified, 14 pica line length, with 8 point type on a 9 point leading. How many picas in length will it be? Comp it.

PROJECT
Typographical Illustration of a Poem

Select a poem, or an interesting and emotive piece of prose that is five to ten lines long. Set it twice, using primarily 12 point type. Use pressure graphics or a typesetting system if it is available to you. The first time, follow the standard guides for type design to enhance legibility. Select your type style and format. Pay close attention to leading, line length, and spacing. Create two variations.

Set it again, breaking as many rules as you can, while creating an effect appropriate to the piece and your feelings about it. Figures 168 and 169 are student designs based on a similar project.

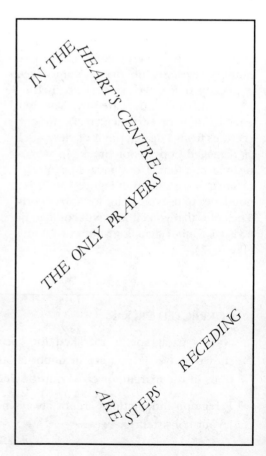

169. *Mari Lunde (UW–Whitewater student designer). Poem illustration.*

IN THE HEART'S CENTRE
THE ONLY PRAYERS
RECEDING
ARE STEPS

Part A: Combine one large letterform, one paragraph of type cut from a magazine, and one bar into a design.

Part B: Combine one large word (paying attention to letter spacing), a comped version of your paragraph from part A, and one bar.

Part C: Combine one large word, one paragraph comped type, one word, one bar, and one photo. This layout must illustrate the mood in the photograph.

Objectives

Learn to apply gestalt unit-forming principles to layout design.

Learn to integrate text and display type, while carefully orchestrating eye direction.

Learn to integrate typography and photography to communicate a point of view.

above left: 170. *Candy Thieme (UW–Whitewater student designer). Layout with text type.*

above right: 171. *Candy Thieme (UW–Whitewater student designer). Layout with text type.*

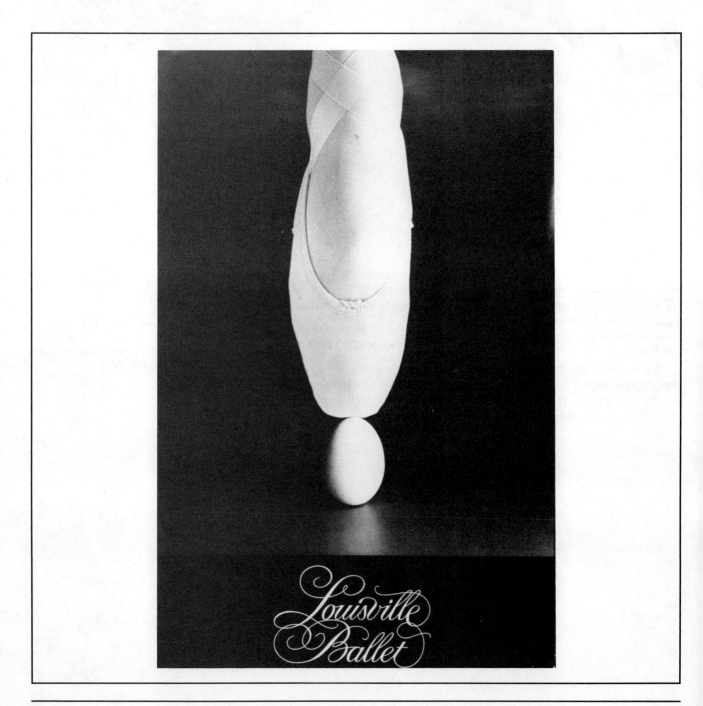

7

LAYOUT

THE BALANCING ACT

Layout is a balancing act in two senses. First, it relates the diverse elements on a printed page in a way at once communicative and aesthetic. Ideally, the form enhances the communication (Fig. 172).

Second, as in all design, every element on the page affects the other elements, changing how they are perceived. Layout is not simply the addition of photographs, text type, display type, or artwork. It is a careful balancing of elements.

The layout artist must select from the vast array of available typefaces one that is appropriate. The format, size, and value contrast of the typographical elements must be closely related to accompanying photographs and illustrations. Layout may be the most difficult balancing act a designer is ever called upon to perform.

Everything you have studied so far about how unity must be accompanied by contrast holds true for layout design. The continuation of a line or curve into an

172. *Terry Koppel (Koppel & Scher, New York). Layout for* Fear of Flying *in "Great Beginnings" brochure.*

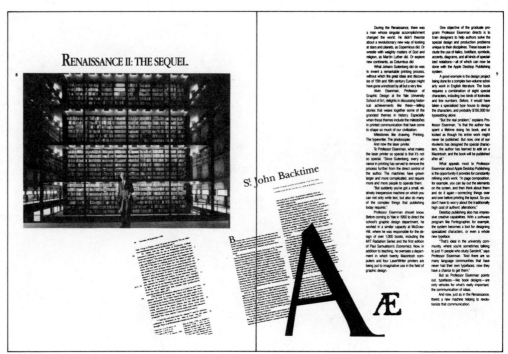

right: 173. *Page layouts from* For Every Voice, a Means to Be Heard. *Apple Computer, Cupertino, CA.*

below: 174. *Albrecht Dürer. Fifteenth-century type design based on the "golden section."*

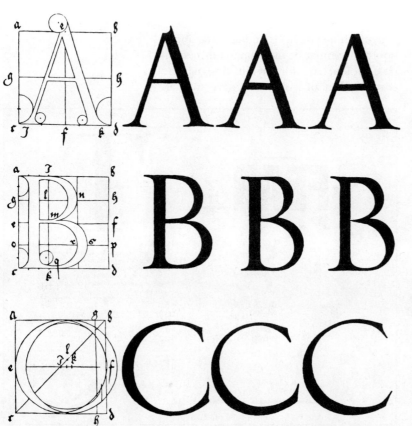

adjoining object is important in guiding the eye over a page. A good relationship between figure and ground is essential in page design. The careful shaping of the white ground of the page gives cohesion and unity to the figures or elements placed upon it. There should be no "leftover" space that is unshaped, undesigned. Open white space functions as an active, participating part of the whole design. Page design can be symmetrically or asymmetrically balanced. In either case, careful figure/ground grouping will enhance the readability of the page. Figure 173 demonstrates these points.

A careful balancing of contrast can give the page dynamic, unpredictable energy that will draw the reader's eye. Chapter 4 discussed contrasts in size, shape, value, and texture. A combination of unit forming and contrast creates a balanced and successful layout.

SIZE AND PROPORTION

This difficult balancing act calls for sensitivity to proportion—the organization of

several things into a relationship of size, quantity, or degree. Artists have understood the importance of size relationships for centuries. The Parthenon expressed the Greeks' sense of proportion. It was based upon a mathematical principle that came to be known as "the golden section." Albrecht Dürer used the golden section in the fifteenth century to analyze and construct his alphabet (Fig. 174). Ultimately, however, no mathematical system can take the place of an intuitive feeling for proportion. You must be able to sense the tension and energy in contrast. You must feel when the contrast between elements is so great that harmony and balance are lost.

The division of a page into areas in harmony with one another is at the heart of all layout design (Fig. 175). The relationships between type sizes, between printed and unprinted areas, and between various values of gray must all be proportionate. In addition, the typography must be in proportion to the other components of a layout.

When we refer to size, we usually use words like "big" or "small." These terms are meaningless, however, unless we have two objects to compare. A 36 point word on a page with a lot of text type will be large. On a spread with a 72 point headline, it will be relatively small. An element large in proportion to other elements on

175. *Emil Ruder. Page areas in harmonious proportion. Diagrams courtesy Arthur Niggli Ltd, Niederteufen, Switzerland.*

the page makes an obvious visual impact and a potentially strong focal point. Do not be afraid to use an element really LARGE, as in Figure 172, where the letter *T* makes a bold graphic statement. Several magazines use a larger format size than is standard. Next to other magazines on the newsracks, they have the impact of a comparatively large and impressive display.

Another way of determining size is to have a standard expected size in mind. If we refer to a large household cat, "large" means over 12″ (30 cm) high. If we refer to a large horse, we have a different size in mind. Deliberately violating this expectation can create a dynamic, unusual effect. The surrealist painter René Magritte used this technique in Figure 176. Mixing up standard relative sizes creates strong tension and compelling interest (Figures 177 and 178).

Another approach to confusing our sense of size and scale is by showing objects larger than life. On the printed page, viewers have come to expect things to be shown smaller than they really are. We have no problem accepting a photograph of the Empire State Building 3″ (8 cm) high; but magnify a tiny object, and we get a visual jolt that makes us pay attention. Imagine the photograph of a common housefly, used 20 times actual size.

VISUAL RHYTHM

Another important consideration in layout design is visual rhythm. Life itself is based upon rhythm. There is a rhythm to the passing days and seasons. The "tempo" of our days may be fast or slow. The growth and gradual decline of all natural life forms has a rhythm. Cities have particular pulsing rhythms. Different periods in our history have seemed to move to various beats. Our current age has an eclectic/quickened tempo compared with 100 years ago.

176. *René Magritte.* Tomb of the Wrestlers. *1960. Oil, 35″ × 46″ (89 × 116.8 cm). Copyright Charly Herscovici 1987.*

Some of us have more finely developed nesting instincts than others.

Some of us have more finely developed nesting instincts than others.

177, 178. *Tom Wolsey/Ally & Gargono (Art Director), Henry Wolf (Photographer). Ads for Karastan Rug Mills.*

Visual rhythm is based upon repetition of shapes, values, colors, and textures. Recurrences of a shape and the spacing between them set up a pattern or rhythm. It can be quick and lively, with small closely placed shapes, or solemn and dig-

---

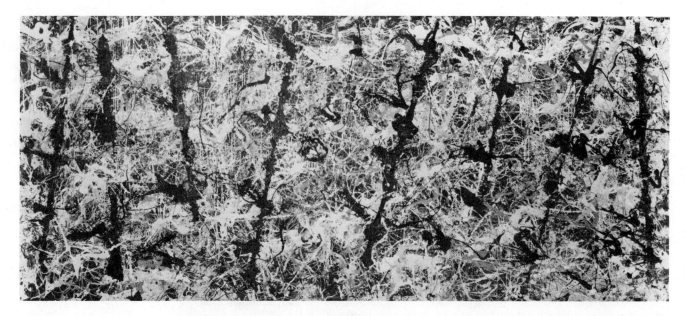

179. *Jackson Pollock. Blue Poles. 1952. Oil enamel and aluminum paint, glass on canvas 6′ 11 1/2″ × 16′ 1/2″ (2.1 × 4.9 m). Collection, Australian National Gallery, Canberra.*

nified, with large solo shapes. Rhythm is crucial in the work of many visual artists (Fig. 179).

There are many ways to use rhythm in typography. Within a single word, a rhythmic pattern of ascenders and descenders, curves and straight lines is created. The rhythm might be symmetrical or asymmetrical in character. Word and letter spacing can set up a typographical movement of varying tempos, as can changes in value and size (Fig. 180).

temp*o *tempo

t e m p o

180. *Letter spacing affects tempo.*

181. *Type position creates rhythms.*

The total layout of the page is another opportunity to form a rhythmic pattern. The lines of type can form a rhythm of silent pauses and rests, of leaps, of slow ascents and descents. Endless rhythms can be created this way (Figure 181).

The spacing and size of photographs can intermingle with typography. An alternating visual rhythm may reserve every left-hand page for a full page photograph, while the right-hand page is textured with smaller units of text and other elements.

Another form of rhythm is progressive rhythm. The repeated element changes in a regular fashion. Text type might be used in changing values from regular to bold to extra bold and back again. A photograph might be repeated, each time with more of the image displayed. This rhythmic movement can take place on one page or on successive pages. Change in a regular manner is at the heart of a progressive rhythm (Fig. 182).

GRID LAYOUT

A sense of pacing and rhythm can be set up throughout an entire publication with the aid of a grid. A grid is an invisible structure underlying the page that is used as a guide for the placement of layout elements.

When and why is [a] grid? Large publicat[ion] one to keep order. G[rids] used in single-page des[ign] as advertisements and posters. They are also used to bring continuity to the separate pieces of a design series (Fig. 183). A grid is most useful when it brings an organized unity not only to a single page, but also to facing

183. *Three-part series of advertisements for 3-M Corporation.*

a.

b.

c.

pages, an entire publication, or a series of publications.

Layout design that utilizes a grid is as flexible and creative as its designer. The grid has been accused of bringing a boring conformity to page design. Grids, however, can help generate distinctive, dynamic images. They allow for experimentation with all the forms of contrast. A grid functions like a musical instrument. A piano, for instance, has a limited number of keys of fixed tone and position. It is possible, however, to play many different musical compositions through placement, rhythm, repetition, and emphasis.

Keeping the Beat

A musical composition has a timing or beat that pulses beneath all the long and short notes. In a visual composition, this beat is often kept by a grid. Just as a four-beats-to-the-measure musical score would not be cut off at 3.5 beats, a grid layout that has four sections across will not end at 3.5.

Whether the fourth unit is filled with an element or left as a white ground, it gets its full count and full visual weight. Within these four musical counts, there might be a mixture of quarter notes, half notes, or whole notes. The four-unit grid might hold one large four-unit element, two half-unit elements, or four quarter-unit elements. The beauty in any composition, whether visual or auditory, comes once the structure is set up, and the variations in pacing, timing, and emphasis begin.

Playing the Theme

An underlying musical theme, like the one in Beethoven's Sixth Symphony (the "Pastoral"), will appear over and over in different guises, tying the symphony together into a whole. An underlying visual theme will accomplish the same for a visual composition. A layout for a publication unfolds through time, just as a musical concert does. Each page must be turned before the next is revealed. It cannot be seen

184, 185. *Layouts for "What's Your Destination?" Courtesy Apple computer, Cupertino, CA.*

184.

WHERE WE'VE BEEN

Our effort to provide the education community with computers didn't begin with a marketing strategy or a directive from The Board.

It began with a vision. A belief that the power of personal computing could help educators to teach and students to learn in new ways. A belief that has put millions of computers at the fingertips of both educators and students.

Our efforts began immediately, when Apple Computer and the personal computer industry were still in their early years. In fact, many of our first customers were teachers and professors. Through their innovations and efforts, computers began appearing in classrooms across the country. In 1979, through the Apple Education Foundation, we began helping those early innovators with special grants.

In the years that followed, our efforts grew, taking direction from the needs of the education community. In 1983, our Kids Can't Wait program gave over 9,000 California schools an Apple® computer system, free of charge and full of power. The program provided students with immediate access to computers—no waiting for budget approvals to learn the skills that a changing world would demand they know.

Finding ways to provide more educators with computers has also been central to Apple's commitment to education. Toward that end, our An Apple for the Teacher program gave educators access to computers outside the classroom, where they could develop better ways to use the computer inside the classroom.

Building Bridges with Higher Education

In January 1984 we introduced the Macintosh computer, and our commitment to educators expanded with new networks of programs and support.

Like the Apple University Consortium, a partnership of universities and colleges brought together to share and explore the integration of technology and education. Our efforts quickly broadened to include hundreds of other colleges and universities.

In 1985 we created the Office of Special Education, which works with educational institutions and human service organizations across the country to identify and help meet the computer-related needs of disabled individuals.

In 1986 Kinko's Graphics, in collaboration with Apple, announced the Academic Courseware Exchange, a program that lets colleges and universities share university-developed software throughout the world. Through the Academic Courseware Exchange educators are able to order courseware in the volumes they need and at prices students can afford.

Our commitment doesn't begin with an appointment and end with a warranty. It is a total effort by professionals dedicated to helping educators make technology work for education.

Kids Can't Wait: Putting technology in the hands of educators and students.

The Office of Special Education was formed to identify and assist disabled individuals through computers.

---

and grasped at one viewing like a painting, an advertisement, or a poster. Unifying it requires a theme. Often this theme will include both a purely visual *design* theme, and an editorial *content* theme (Figs. 184, 185).

The editorial theme could be the repetition of quotations on a particular topic. It could be a contrast of "then and now," a set of interviews—anything that seems to tell an interesting story related to a common topic. Advertising campaigns are usually based upon an editorial theme. Specialty publications such as annual reports, which revolve around one company, may also use an editorial approach.

A visual theme almost always accompanies the editorial theme. It might be the repeated use of a single thematic photograph on several pages throughout the publication. It could be a particular repeated arrangement of typography—or the grid itself. Many people consider the most creative activity of the layout artist is in the highly conceptual activity of establishing a visual and sometimes an intellectual theme.

Grids in History

The grid is by no means a new invention. It has been used for centuries by various cultures to design ornamental screens and textiles (Fig. 186). It has been the basis for quilt design, architecture, and navigation. It has been used by Pakistanis, native Americans, isolated African tribes, contemporary designers, and a host of others. The squared grid, in which each of the

186. *An ornamental grid design.*

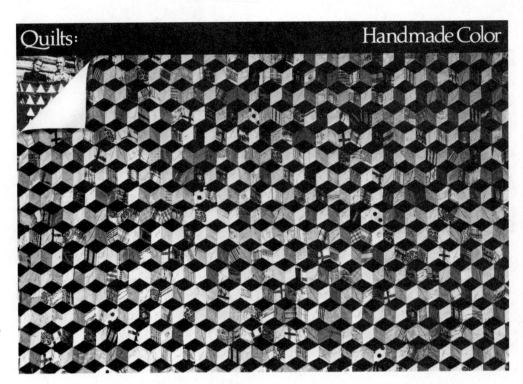

187. *Julius Friedman/ Walter McCord (Designer), Craig Guyon (Photographer). Quilts: Handmade Color.*

four sides of the unit is equal to the others, is the simplest variation; but it is capable of producing sophisticated results (Fig. 187).

Renaissance artists developed a method of examining a subject through a grid network of strings and drawing onto a paper similarly divided into sections. In the twentieth century the grid has become of interest to artists as a shape in itself. Frequently drawings, illustrations, and paintings allow the grid structure to show through, just as Bauhaus architects insisted that the structure of their buildings show through.

Many layouts today that have a strong grid structure have their origins in the de Stijl movement (see page 22). Van Doesburg and Mondrian were both using dark lines to divide their canvases into asymmetrical patterns by 1918.

A more recent figure associated with the grid layout is Swiss designer J. Müller-Brockmann. He has had tremendous influence on the structure and definition of graphic design. "The tauter the composition of elements in the space available, the more effectively can the thematic idea be formulated," he has written. Copy, photographs, drawings, trade names are all subservient to the underlying grid structure in what is called "Swiss Design."

Choosing a Grid

There are as many different grids as the mind can create. They vary from the familiar three-column format, to a Swiss grid based on overlapping squares, to an original creation.

The first consideration when choosing a grid is the elements it will contain. Consider the copy. How long is it; how long are the individual segments; how many inserts and subheads? If the copy is composed of many independent paragraphs, the underlying grid should break the page area up into small units. On the other hand, if the copy is a textbook of long unbroken chapters with few visuals, a complex grid is wasted; most of its divisions will be seldom used.

Now consider the art. A publication that uses many photographs will call for a different grid than one that is copy-heavy. Whenever many elements need to be incorporated into a layout, a more complex grid, broken down into many small units, is the most useful. It will give more possibilities for placing and sizing photographs.

You can create your own grid that corresponds to the number of elements and size of your page. The tinier the grid units, the more choices will need to be made about placement. The more placement options there are, the greater the chance that the underlying unity will be lost. In other words, sometimes a simple grid is the best choice.

Both the vertical and the horizontal divisions in a grid are important. The vertical dividers determine the line length of the copy. Both the vertical and horizontal lines determine the size of photographs or artwork. Remember from Chapter 6 to relate line length and type size to make it easy for the eye to read and keep its place. Forcing large type into small grid units makes for slow, difficult reading.

Constructing the Grid

The vertical divisions of the grid are usually expressed in picas, as is the line length of copy measured for typesetting. The horizontal divisions are most frequently measured in points, as is leading. A 10 point type, for example, with 2 points of leading between lines would be set on 12 point leading. Working out grid measurements this way will ensure that the copy from the typesetter will correspond to the structure of the ad layout.

You may draw in some of the grid units, although the structure is usually sounder if the elements themselves align with the grid edges and merely suggest the presence of the grid. With precise alignment, our eyes will draw an invisible line of "continuation" between elements that is a much stronger bond than the physical, inked line.

A subtle echoing of shape occurs in the advertisement in Figure 188. The keyboard, the long thin rectangle of the photograph, and the columns of type all reinforce one another. Such a continual, dancing repetition of placement and measurement will bring a layout alive.

Grid structure gives results similar to another approach, the "path" layout. Both depend on the eye and mind detecting such unit-forming factors as repetition and continuation, tempered with a deliberate contrast or variation for effect.

PATH LAYOUT

The path layout assumes no underlying, unifying structure. Rather, the designer begins with a blank white sheet of paper and attempts to visualize the elements on it in various arrangements. This complex approach can yield tremendously varied results. The underlying unity comes from a direct reliance on unit-forming factors. This reliance is sometimes unconscious, but beginning designers should learn it on a conscious level. It will lead to excellent results.

188. *Don Harbor (Art Director), Jeff France (Designer), Ken Hines (Copywriter), Don Woodlan (Type Director), and Jamie Cook (Photographer). Newspaper ad for Norfolk General Hospital. Lawler Ballard Agency, Norfolk, VA.*

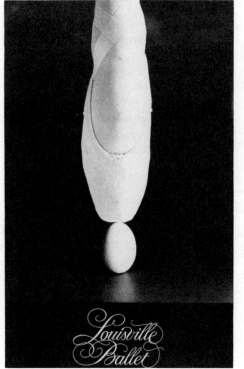

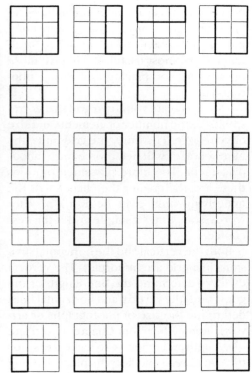

The word "path" describes this less structured, more spontaneous approach because the designer is attempting to set up a path for the eye. The goal is to guide the eye skillfully through the various elements. In order to do so, there must be a clear entry point or "focal point" and a clear "path" to the next element and the next.

Focal Point

The focal point, or the point of entry into a design, is the first area that attracts attention and encourages the viewer to look further. If at first glance, our eye is drawn equally to several different areas, visual chaos results and interest is lost. A focal point can be set up in many different ways, but they all have to do with creating difference or variety. Whatever disrupts an overall visual field will draw the eye. These differences could be:

A heavy black value set down in a field of gray and white.

A small isolated element in a design with several larger elements in close proximity to one another.

An irregular, organically shaped element set next to geometric ones.

A textured element set next to solid areas. Text type can often function in this manner.

A pictorial image or word that is emotionally loaded, such as "sex."

The focal point should not be so overwhelming that the eye stops.

Path

The eye is guided from element to element through grouping of elements, continuation, one element pointing to the next, the echoing or repetition of a shape, angle, or color, or careful balanced contrast of size and value. A simple path layout is used effectively in Figure 189, a poster design for the Louisville Ballet. The eye follows down the foot to discover the typography.

Photography in a Layout

An important element in layout design is the photograph. Learn what makes a good photograph and how to use it to best advantage. (Chapter 11 will help you do so.) Copywriters, photographers, and designers depend on one another's skills. Poor page design can make a beautiful photograph lose all its impact and appeal. Sometimes, also, a poor photograph may be strengthened by a good design.

Dynamic photos strong in design and human interest can look lifeless with certain design mistakes. One is the paper. If it is too absorbent, it will ink poorly, so the value contrast in the reproduced photos will be muddy. Another common mistake is with size contrast. Photos at similar sizes compete for attention; the eye will be drawn to none. Other elements on the page may also point away or detract.

Figure 190 shows some different ways of placing a photograph on a grid layout. Practice some variations yourself, attempting to establish a visual pacing.

Cropping

Many photographs can be improved by careful cropping. Cropping is eliminating part of the vertical or horizontal dimension of a photograph to focus attention on the remaining portion. Cropping is also used to fit a photograph into an available space, by altering its proportions. When cropping to fit a space, use discretion. Cropping too tightly will destroy the mood of the image.

Sometimes a photograph, like an overwritten paragraph, can be improved by deleting excess information. The format is fixed in a camera, but the action that is being photographed might be taking place within a compact square area or a long thin vertical. Trimming away the meaningless part of the image on the sides will improve the impact (Fig. 191).

Sometimes cropping a photograph makes it dramatic. If you wish to emphasize the height of a tall building, for example, cropping in on the sides to make a long, thin rectangle will increase the sense of height. Cropping the top and bottom of a long horizontal shot will increase the sense of an endless horizon.

Cropping causes us to focus on the dramatic part of the image in Figure 192, a poster for the Cincinnati ballet company.

Resizing

There are three ways to figure out the new proportions of a photo you resize—a simple algebraic equation, a proportion wheel, or a visual aid.

The algebraic formula is

$$\frac{\text{original height}}{\text{original width}} = \frac{\text{new height}}{\text{new width}}$$

$$\text{or } \frac{x}{y} = \frac{x^{\text{new}}}{y^{\text{new}}}$$

above: **191.** *Gordon Baer (Louisville, KY). Pepsi-Cola Diving Competition.*

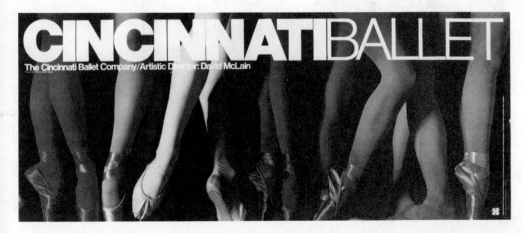

left: **192** *Dan Bittman (Designer), Corson Hirschfeld (Photographer), and the Hennegan Company (Lithography). Poster for the Cincinnati Ballet Company.*

193.

will give the percentage of enlargement or reduction.

A proportion wheel is shown in Figure 193. Following the directions printed on the wheel will give you the same information without any mathematical computations on your part.

Layout artists sometimes leave the percentage calculations to the printer, and instead only figure visually whether the proportions of a resized photo will fit the layout. Simply draw a diagonal from a lower corner to an upper corner of the cropped photograph. Then select either the vertical or horizontal dimension as the given new measurement. Draw a line from that edge to the diagonal. Then draw a line at right angles to the intersection. The resulting rectangle has the proportions of a correctly resized photo (Fig. 194).

Selecting

A designer may be given the photographs to work with or have the opportunity to order specific photos shot. You might also elect to shoot them personally. It is a wise idea for anyone considering a career in

One new dimension is unknown. Crossmultiply and divide to find it. Dividing the new width or height by the old one

194. *One way of resizing.*

graphic design to take a course in photography.

Choose photographs for your layout on three grounds: the quality of the print, the merit of the design, and the strength of the communication.

MULTI-PANEL DESIGN

Folders and brochures present a slightly different layout problem than magazines or books. A brochure is actually more a three-dimensional construction than a two-dimensional layout. Nevertheless, a grid may be used. Contrast of size and visual rhythm remain important.

The additional element of the fold complicates matters. Brochures may fold and unfold into unusual shapes (Fig. 195). They may unfold several times, and at each successive unfolding present a new facet of the design. Use this opportunity to tell a story. Each panel can give additional information, with the front panel acting as a "teaser." Never give your punch line on the front panel. Lead up to it. An example is the brochure in Figures 196 and 197. Designed by a graduating senior, it

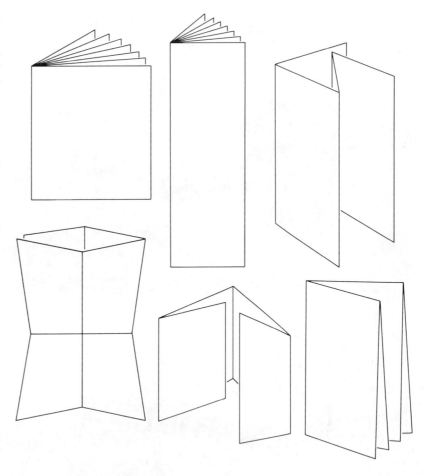

above: 195. *Brochure construction.*

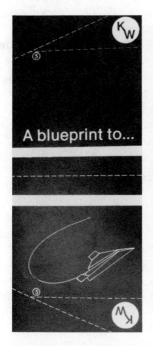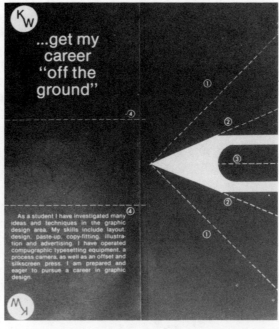

196, 197. *Kim Werner Block (UW–Whitewater student designer). Brochure.*

information (Figs. 198, 199). The back panel will usually remain almost blank. If the brochure is a self-mailer, address and stamp go directly on the back.

Other special decisions go into a multi-panel design: the size of the piece, the number of folds and their direction, and the flexibility of the paper. Usually when preparing a comprehensive, the designer will not mount the piece, but execute it on the same paper it will be printed on. Then the client can hold and unfold the design.

The brochure or flyer will often be part of a unified publication series. Then you must sustain the visual and intellectual theme of the series.

CONCLUSION

Layout is a balancing act, creating unity among the diverse elements on a page. An underlying grid can unite the many pages of a large publication. When you combine copy, illustration, and photography, you can also establish unity by finding similar shapes, angles, values, and type styles. Like a musical composition, a layout needs pacing, rhythm, and theme.

Variety or contrast is important, too. Many kinds of contrast—visual texture, value, shape, type style, and especially size—can create a focal point for a path layout.

Your layout should do justice to the intentions of the copywriter, photographer, and illustrator. Balance their contributions to achieve the strongest visual communication.

EXERCISES

198, 199. *Erica Green. Brochure for the YMCA of Milwaukee.*

was mailed to prospective employers. An inside panel explains how to fold on the dotted lines to create a paper airplane.

A successful front panel will lure the reader inside. The next panel will build interest and develop a theme, while the inside spread will hold the bulk of the

1. Use the full-page sample grids in Figures 200–203 to do several rhythmic layouts, with black or gray rectangles to signify photography or illustration. Comp the text type with lines, creating a rhythmic effect with their placement. Experiment with the different effects it is possible to create from a single grid.

200.

2. Select several magazines and figure out their grid structure. Which are successful and which unsuccessful? Why?
3. Using old magazines, cut out photographs to use in practice layouts. Try cropping large photos down for use in these exercises. Create a layout that uses the different contrasts of size discussed in this chapter.
4. Save samples of brochure design that appeal to you and study them for future inspiration. Look for interesting multipanel folders that unfold the message in sequential steps.

200, 201, 202, 203.
Sample grids (see pp. 115–118).

2.

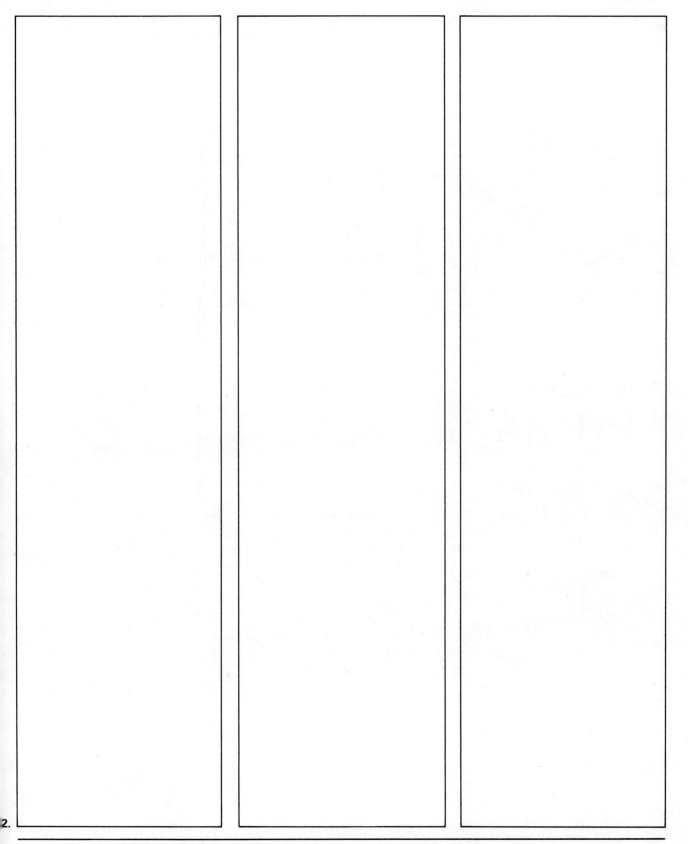

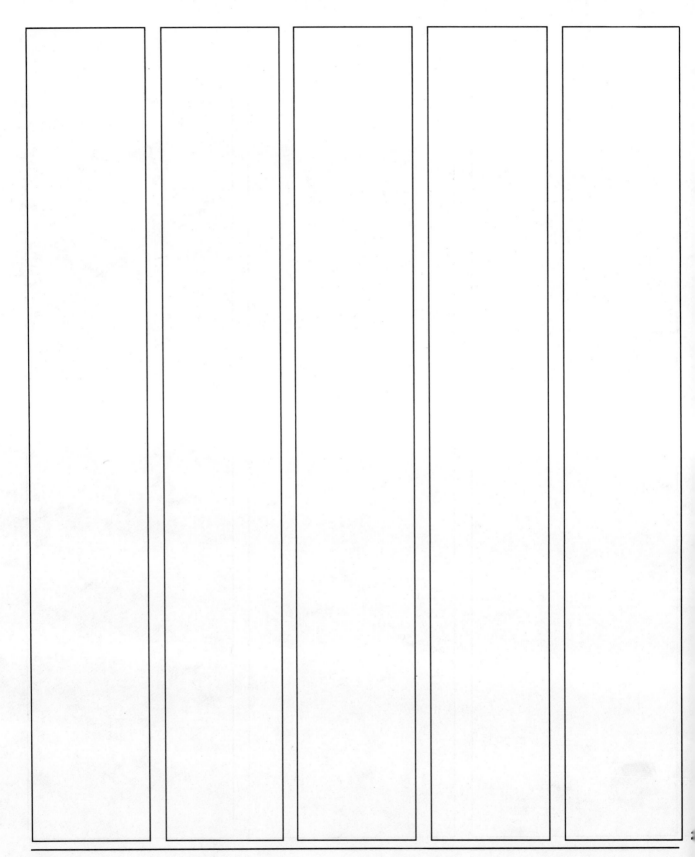

PROJECT
A Two-Page Layout

Redesign one of the unsuccessful layouts you found for Exercise 2. You will want a two-page spread. Each page should be 8 ¹/₂″ × 11″ (20 × 28 cm). It must have a headline, from three to five photographs, and a minimum of 4″ (10 cm) of body copy. Retain all the elements, but change their size, format, cropping, and placement. Establish a grid that suits your copy and fit your layout into it. Comp the text type and draw in the artwork and headlines on layout bond or marker paper with markers or a technical pen. An opaque enlarger is useful at this stage. You are preparing a polished "rough" layout. Figure out the percentage of enlargement or reduction for your photos and keep notes to present to the instructor.

Prepare a "comprehensive" of your layout. Pressure graphics, typesetting equipment, stat camera or process camera, and enlarging and reducing copiers are useful at this stage. If they are not available, content yourself with a polished rough. Figure 204 is a student layout from a similar project.

204. *Lynette Schwartz (UW–Whitewater student designer). Two-page layout.*

Objectives

Learn to choose an appropriate grid and fit layout elements into it.

Practice resizing photographs and comping type.

Use all the information so far on balance, rhythm, unity, and contrast to create a dynamic and compelling layout.

Bring typography and pictorial elements into a unified, balanced whole.

8

PREPARING CAMERA-READY ART

THE PASTEUP ARTIST

The first step in preparing art for the printer is the job of the graphic designer. It is the designer who makes decisions about the placement of elements, the location of color, and the type style. Once the rough layout and more polished comprehensive are approved, preparation is turned over to a pasteup artist, who prepares a "mechanical." Many entry-level jobs for artists are in pasteup.

The pasteup artist prepares a black and white version of the design that is "camera-ready." All of the components of the design have been assembled and prepared for reproduction by a process camera. If any artwork is to be reproduced in full color, it must be color-separated by a laser scanner or a process camera. A process camera will produce negatives of the black and white pasteup. These negatives are prepared for plate-making by a technician called a stripper. The plate is put on the printing press, where the final printed copies of the original layout are produced.

This process requires high standards from everyone involved. The pasteup artist must be a perfectionist. You also need a printer you can rely upon. Often the printer can answer questions about the equipment your job will be run on that will influence how you prepare the artwork. This chapter will discuss the preparation of artwork for the offset press, the commonest method of reproduction.

PARTS OF THE MECHANICAL

To the printer, the terms "art" and "copy" refer to all material to be reproduced. The copy is your typeset material, whereas art is everything else. All photographs, illustrations, and diagrams are called art. In general, they fall into two classifications: line art and continuous-tone images. The latter are prepared differently depending

205. *Line art.*

206. *Jeff Larson. Logo for "The Works" using shading films.*

India ink solids, and pen and ink stippling are all forms of line art. Special shading films that bear a printed pattern of dots or lines on adhesive acetate are forms of preprinted line art screens (Fig. 206). Zipatone, Letraset, and other manufacturers offer this product. They are not as accurate or clean as asking your printer to strip in a screen at the negative stage, so use them for special effects only.

Art with Gray Tones

Art that produces a graduated or blended variety of values is called continuous-tone art. It includes black and white photographs, illustrations or diagrams done with pencil or paint, and any other method that produces a variety of values. The position of these elements must be indicated on the pasteup, but the actual art is sent separately. It will be converted into line art and stripped into position on the negative. Continuous-tone images are converted into a special dot screen called a halftone screen (Fig. 207).

Multicolor art must also be broken into black and white for the printer. Each color must be prepared in black on its own separate acetate overlay. The flat color areas of these overlays are usually cut from a masking film like Rubylith. All of these overlays must be positioned in perfect registration with one another. Color printing is done by making a separate negative and plate for each necessary color. The different inks will be laid on the paper by the press in succession.

Because all camera-ready art except full-color images must be sent to the printer as black and white, there are two tricks it is useful to know. The camera will see and photograph red as black. It will see and photograph light blue as white. These exceptions are used extensively in pasteup.

PREPARING THE BOARD

The illustration board for the pasteup should be rigid enough to prevent the

on whether they are to be reproduced in one color or many (process color).

Line Art

Line art is made up of a black and white image with no variation in grays except those created by optical mixing (Fig. 205). Anything that is line art may be pasted up directly onto a board. It is ready to be photographed for reproduction. Anything that is not line art must be handled separately, because it must be converted at the printer's. The printing press will only reproduce line art.

Typeset copy, pen and ink drawings or diagrams, high contrast photography, copy from being damaged by popping off a thin baseboard as it bends. It should also have a smooth hotpress or clay-coated surface. There are many excellent pasteup baseboards available. The clay-coated are especially good for inking.

Cut the illustration board to about 2″ (5 cm) larger on all sides than your pasteup will be. Using your T-square and triangle, arrange the illustration board on the drawing board and tape it securely at the corners with masking tape. A pasteup will be more accurate if it is not moved until all copy and art has been positioned.

Use your triangle and T-square throughout the pasteup. Use the T-square for the horizontals and the triangle for the verticals, resting it on the top edge of the T-square (Fig. 208). Carefully measure the size your finished piece will be. Draw that onto the board in a well sharpened non-photo blue pencil. This outline forms the trim line. Leave several inches of "matte" outside the pencil line for writing instructions. Next, draw in the crop marks and fold lines using a technical pen with a fine point. They should be about $1/8″$ (0.3 cm) outside the trim dimensions indicated by your light blue line, and about $1/2″$ (1.2 cm) long. Fold lines are indicated by a dashed line. If the mechanical must be removed for a time and later repositioned, use the crop marks to realign it. These crop marks are what the printer will use to position the image for printing and to trim your paper. They must be as precise as a hairline (Fig. 209).

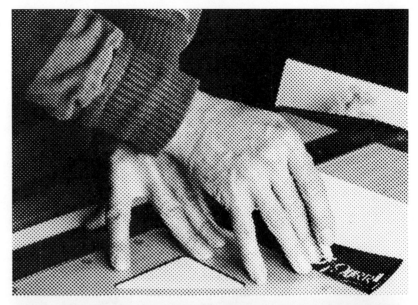

above top: 207.
Halftone dots enlarged.

above bottom: 208.
Pasteup tools.

209. *Crop marks.*

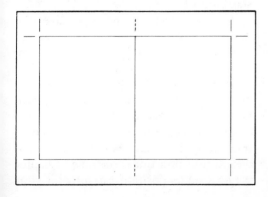

Assemble the original layout and all of the finished units that are parts of the layout. Check them for cleanliness and accuracy. Using non-photo blue pencil, draw in position lines for your copy and art based on the layout. Make certain that all the tools you will need are gathered around you, and that the waxer is turned on, or the rubber cement jar is full.

Check whether the type proofs require a fixative spray to prevent smudging. Photographic type proofs probably will not, but ink-printed proofs damage easily.

PASTING UP LINE COPY

Before beginning the actual pasteup, determine if any areas will be inked directly onto the board. If so, it is best to do them first, before the surface of the board gets wax or rubber cement or oil from your hands on it. If the pasteup calls for a black border, you can ink it yourself or use black adhesive tape. The tape is not as accurate, nor will it last as long as an inked line.

Inking mistakes can be covered over with opaque white, as long as they were not executed in water soluble ink. If a large area needs to be blocked out, paste opaque white paper over it rather than attempting to cover it with paint. As long as the black line copy itself stays sharp and precise, the retouching with white opaque and pasted paper will not harm the reproductive quality of your pasteup. If you plan on putting it in your portfolio, however, redo it so that all parts are neat and clean with no retouching.

If you will be using a waxer, run your copy through it before cutting it up to minimize the chance of catching it in the waxer. Trim all line art, using T-square, triangle, and X-acto knife. The edges of everything except free-form shapes should be kept precisely squared up to make it easier to judge whether the pasteup is crooked (Fig. 210). Cut your copy leaving an extra $1/16''$ (0.2 cm) of paper around all images. Cut marks sometimes show up on a negative, and the stripper will opaque them out. Leave room for an opaquing brush. Be certain to do your trimming on a surface that will not be damaged, or on a piece of board that will later be thrown away. It is a good idea to throw away scraps immediately to avoid a confusing, messy work area.

210. *Crooked edges make alignment hard.*

If you are using rubber cement, apply it to the back of the copy, putting a piece of scrap paper underneath to catch any excess. Allow it to dry slightly before pasting it down. For an extra firm hold, let the back of the copy dry, and apply a wet coat of cement to the board before positioning the copy.

Use your positioning guidelines. Begin from the top of the page and work down. This method decreases the number of times the T- square will be drawn over the pasted copy. Square the copy carefully vertically and horizontally with triangle and T-square. If it is important to follow the layout precisely, use a divider to measure small areas, or transfer the measurements from the layout to the mechanical with tick marks placed along the edge of a scrap of paper.

Place a clean sheet of paper over the pasted up copy and burnish it down, paying special attention to the edges. Use a rubber cement pickup to clean up all excess rubber cement. Should you need to reposition these elements later, rubber cement thinner will loosen the bond. Waxed copy can be repositioned at any time.

VARIATIONS WITH ONE-COLOR LINE ART

Reversals and tint screens are some variations that can add interest to your one-color line art pasteup. They should be planned out at the design stage. Sometimes, however, when a rush job comes through, the design stage and the pasteup stage are the same.

You can attach tracing paper over the pasteup and mark it for reversal at the printer's. If you have access to a stat camera or a process camera, you can prepare your own reversal. If you do, be sure to blacken its cut edges with a marker before pasting down (Fig. 211).

A tint screen can also be indicated on a tracing paper overlay. (For a more detailed description of a tint screen, see Chapter 9.) Keyline its position carefully for your

211.

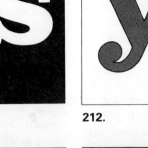

212.

213.   **214.**

211. *Line art reversal.*

212. *Specify percentages for screen tint.*

213. *A dropout—line art reversed out of a tint screen.*

214. *A surprint—line art superimposed over a tint screen.*

215. *Create a "window" for a halftone.*

printer's reference. Mark which percentage screen should be stripped into position. The pasteup artist may instead provide a solid black or solid red shape for the tint screen. It can be on the board itself if no other copy or artwork lies beneath. The area for the screen may also be placed on an acetate overlay. The screen tint to be stripped in must be specified by a percentage, such as 20 percent (Fig. 212).

A reversal can also be marked for conversion to a tint screen, as can any line art copy. When line copy is reversed out of a tint screen or a halftone it is called a *dropout* (Fig. 213).

Line copy superimposed over screened copy is called a *surprint* (Fig. 214). The positive line copy is pasted directly on the board. The tint screen area, a solid area of masking film on an acetate overlay, is placed over the line art on the board. The tint screen area can also be indicated with a red holding line accompanied by blue pencil instructions to the printer.

Shading film can be applied to a line drawing on the mechanical. Only coarse

dot patterns are available using this method, but the designer can rework the dot pattern if desired.

All of these variations still require only one ink color and one plate; they are all line art.

215.

CONTINUOUS-TONE ART

Continuous-tone art is any original art containing graduated or blended values. Photographs are the most common form of continuous-tone art, but illustrations are prepared for reproduction by the same process. As mentioned earlier, continuous-tone material is indicated for position on the pasteup, but it is sent separately to the printer to be converted into line art before printing. The printer will photograph it through a halftone screen that converts the tones to tiny dots of varying sizes. Because the screen reduces contrast and makes details less distinct, continuous-tone art for reproduction should be bold, with greater value distinctions than normal.

If the continuous-tone art has a geometric outer shape, like most photographs, it is indicated on the pasteup with a "window." This window is cut from red masking film such as a wax-backed Paropaque.

An area larger than the photograph is cut and lifted from its backing, then burnished into position on the board. It is then trimmed precisely to size (Fig. 215). Windows must be keyed with an identifying number or letter so that the stripper knows which halftone to place in them. Keying can be done on the tracing paper overlay or in black ink on the window itself. If the shape of the continuous-tone image is not geometric, cut a specially shaped dropout window for it. If it has a complicated outline, attach a photostat of the image to the pasteup, marking it "for position only." The printer will make the window (Fig. 216).

A special kind of overlay material for cutting a window is a red or orange masking film laminated to a clean acetate backing. The backing sheet serves as an acetate overlay hinged to the mechanical. The window is cut in the film, but not through the acetate backing. The unwanted red or ruby film is peeled off and discarded, leaving a clear acetate cover for your pasteup, with the masked out areas left on it. This method is often referred to as "cut and peel." Amberlith and Rubylith are brand names for this product.

ACETATE OVERLAYS

An overlay permits superimposing units that cannot be put together for one reason or another. As we have discussed, acetate overlays are used when two images occupy the same space, when more than one color is being used, and sometimes when tint screens or continuous-tone images are to be stripped into windows (Fig. 217).

The overlay should be taped along the top front of the pasteup so that it lies flat. It should extend beyond the trim lines. Accurate positioning is important. Ensure it with registration marks placed on the board and on the overlay so that they line up over one another precisely. You may draw your own, but purchasing preprinted ones is easier and probably more accurate. If you draw your own, you will need

216. *A photostat of a halftone can be attached to the pasteup and marked "for position only."*

acetate ink that will not crawl or bead on acetate. At least three registration marks are necessary, on different sides of the pasteup.

If more than one overlay is required, attach them to different sides of the board. This way any overlay can be brought into direct contact with the board for accurate registration (Fig. 218).

When the printer makes the negative, a sheet of white paper is positioned behind each overlay. A photograph is taken of each overlay without the rest of the paste-up showing. In that way, each overlay can be treated separately for screening, reversals, or separate colors.

MULTICOLOR MECHANICALS

Preseparated Art

There are two approaches to multicolor reproduction—preseparating and keylining. In the first, the art for the primary color is pasted to a piece of illustration board, and the art for the other colors registered on acetate overlays. The primary color on the board is either the most complicated color of the most prevalent. Acetate overlays are hinged to the top of the board with drafting tape. They have registration marks corresponding to those on the board, but no crop marks or fold lines. Color and screened percentages should be marked in the margins of each overlay. This method is called preseparated art, because it is done by the pasteup artist before being sent to the printer. Usually a marker indication of color is done on a final tissue overlay with special instructions for shooting.

For precise hairline register, it is better to keyline the positions of the second and third color, and let the printer separate it photographically.

There are three types of color register: nonregistered, commercial register, and hairline register. Nonregistered colors do not abut. Commercial register (sometimes called lap register) means that slight variations in placement of color of about one

row of dots are not important. Hairline register is a term for extremely tight register, where the tolerance is not greater than half a row of screen dots. Acetate overlay separation is generally used for nonregistered or commercial registration. It is not suitable for a hairline registration.

Keylining

In overlay separation, the pasteup artist prepares copy for each color on separate

217. *Acetate overlays have various pasteup applications.*

218. *Accurate registration marks are important.*

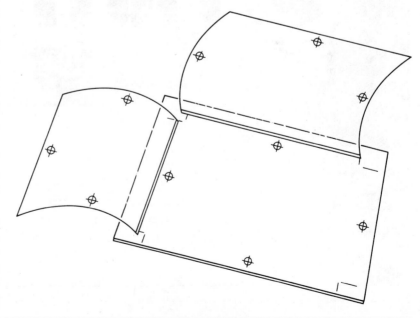

sheets, which the printer photographs to make plates. In keylining the printer performs the separation. It is quicker, more precise, and more expensive.

In keylining, the copy for all the line art, regardless of color, is placed on the baseboard. The black is inked in, but the other color areas are indicated by a red outline. The printer will make as many negatives as there are colors, removing or completing shapes on each negative as necessary to obtain a separation negative for each color.

Final Touches

After all overlays have been completed, tracing paper is attached to the pasteup for specifications. Positions of continuous-tone photos are marked on this tissue, as are color areas and special instructions about reversals or tint screens. A rough marker indication of color is usually drawn

on this tissue, unless a comprehensive or rough is being sent with it (Fig. 219).

The bottom of the pasteup board is marked with the dimensions of the printed piece, and with "SS" (same size) or percentage of reduction or enlargement.

Above all, your pasteup must be perfectly clean, with sharp edges, straight lines. There is no "B" grade in pasteup. It is perfect or it is a failure.

EXERCISES

Find a black and white magazine layout with a photograph, a headline, and text or body copy. Carefully cut it apart, trimming away excess white areas. Paste it up on board, keeping the layout the same. Cut a window for the photograph. Set the headline in pressure graphics, to practice letter and word spacing.

PROJECT
Camera-Ready Art

Make your project from Chapter 7 camera-ready. Prepare it for the printer, including all pasteup, all hand-separated acetate overlays, and instructions for the printer. If you do not have access to typesetting equipment for the body copy, your instructor may be able to have several copies of generic text run off by a local typesetter in varying styles and sizes.

Objective. Practice pasteup skills.

Quality Checklist

1. Does your finished pasteup look good to the eye? There should be no rough edges (cut or drawn), fingerprints, or imprecise lines.
2. Does every horizontal line align with your T-square?
3. Does every vertical line align with your triangle?
4. Is the letter spacing in the headline exactly what you intend?
5. Do the crop marks measure *precisely*?

219. *A marker rough will indicate color on the tissue overlay.*

6. Is all rubber cement or wax cleaned off the board?
7. Are all overlays marked for tint screens and color?
8. Are the edges of your "windows" *perfectly* square?
9. Are your registration marks cleanly placed over one another?
10. Is the tracing paper overlay clearly marked for color and tint screen?

Are all possible questions concerning your pasteup answered by the information provided on the board itself?

Congratulations! If you passed this checklist, you are on the way to becoming a good pasteup artist. That means you are beginning to understand design problems from the printer's point of view (an important perspective for a future art director).

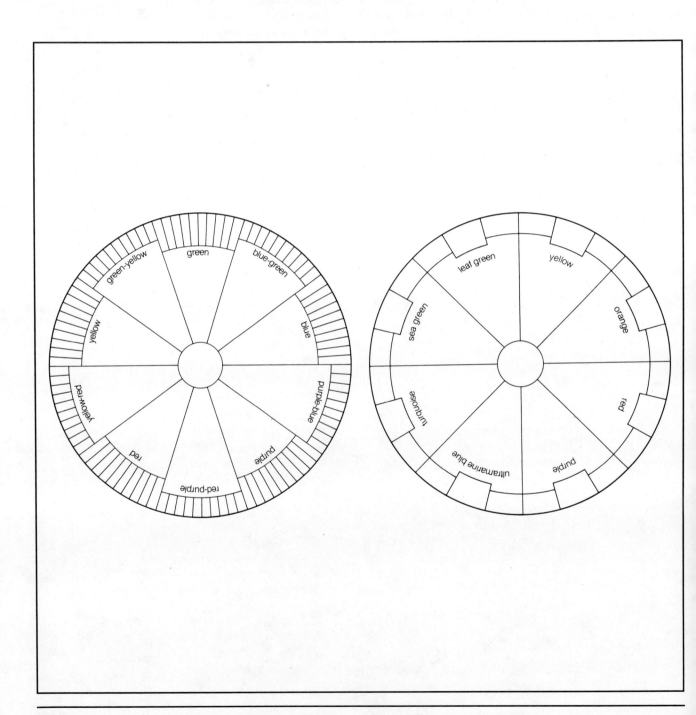

9

THE DYNAMICS OF COLOR

Color for the designer and color for the fine artist are much the same at the creative stage. Later, in preparing art for printing, the designer has to know how color is influenced by printing technology. A great deal of new terminology has to be understood. Let us first brush up on color as a creative and expressive communication aid (Pl. 1, p. 133). (For more detailed information, a number of excellent basic design books are included in the Bibliography at the back of this book.) Then we will consider color from the printer's perspective.

UNDERSTANDING COLOR

Every student who has completed an elementary course in art has heard that color is a property of light. Many people do not fully understand those words, however, until years after their art degree is completed. A young painter several years past her B.F.A. degree tells a story of looking around her living room for a composition to paint. "I considered the objects in the room and the space they occupied; the corners of the ceiling and the negative spaces in the staircase. I looked at the carpet and saw the standard 'landlord green.' And then I looked at the carpet again and realized that my mind was processing 'landlord green,' but my eyes were actually looking at black geometric shapes beside a shining pastel/fluorescent color like fresh spring leaves. The sun was shining in the window of my dark living room and transforming my carpet. Color

220. *Claude Monet. La cathédrale de Rouen. 1894. Chichés des Musées Nationaux. Monet was fascinated by the everchanging effect of light on color. He painted the Rouen Cathedral at several times of day, in varying light conditions.*

221. *Light waves of many colors join to make white light.*

Isaac Newton first passed a beam of white light through a prism and saw it divide into several colors. The colors of the light wave spectrum are red, orange, yellow, green, blue, and indigo (Fig. 221). In physics, mixing the colors of the light wave together will produce pure white light. It is these light waves, bouncing off or being absorbed by the objects around us, that give them color.

The three primary colors in white light are red, blue, and green. They are called "additive" primaries because together they can produce white light. The eye contains three different types of color receptors, each sensitive to one of the primary colors of the light spectrum.

The designer has to understand that color is dependent on light. Color is not an unchanging, absolute property of the object. It is dynamic. It is affected by its environment.

The Color Wheel

For the designer, unlike the physicist, mixing pigments will never produce white. Black is the sum of all pigment colors. Several color wheels have been developed to help us understand the effects of combining pigments.

The traditional color wheel, developed by Herbert Ives, begins with "subtractive" primary colors of red, yellow, and blue. Mixing these hues produces secondary colors. Mixing the secondary colors with the primary produces a tertiary color.

is a property of light, I thought. Oh!" (Fig. 220).

Color has been described as both "the way an object absorbs or reflects light" and "the kind of light that strikes an object." The painter's carpet would appear to have a different color had it a deep shag texture or a slick, shiny surface. It would appear to have a different color under an incandescent or fluorescent light, under bright natural sunlight or light overcast cloud cover. Even the angle from which it is viewed would have an effect.

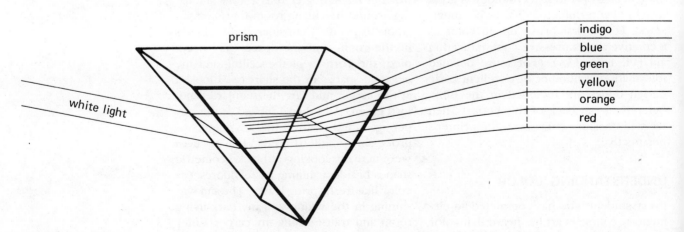

prism

white light

indigo
blue
green
yellow
orange
red

The Dynamics of Color

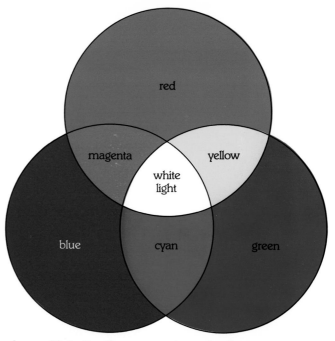

right: Plate 1. *Julius Friedman (Designer), Warren Lynch (Photographer). Fresh Paint. Poster for Kentucky Arts Commission Painting Show.*

below: Plate 2. *Susan Foster (Designer), John Coppola (Art Director), Lang Photo Services. Poster for traditional American Dance. Torn paper. Complementary colors here are exciting.*

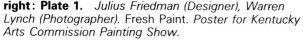

above: Plate 3. *Cyan, magenta, and yellow are subtractive primaries left after one primary has been subtracted from white light.*

PI. 4.

PI. 6.

Four-color pre-separated art

PI. 5.

Pl. 7.

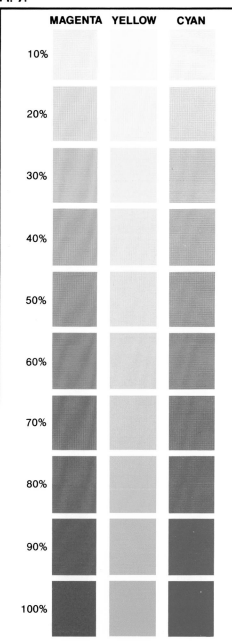

	MAGENTA	YELLOW	CYAN
10%			
20%			
30%			
40%			
50%			
60%			
70%			
80%			
90%			
100%			

Pl. 8.

Black and blue duotone

Black and yellow duotone

Black and red duotone

far left: Plate 6. *Tint screen percentages of the four process colors are combined to create this illustration.*

left: Plate 7. *Changing tint values with screens. Material furnished by Hammermill Papers Group for Plates 6, 7, 8, and 9.*

near left: Plate 8. *Duotones created by combining black with a second color.*

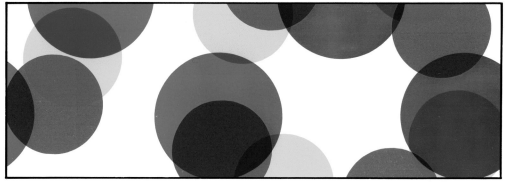

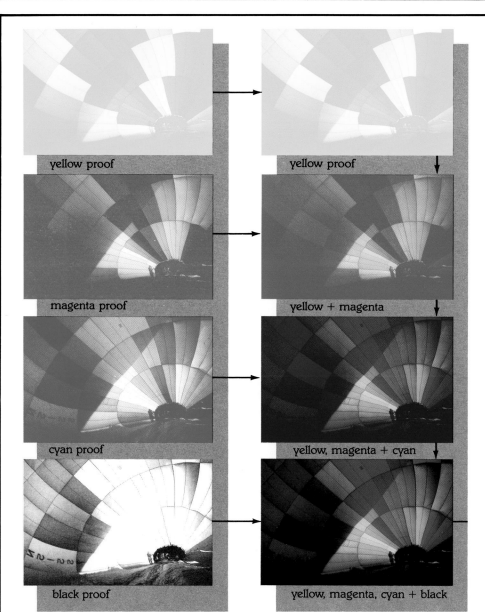

above: Plate 9. *Dots in process color vary in density.*

right: Plate 10. *Yellow, magenta, cyan, and black proofs and their combinations.*

yellow proof

yellow proof

magenta proof

yellow + magenta

cyan proof

yellow, magenta + cyan

black proof

yellow, magenta, cyan + black

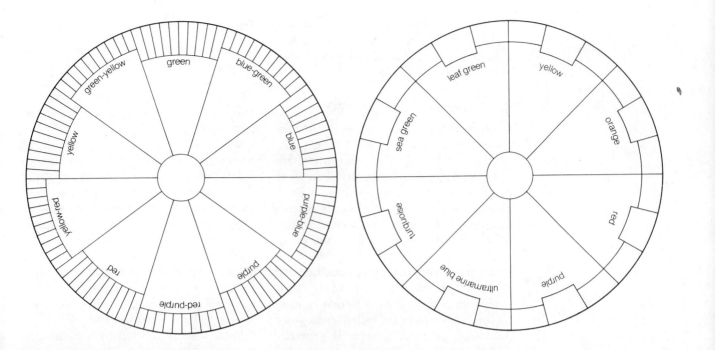

The Munsell color wheel is based on five key hues—red, yellow, blue, green, and purple. Secondaries are formed by mixing these primaries. Although these two classification systems differ, the basic "look" of the resulting colors is similar. The color wheel is only a workable system, not an absolute (Fig. 222).

Properties of Color

Every color has three properties: hue, value, and intensity. Hue is the name by which we identify a color. The color wheel is set up according to hue.

Value is the degree of lightness or darkness in a hue. It is easiest to understand value when looking at a black and white image. The darkest value will be close to black, the lightest close to white, with a range of grays in between. Value also plays an important role in all color images. Every hue has its own value range. Yellow, for example, is normally lighter than purple. Its "normal" value in the middle of a yellow value scale will be lighter than purple. In a value scale, the color values that are lighter than normal value are called *tints*; those darker than normal value are called *shades*. The addition of white will lighten a value, whereas the addition of black will darken it (Fig. 223).

The third property of color is intensity or saturation. It is a measure of a color's purity and brightness. In pigments there are two ways of reducing the intensity of a color: mix it with a gray of the same value, or mix it with its complement (the color opposite on the color wheel). Low

222. *Two possible color wheels.*

223. *Changes in value.*

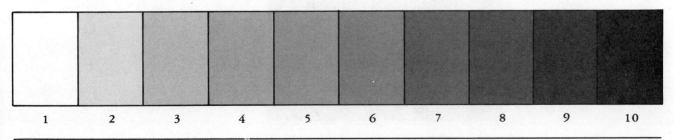

intensity colors have been "toned down" and are often referred to as tones. Colors that are not grayed are at their most vivid at full intensity.

Color Schemes

Color combinations are grouped into categories called color schemes. Colors opposite one another on the color wheel are called *complements*. Art that combines these colors is said to be using a complementary color scheme. Complements heighten and accent one another. They often are used to produce a bold, exciting effect (Pl. 2, p. 133). A split complementary scheme includes one hue and the two hues on either side of its direct complement. Colors next to one another on the color wheel are called *analogous*. An analogous color scheme is generally considered to be soothing and restful. A *monochromatic* color scheme is composed of one hue in several values. It also is often used for a quiet, soothing effect (Pl. 5, p. 134).

In color there are no real absolutes. That is why this information is often called "color theory." It is unusual, but quite possible, to produce a tense, dramatic effect using analogous colors or a soothing, harmonious effect using complementary colors. Remember that these principles are not rules, but useful guidelines. You may deliberately violate them for effect.

THE RELATIVITY OF COLOR

Our perception of color is "colored" by many considerations. For example, the way each color looks to us is strongly affected by the colors that surround it. This phenomenon is known as simultaneous contrast.

We automatically compare and contrast colors that sit side by side. When complements (such as red and green) are placed side by side, they seem to become more intense. They "complement" one another. A gray placed beside a color will appear to have a tinge of that color's complement in it because our eye automatically searches for it. Therefore a neutral gray beside a red will appear to be a greenish gray, while the same neutral gray beside a green will appear to have a reddish cast.

Value also is affected by simultaneous contrast. A gray placed against a black ground will appear to have a lighter value than the same gray placed against a white ground (Fig. 224). Our eye makes a comparison between the black and gray and judges the gray as much lighter. In the other sample, our eye looks at the white and judges the gray as much darker.

One designer first experienced this effect when she was a child, visiting her aunt for dinner. Butter in her own home was a yellow stick brought home from the store. On the aunt's farm it came straight from the cows, after a little churning. This fresh

224. *Simultaneous contrast gives two boxes of the same gray different apparent values.*

butter did not have a yellow food coloring added to it. When her aunt placed it on the table on a yellow plate, the niece would not eat it. It looked white, and could not be the "real thing." Who would eat white butter? The aunt, however, knew about simultaneous contrast, although not by that name. She whisked the butter plate away, and returned with the same butter, this time on a white plate. The young girl was delighted with the "new" butter. This time, compared with the white plate it sat on, the fresh butter looked yellow.

Simultaneous contrast means that color is relative to the colors surrounding it. This fact was first discovered in the nineteenth century when a French chemist named Michel Eugene Chevreul, a merchant who dyed fabric, was disturbed by apparent inconsistencies in his bolts of cloth. He discovered that his dye remained consistent, but the viewing conditions did not. Bolts of the same color appeared to be different colors depending on the color of the fiber samples around them. He went on to research this phenomenon. In the twentieth century, Josef Albers made a further, intensive study of color. Albers experimented with simultaneous contrast and contributed to our understanding of that effect.

THE PSYCHOLOGY OF COLOR

Relativity also holds true in the psychology of color. Colors have the power to evoke specific emotional responses in the viewer—some personal, and some more universal. In general, for example, warm colors stimulate, whereas cool colors relax most people. Interior decorators pay close attention to this relationship when they consider the color schemes for a dentist's waiting room or the newsroom of a daily paper. Can you imagine sitting in a dentist's chair while staring at a bright red wall?

Red, yellow, and their variations are referred to as warm colors, perhaps because we associate them with fire and the sun. Blue and green are considered cool colors. They also happen to be the colors of sky, water, and forests. The difference in the wave lengths of these colors may account for our reactions to them.

Associations

Personal memories play a part in color perception as well. If your mother usually wore a particular shade of blue, and you loved your mother (and she loved you), then that shade of blue would have good associations for you. It would seem a warm, friendly color, although to other eyes it might look cool.

Along with personal associations, we have cultural associations with color. They often appear in our language: "black anger," "yellow-bellied coward," feeling "blue," and "seeing red" are a few examples. To a wedding we wear white, the color of purity; to a funeral we wear black, the color of mourning. These are not absolute; they change from culture to culture. For example, people in India wear white to a funeral. For a wedding, they favor yellow.

We can describe our culture's general color associations. It is by no means a description to be memorized and taken as "gospel." Color psychology is complex, affected by many considerations, but if you can combine this information with a light hand and sensitive eye, it may prove useful.

Red   Red is a dramatic, highly visible hue. It is associated with sexuality and aggression, with passion and violence. It is also an official hue that is found in most national colors. Red is often the favored color for a sports car or a sports team. A dignified, conservative executive, however, is unlikely to choose red for a car or a corporate logo unless its intensity is toned down or its value darkened toward black.

Blue   In its darker values, blue is associated with authority. Our executive might likely favor a navy blue car, suit, and logo.

A middle value blue is generally associated with cleanliness and honesty, and has a cooling, soothing effect. It is used as a background color in package design because of its quiet, positive associations. Even at full intensity blue retains a calm quality.

Yellow Yellow is used in food packaging a great deal because it is associated with warmth, good health, and optimism. There remain in our language reminders that yellow also has been associated with cowardliness and weakness. That does not appear to be case currently, however. Even our cultural associations are subject to change.

Green Green is associated with the environment, cleanliness, and naturalness. It is soothing and cooling and consequently a favored color among manufacturers of such products as menthol cigarettes and non-cola beverages.

Selecting Color

Consider the psychology of your audience in your choice of color. A game or toy intended to appeal to children should have different color than one intended to reach adults considering retirement plans (Pl. 4, p. 134). Our color preferences change as we grow older. In general, youth prefers a more intense color that signals urgency and excitement. The subtle color preferences of age are associated with restraint and dignity.

The institution you are designing for should also affect your selection of color. Banks tend to prefer the darker values and the blues and grays that are associated with authority and stability. A physical fitness club would probably want more vibrant and intense colors. A restaurant may choose complementary colors that are toned down to an attractive and intimate level.

As a designer, your individual color preference is not the only or even the primary consideration. Your choice of color should reflect four psychological factors:

1. Cultural associations with color.
2. The profile of your audience and its color preferences.
3. The character and personality of the company you are representing.
4. Your personal relationship with color.

COLOR IN PRINTING

In addition to applying the psychology of color, the designer must work within restrictions imposed by the technology of mass reproduction. Designs must be created within the limitations of the budget, equipment, expertise, and time available for a particular project. The designer's use of color must be not only creative and appropriate, but practical. The first step to understanding color in the printing industry is to study the difference between the artist/designer's mixed pigment color and color as it is used in the printing process.

Mixed pigment color is changed by the addition of a different color. Black is altered to gray by the addition of white; white is altered to gray by the addition of black; red is altered to a lighter pink-red by the addition of white, and so forth. In printing, however, color is changed by combining screened percentages of hues. Whereas the artist makes gray from black by adding white paint, the printer makes gray from black by subtracting part of the density of the black ink.

There are two types of screens used by a printer to achieve color variety: tint screens and process color separations. In Chapter 8 you learned to handle both in pasteup. Now you will learn to see them from a printer's viewpoint.

Tint Screens

To create a tint or light value of a hue, the printer cuts back on the density of the ink through varying screens. Screens are available in gradients from 10 percent to 90 percent. A zero percent screen means no ink coverage; the white of the paper shows through. One hundred percent coverage means solid inking. There is a similarity between the tint screens of printing inks and the application of transparent watercolor. In both cases, white is made by allowing the white of the paper to show through, and lighter values are made by applying less pigment or ink.

In appearance the value scale of a printer's screens is similar to a value scale mixed by an artist combining pigments. However, if you look at the printer's scale under an industry magnifying glass called a linen tester, the screened dots will show up (Fig. 225). All of printing is a form of optical illusion achieved not by sleight of hand, but by dot screens. The same black ink is applied to paper for a 90 percent gray or a 10 percent gray, but the dot screen fools the eye into believing it is different. Where there are more dots, the ink looks blacker.

Screens change the tint value of a color. Plate 7 (p. 135) shows 10–100 percent tint screens of the three process colors: yellow, magenta, and cyan. Changing the hue or making an ink appear darker is done by combining screened percentages of different colors. To change a blue to purple, for example, a tint screen of red could be laid over it. Plate 6 (p. 134) shows the three process colors plus black combined in screens of various amounts.

Color Reference Guides

It is important for the designer to visualize these screened color combinations in advance. Probably markers or cut paper colored the original artwork for the client. How do you translate these colors for the printer?

You could just ask for candy apple red, bright red, or pure, true red. If you did, only your printer would know what color you would get. It surely would not match the picture in your head. You could give in your artwork, done up in markers or colored pencils, and hope for a match. Fortunately, there is a much more precise method: numbers.

Several numbered guides to color are available. The most complete, the PANTONE®* MATCHING SYSTEM, consists of a full line of color specification books, coordinated by PANTONE Color numbers. The PANTONE Color Formula Guide, first developed in 1963, presents the full range of printer's ink colors on both coated and uncoated paper (Fig. 226). Each ink color has its own number. You choose your ink color from the guide and tell the printer its PANTONE Number. The printer looks at the guide and prepares the ink you have specified. To get the desired blue for your design, you might specify PANTONE 313 with a 20 percent screen of black. You can now buy paper

*Pantone, Inc.'s check-standard trademark for color reproduction and color reproduction materials.

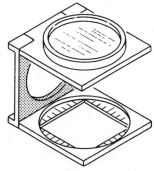

225. *A linen tester magnifies screened dots.*

226. *The PANTONE Color Formula Guide.*

and markers that correspond to the PAN-TONE MATCHING SYSTEM. This system increases the likelihood that the original comped design and the printed piece will closely resemble one another.

A variety of reference books show screened percentages of these ink colors. They also show what happens when you combine two different ink colors in screened percentages. The commonest guide available will show black ink added in varying amounts to the other printer's inks. The *PANTONE Color & Black Selector* is a good guide of this sort.

Cutting Costs

Each additional ink used in a design means the printer must do additional work preparing plates, negatives, and the press. The more ink colors you use, the more printing the design will cost. Combining screened percentages of inks will enable you to get the most out of each color you pay for, and can decrease the cost of the job.

Ink colors can also enhance black and white photography. Plate 8 (p. 135) shows three identical photographs, each printed in two colors. This two-color effect with black and white photography is called a *duotone*. It is less costly than reproducing a full-color photograph.

Another way to get more color into a job without increasing the cost is by printing on colored paper. There are also excellent reference books (often from paper companies) on using colored inks on colored papers. The color of the paper will show through, subtly altering the look of the ink. (For this reason white ink is rarely used in the printing industry. There is not an opaque white available in printer's inks. The paper will always show through. Sometimes this subtle, ghosting effect is what the designer wants.)

Study how tint screens and ink and paper interact. Then you can achieve the effect you desire at a minimum cost and avoid surprises when the job comes back from the printer.

Process Color Separations

Reproducing a full range of color rather than just two or three colors is done with process colors. This method is easier for the designer, but more complex and expensive for the printer. The three primary colors in process printing are yellow, magenta, and cyan. The addition of black as a fourth color gives depth and solidity to the image. These four inks produce the effect of full color.

Once the designer has given the printer a full-color illustration or photograph to reproduce, the printer separates out the process colors photographically. The artwork is photographed on a process camera or a laser scanner at least three times, through red, green, and blue filters corresponding to the additive primaries of the light spectrum. Each filter subtracts certain hues. The red filter, for example, produces a recording on the negative of all red light reflected from the image. When a positive is made, it will drop out all red and record only the blue and green present. This recording of blue and green will print as cyan. The green filter produces a magenta positive image, whereas the blue filter produces a yellow positive called the "yellow printer."

These three colors—yellow, magenta, and cyan—are called *subtractive primaries* because each represents the two additive primaries left after one primary has been subtracted from white light (Pl. 3, p. 133). These three exposures are the three color separations from which the printing plates will be made. A black separation is also made from a separate modified filter. When the press is inked with each of these four colors, and the color is laid down from the plate onto the paper, an illusion of full color results. The varying densities of dots overlap and lie beside one another, mixing optically. It is a truly effective illusion.

As with tint screens, the mixing happens not within the pigment, but within the eye of the viewer. Unlike the even dot coverage of tint screens, a process color separation is made of dots of varying densities that correspond to the color density in the original image (Pl. 9, p. 136). This variation is why such a complex range of color can be produced from only four process colors.

Plate 10 (p. 136) shows a proof of each of these four colors in the left column. The right column shows the effect created when these colors are printed over one another in sequence.

EXERCISES

1. Find printed samples of monochromatic, analogous, and complementary color schemes. Search for samples of color used in graphic design, advertising, or packaging that convey a particular mood and reach a particular audience.
2. Find an example of simultaneous contrast that uses value. Now find one that uses hue.
3. Find an example of a two-color design that uses tint screens to achieve a multicolor effect. Analyze how this design was prepared for printing. Make notes and discuss them with your instructor.

PROJECT
Word and Image Poster

Prepare two full-color posters that combine the image of a famous person with a related word. Select two people who are extremely different. The word related to each image can be a name or an association the image brings to mind. Pay close attention to integrating the typography with the image through various gestalt unit-forming techniques.

Choose a complementary, split complementary, or analogous color scheme for both posters. Use tint, tone, and shade to give your color schemes different personalities appropriate to their images.

Make the poster 11″ x 17″ (28 x 43 cm) with approximately 3″ (8 cm) white "matte" left around the image. Execute the design in either cut paper or opaque paint such as designer's gouache. Present it on illustration board, properly flapped.

Figure 227 is a student album cover design produced in warm, mellow reds and yellows. It demonstrates the careful integration of typography with illustration this project requires.

Objectives

Learn to use color to express a mood appropriate to an image.

Control hues through tint, tone, and shade to express different emotive qualities.

Practice integrating word and image from the standpoint of both pure design and content.

227. *Candy Thieme (UW –Whitewater student designer). Album cover.*

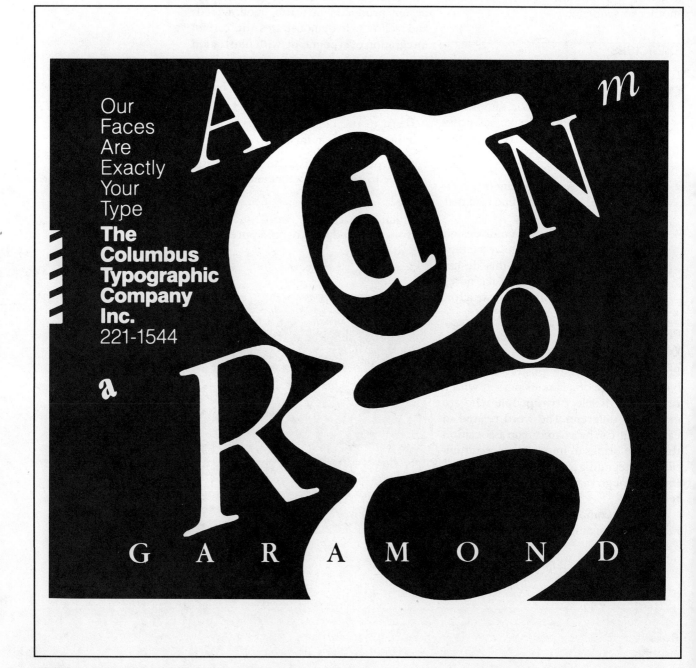

10

ADVERTISING DESIGN

THE PURPOSE OF ADVERTISING

Advertising differs from pure graphic design in intent. It seeks to persuade, not primarily to inform. Both purposes involve communication. As Figure 228, a poster for Heritage Color, boasts, "Sometimes your whole image rests on a piece of paper."

The successful advertisement (1) attracts attention, (2) communicates a message, and (3) persuades an audience. Advertising can have many different looks. It may appear in television, newspapers, direct mail, magazines, billboards, outdoor displays, and point-of-purchase displays. Whatever the medium, it is characteristized by an attempt to persuade an audience, with the intent to boost sales, profits, and share of the market.

There are elements of information in an advertisement and elements of persuasion in pure graphic design. Among the current issues in advertising theory is the argument about how much advertising should be informational and how much persuasive. The proponents of the "advertising as information" school assume the consumer initially buys the product based on information supplied by advertisements. Future purchases are based on first-hand assessment of the quality of the product (Fig. 229). This theory states that the persuasive element in advertising is secondary to the information supplied.

To what extent is this view of advertising true? Probably the ads that are most useful in informing consumers are those on a regional level announcing events such as plays, concerts, and meetings. The consumer might miss an opportunity to participate without an advertisement.

Those who believe the function of advertising should be persuasion maintain that advertisements exist to change perception. Advertising induces the consumer to believe the product has certain desirable qualities or associations. Soda

above left: 228. *Clint Clemens (Photographer), Woody Kay (Art Director). Promotional poster for Heritage Color. (Leonard Monahan Saabye Agency.)*

above right: 229. *Advertisement for Apple Computer. Copyright 1986.*

pop and blue jeans become associated with youth, zest, and popularity. Ads for them "sell" an attitude and a lifestyle.

The purest example of advertising for persuasive purposes can be found in national advertising, especially of long-standing and leading products. The public no longer needs pure information on these products. What sells such a product to the public is the associations they have with it. Many of these associations are generated by advertising, rather than by experience. The three photographs in Figures 230–232 are from a storyboard for a Pepsi Cola commercial.

Most advertisers want both persuasive and informative qualities in their advertising. The closer an advertisement comes to pure information, the closer it comes to pure graphic design. The closer a graphic design such as a poster comes to not only announcing an event, but persuading ticket purchases, the closer it comes to pure advertising (Figs. 233–234).

TYPES OF ADVERTISING

Retail and national advertising are the two major categories of advertising. Each of them can be divided into three major areas according to dollar volume: television, newspaper, and direct mail.

Retail advertising is so named because it is often sponsored by a retail establishment. It tends to be informational in nature, especially when announcing special discounts or availablity. It often attempts to get people to go to sponsoring stores to buy items they have seen advertised nationally. Studies have shown that retail advertising encourages price competition.

National advertising is advertising run by manufacturers with a nationwide distribution network for their product. It tends to be persuasive in nature. It began when manufacturers wanted to differenti-

below: 233, 234. *Eric Rickabaugh (Columbus).*

Our Faces Are Exactly Your Type **The Columbus Typographic Company Inc.** 221-1544

L U B A L I N

Our Faces Are Exactly Your Type **The Columbus Typographic Company Inc.** 221-1544

G A R A M O N D

above: 230, 231, 232. *Harvey Hoffenberg (Art Director), Susan Procter (Copywriter), Ed Pollack (Executive Producer) for BBDO Agency, New York City. Tony Scott (Director) and Jordan Kalfus (Executive Producer) for Sunlight Pictures, Los Angeles. Three photos for a Pepsi-Cola commercial.*

below: 233, 234. *Eric Rickabaugh (Columbus).*

Types of Advertising   **147**

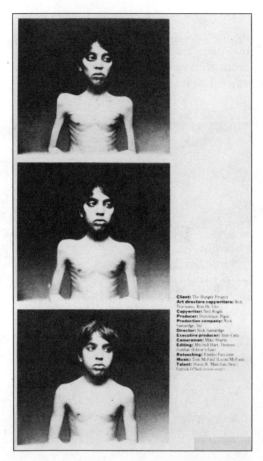

Client: The Hunger Project
Art directors copywriters: Rob Trasvanto, Ron De Vito
Copywriter: Neil Rogin
Producer: Dominique Bigar
Production company: Nick Samardge, Inc.
Director: Nick Samardge
Executive producer: Stan Carp
Cameraman: Mike Shapiro
Editing: Mitchell Hart, Dedeen Zumbar (Editor's Gas)
Retouching: Emelio Paccione
Music: Tom McFaul (Lucas McFaul)
Talent: Shaun B. Manchan (boy), Patrick O'Neil (voice-over)

235. *Ron DeVito (Art Director). Storyboard for a World Hunger Project commercial.*

ate their brands from similar or identical brands.

Television

The description of television will be brief, because it is outside the scope of this text. The majority of advertising dollars are spent on television. The content of national television advertising is strongly persuasive. Commercials may be a network advertisement, shown on national shows, a spot advertisement, prepared nationally and shipped to local areas, or a local advertisement, prepared and shown locally.

Market research is an important part of all advertising, especially in heavily persuasive advertising. The two primary marketing considerations in television advertising are program attentiveness and viewer volume.

Program attentiveness is how strongly viewers concentrate on a show. The maximum attention assures maximum recall. Unlike newspaper, direct mail, or other print media, the television ad occurs in time and cannot be reread.

The second marketing consideration is the number of persons viewing television programming. In the average home, a television set is on for almost seven hours a day. Certain hours are considered peak viewing periods. These prime time slots cost prime dollars. Because so much money is at stake, there is a great deal of research into ad effectiveness.

The television advertisement is usually prepared initially in the form of a storyboard (Fig. 235). It consists of two frames, one carrying a visual depiction of the scene, the other carrying words being spoken by an announcer or cast. The storyboard will depict only key scenes. There are usually no more than five scenes in a 30-second commercial. The visual is often prepared so that it will carry the message even if the volume is turned down. The product name is often superimposed over the screen at the end of the ad. The audio is also written to carry the message alone, in case the viewer is temporarily out of the room or unable to see the screen.

Newspapers

Newspaper advertising carries both regional and national ads. National advertising will often arrive as an "ad slick" ready for insertion. The creative work has been done at the company's ad agency. Regional display advertising usually requires designing by the newspaper's staff of artists and copywriters.

Advantages and Disadvantages

There are some disadvantages for the designer in newspaper advertising. First, the designer often must include diverse art elements and typefaces into a single ad. The logo and elements relating to a national campaign must often be incorporated into an ad for a local sale. Often the cost of an advertisement will be shared among manufacturers if their logos appear in the ad. This diversity can make the task of creating a well designed, attractive ad a real challenge. Second, the designer must also create around the limitations of cheap, absorbent newsprint and hurried printing to meet daily, sometimes hourly deadlines.

Single-item ads or large institutional clients like banks may use a full page with room for white space. These ads allow more leeway for pure design. No matter how many elements are in your advertisement, whether it is a national or retail ad, whether it is reproduced on newsprint or expensive glossy paper, good design will always aid communication. Given some creativity, it will also attract attention and help to persuade the audience.

The advantages of newspaper advertising are many. The paper is widely read. Circulation rates are available to help advertisers plan the number of people their ads are reaching. Moreover, the circulation is localized. It is therefore easy for a retail outlet to reach those people most likely to be interested in and able to travel to a sale. Finally, the copy may be changed daily, and the updated ad will still reach its audience within a day.

The Audience

Newspaper readership is varied in character. Young and old people from every social and economic group read the paper. When a product is of interest to a limited group, newspaper advertising is not advisable, because so small a percentage of readers would be potential buyers.

Newspaper advertising can be targeted to a limited extent, however, by considering the type of reader attracted to a certain type of paper. The *Wall Street Journal,* for example, has a different readership than the *New York Daily News.*

Advertising rates are based on the size of the ad, the circulation of the paper, and the position of the ad within the paper. The sports page, the women's page, the home section, and the financial section are areas where advertisements allied to spe-

cial subjects are likely to be seen by the desired group of readers. Advertisers will pay extra dollars to ensure that the appropriate audience sees their ad. Other positions within the paper that are worth extra money are on the outside pages, at the top of a column, and next to reading material.

Direct Mail

Direct mail advertising comes in many forms. It is an exciting and growing area of advertising that has boomed partly as a result of credit cards and partly as a result of today's busy lifestyle. Direct mail accounts for most third class mail and a considerable amount of first class mail.

Direct mail is advertising in which the advertiser acts as publisher. The advertiser produces a publication rather than renting space or time, selects the mailing list, and sends the publication directly to the prospects through the mail (Fig. 236).

Advantages and Disadvantages

The advantages of direct mail are substantial. First, the advertiser can use a mailing list that has been compiled to reach a specialized audience. Businesses usually develop their own mailing list. The pri-

236. *The University of Pittsburgh conducted an eight-step sequence of mailings to increase student enrollment.*

mary source of names, however, is mailing list brokers. They are in the business of building and maintaining lists of individuals likely to have an interest in a given topic. Lists are usually rented for one-time use because they go out of date quickly and must be constantly updated. Second, direct mail does not have to compete for attention with other ads on a newspaper page or surrounding a television commercial. Third, it is flexible in its format. This feature makes direct mail challenging to the designer. The size, paper, ink color, and folding characteristics are all additional variables to be designed. A piece that folds is a three-dimensional problem. It must succeed visually from a variety of positions (Fig. 237). The design develops from front to back, building interest and encouraging the reader to continue.

One of the disadvantages of direct mail is that people are often hostile to it. If the audience throws away the envelope without even opening it, communication has failed. Studies have shown that a mailing that requires participation, such as a lottery, will increase effectiveness. Copy and graphics that present specific offers and a clear, simple message succeed well.

237. *Lois Ehlert. Invitation for the Milwaukee Art Museum. Pieces prepared through a hand-fed Xerox machine, then trimmed and folded by hand.*

Forms

Forms of direct mail include letters, flyers, folders or brochures of varying dimensions and formats, catalogs, and booklets. A single mailing may consist of several pieces, such as an outside envelope, a letter, a brochure, and a business reply card. It might be part of a campaign of related pieces that are mailed out over a period of weeks.

Other Forms of Advertising

Magazines also offer a forum for advertising. There are a wide variety of magazines. There are general interest magazines, such as *Newsweek* and *Life,* and specialty or "class" magazines, such as computer, religious, sports, and health publications. There are trade and professional magazines, such as *Print, CA,* and *Art News,* as well as professional publications for doctors, engineers, and so on. An advantage to magazines is that it is possible to target a specific interest group with your ad. Also, if you have a national product, you may choose magazine advertising, because many magazines have national circulation.

Another form of advertising is billboard display (Fig. 238). When designing for billboards, it is important to remember that the message will be seen from a moving vehicle at a distance of at least 100 feet (30 m). The visual and the copy must be kept simple. It is surprising how many billboards violate this principle. Type for billboards should be at least 3 inches (8 cm) high at 100 feet (30 m) and 12 inches (30 cm) high at 400 feet (120 m). A message of more than seven words is difficult to read. A single image is easiest to grasp. The problems presented by transit advertising and outdoor advertising in general are similar to those for billboards. The audience is always in motion. The form of the appeal must be bold and simple, with details eliminated.

Point of purchase advertising is a growing area of importance. It is primarily three-dimensional, however, so it is better suited to study later in your cur-

238. *Duncan Milner (Art Director), Hal Maynard (Copywriter), Rick Gayle (Photographer) for WFC Advertising, San Diego. See Spot Run. 1985. Outdoor board.*

riculum. Point of purchase describes the display that is present along with the product in the store. Studies have shown that purchase of many items is based on impulse. More than one-third of purchases in department stores and almost two-thirds of the purchases in supermarkets result from display of the product. The display in the store, especially supermarkets, consequently plays an important part in advertising products. Package design can be considered a form of point of purchase design. The package design in Figure

239 makes creative use of combinations caused by stacking the product.

CORPORATE IDENTITY

Large companies and institutions often have a master plan that coordinates all their design. This plan begins with the trademark and applies it to the layout of business cards, letterhead, advertisements, product identification, and packaging. Even the company uniforms and vehicles are a part of this identity program.

239. *Allen Porter and Lisa Ellert (Designers), John Payne and Gary Mankus (Photographers) for Porter, Matjasich & Associates. Package design for Lightning Bug, Ltd. Designed to encourage retail display and to appeal to a young, contemporary-minded audience, this packaging program has been received by retail store buyers with enthusiasm.*

a.

b.

d.

c.

240a–240d. *J. I. Case Company corporate logo applied to signage, packaging, vehicles, and stationery. Courtesy J. I. Case, Racine, WI.*

The accompanying illustrations from J. I. Case Company show their strong corporate logo applied to signage, package design, vehicles, and stationery (Figs. 240a–240d).

Corporate identity is a specialized branch of advertising and design. Every aspect of typography, imagery, and application must be considered part of an inte-grated presentation. This integrated image presents the corporation to the public in a positive and memorable light. It not only communicates an image, but attempts to persuade the public that the company, hence the product, is superior.

A graphics standard manual is presented to company personnel detailing the appropriate use and placement of the trademark, and so on. The identity program must be flexible enough to be adapted to future needs. It is one of the most comprehensive applications of design and advertising.

WORKING WITH OTHERS

Advertising takes teamwork. You must communicate closely with copywriters, photographers, clients, and market researchers. Either the visual or the verbal element may be the departure point for developing the message. An integration of form and content, of design and communication is at the heart of good advertising.

Work with others to establish key information. Who is the audience? What is the nature of the product? Where will the ad appear? What is the purpose of the ad? What is the budget? Then you can begin to translate this information into visual form.

A successful ad will attract attention, communicate through its unified arrangement of elements, and persuade through the interaction of strong and appropriate copy and layout.

EXERCISES

1. Find some persuasive ads in a magazine. How do they catch their intended audience? What associations with the product do the ads induce? How?
2. Find an ad that targets different audiences by appearing in two magazines in a different format.
3. Turn off the sound and watch some television commercials. Does the visual convey a complete message?
4. Scan your local newspaper. Which advertisements grab your attention? How do position and design affect their success?

PROJECT
Magazine Advertisements

Design two magazine advertisements in an 8 1/2″ x 11″ (20 x 28 cm) format for a nonprofit, public service organization. Your task is to warn readers of the hazards of alcohol abuse. The primary audience for the first ad is 18 to 24 years old. The second ad should communicate with the under-age drinker. Identify the magazines in which your ad will appear. Research and discuss in class some of the problems that might be targeted, such as drunk driving.

Prepare the ads for black and white reproduction, including an image, a headline, and a few lines of (comped) body copy. Write all copy and attach it to the back of your illustration board.

In your thumbnails, try various approaches, including a path layout, grid layout, and a simple dominant image. Figure 241 is a design solution for a similar project.

Objectives. Experiment with researching and targeting a particular audience. Practice both communicating a message and persuading an audience.

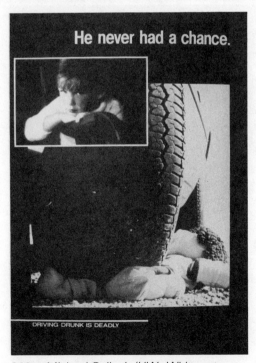

He never had a chance.

DRIVING DRUNK IS DEADLY

241. *Michael Pollock (UW–Whitewater student designer, photographer, and copywriter). Ad campaign against drinking and driving.*

11

PHOTOGRAPHY

PHOTOGRAPHY AS COMMUNICATION

Photography is a strong tool with which to prove a point, explore a problem, or sell a product. Most people believe that the camera does not lie. They believe that an illustrator may change things around and make people or situations out to be better than they really are, but they fail to realize that a camera also represents a point of view. It is this attitude that makes the camera such an effective tool for persuasion and communication.

The artist/photographer behind the camera always produces an *interpretation* of reality. What the photographer chooses to shoot or to leave out, the angle, the filter, and how the image is cropped in the camera can edit the truth even in seemingly unstaged photos. No photograph is truly candid. It is selected, framed, and shot by an individual who is interacting with the environment. Moreover, a situation will change just because a camera is introduced. Another editing and selection process occurs when the contact prints are viewed. Darkroom manipulation may influence the last stages. All of these processes place photography firmly in the camp of an interpretive art. It is not that a photograph cannot tell the truth; but truth is in the eye and intent of the photographer (Fig. 242).

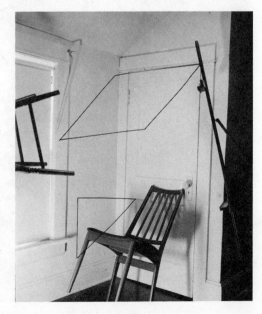

242. *Amy E. Arntson. Off the Wall. 1982. Collection of the artist.*

Keeping this fact in mind, photos fall into two general categories: "candid" and staged. Most photojournalism is candid. It is not shot in a studio or with hired models. Photojournalism attempts to capture a news event on location with honesty. When a feature story is run in a newspaper, it may not concern a fast-breaking news event. There is more time for interpretation (Fig. 243). Still the photographer will usually attempt a candid feeling. An art director or editor may ask for a picture essay that will illustrate a feature story with a sequence of images that give a sense of movement, establish a narrative, or set an emotional tone.

Staged photographs are often used in advertising and product photography. They are tightly directed and require elaborate studio lighting. Hired models can make shooting time expensive, but candid shots can be time-consuming without guaranteeing results. Product photographers are usually less concerned with "truth" telling than the photojournalists and more concerned with presenting a product in the most favorable light.

Designers use photographs and work with photographers throughout their career. You may need a photograph to document an event, illustrate a story, sell a product, or put across a point of view. In all cases the photograph must be evaluated in terms of print quality, design quality, and ability to communicate. The fashion photos in Figures 244a and 244b evoke an atmosphere through design and through soft, grainy texture. To develop a feeling for print quality, study good photos and take a class in darkroom work. The criteria for good design in a photograph are the same as for good design in layout or illustration. This chapter will make you familiar with various types of photography and photographic communication.

THE IMPACT OF PHOTOGRAPHY

Paul Delaroche, a French painter commenting on the invention of photography, exclaimed that "From today painting is dead!" While some artists shared that fear, others embraced the new media as a tool. From its beginning illustrators have

243. *Steven Shames (Visions).* Lafayette/ Chicago. *1985. Selenium-toned, silver-based print. Collection of the artist.*

Photography

244a.

244b.

used photographs as aids. The illustrator Alphonse Mucha carefully posed models amidst studio props and photographed them for reference in his poster designs (Figs. 245–246). Such well known twentieth-century illustrators as Maxfield Parrish and Norman Rockwell have also relied heavily upon posing and photographing models for visual reference in later paintings. Photographer Eadweard Muybridge

244a, 244b. *Nana Watanabee (President, Nana Inc., New York). Spring clothing for Japanese manufacturer. Courtesy the artist.*

245.

246.

far left: 245. *Alphonse Mucha. Studio photograph of model.*

near left: 246. *Alphonse Mucha. Poster design based on Figure 245.*

(1830–1904) is well known among the design community for his photographic series documenting the movement of people and animals. His books remain a valuable resource to illustrators today (Fig. 247).

Documentary Images

Photography became an important visual document of our society in the last decades of the nineteenth century. By 1903 the British *Daily Mirror* became the first daily newspaper to be illustrated solely with photographs. In the 1930s the first issues of *Look* and *Life* magazines opened new markets for artists and photographers. Advertising flourished along with the increase of such publications, providing an additional market for photography.

The French free-lance photographer Eugene Atget (1857–1927) was an innovator in these new markets. He did a photographic survey of Paris to satisfy his personal aesthetic and to meet the needs of his customers. These photos had to appeal to artists and designers as source materials, to libraries and museums for documentary subject matter, and to publishers of books and postcards (Fig. 248). He also created a series of botanical photographs for sale to designers of textiles and wallpapers.

New Ideas

In these early days, the camera was destroying the old visual standards of painting. The picture edge sliced the image in an arbitrary and absolute manner. Unexpected juxtapositions often appeared, because it was difficult to control everything within the frame, as had been possible with painting. Our visual aesthetics and conventions were changing.

247. *Eadweard Muybridge. Excerpt from* Animal Locomotion. *1887.*

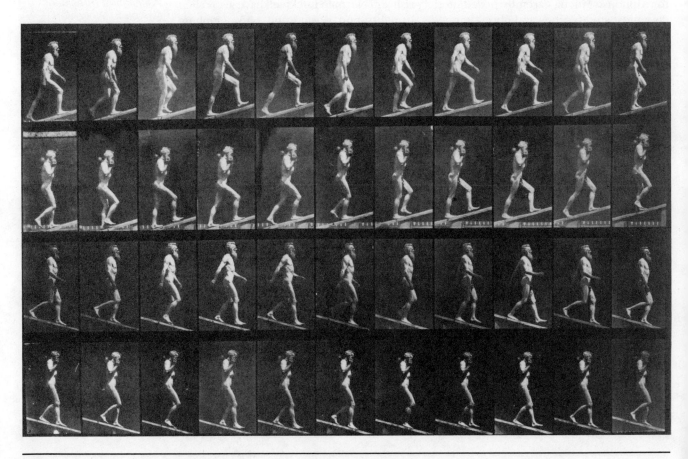

For many artists photography was a medium to be integrated with other media. Photographs from a variety of sources would be collaged with painting, drawing, and assemblage. These artists often did not share the concern of professional photographers with print quality and integrity of materials but were often daring and experimental in their treatment of the image. Darkroom manipulation of the print and/or negative also began to yield creative and often surreal effects. These became useful to the photographic illustrator.

Some of this experimental work originated with László Moholy-Nagy (1895–1946) at the Bauhaus. He experimented with photograms, solarization, and photomontage, and with pure abstract imagery. In *Painting, Photography and Film,* published in 1925, he states:

The most important development affecting present-day layout is photoengraving, the mechanical reproduction of photographs in any size. . . . The inclusion of photography in poster design will bring about another vital change. A poster must convey instantaneously all the high points of an idea. The greatest possibilities for future development lie in the proper use of photographic means.

The many uses for commercial photography today have proven the importance and versatility of the medium.

SPECIALTIES

Product Photography

Any area in which the intent is to promote or sell a product is called product photography. The product can be food, automobiles, furniture, clothing, fine art, or a wide

248. *Eugene Atget. Pontoise, Church of Saint-Maclou. 1902. The National Gallery of Canada, Ottawa.*

range of other items. This metal sculpture is captured in all of its surface texture and complexity through the art of the photographer (Fig. 249). Still lifes enhance the beauty and desirability of many products (Fig. 250). Others involve posing a model.

Whether the assignment comes from an art director at an advertising agency or directly from the client, the photographer is often told what to shoot and how. The photograph will then be combined with typography and turned into a layout. Although product photographers are not free to photograph in any manner they choose, there is still a great deal of difference in their interpretations and expertise. Part of the challenge in this form of photography is to help sell the product but in a way that is personally and aesthetically satisfying.

Most photographers doing this kind of work are free-lance, and many work through an agent who solicits work from clients. The "rep" usually will get a 25–30 percent finder's fee from the assignment. Major catalog houses and department stores have their own in-house photo-

graphic staff and facilities. Regional advertisers often make use of in-house photographic staff, but national advertisers usually hire a dependable free-lancer whose previous work suits the project at hand.

When shooting a fashion layout for a catalog, newspaper, or direct mail piece that calls for a model, the photographer will work with the art director and with assistants who help with the details of clothing, makeup, props, and so on. It is important that all people at a "shoot" show respect for one another's professional abilities.

Corporate Photography

Large corporations need a great deal of photography for annual reports, presentations, and other publications. The company's art director or designer often hires a photographer for an individual assignment and offers suggestions regarding the project. The public relations executive also may become involved in consultations. The corporate photographer often becomes involved in the creative decision-making process. Sometimes there is an in-plant photographer on the staff who does some of the photographic work. This photographer is often a generalist working out of the public relations (PR) department and shooting anything from company parties to news release photos to architecture.

Architectural photography calls for a special skill in handling building interiors and exteriors. Lighting an interior so that the bright chandeliers as well as the detail in dark corners of the room are all properly exposed calls for considerable expertise. Figure 4a in Chapter 1 is an example of such work. Photographing exteriors of tall buildings may call for special equipment that will correct for parallax. A photographer may be asked to emphasize the abstract design qualities of a new building. People who specialize in architectural photography work for a variety of interior design firms, landscape designers, travel firms, and entertainment businesses.

Editorial Photography

Editorial photography illustrates an accompanying story—anything from fiction to a feature article on restaurant dining. Photographic illustrations are sometimes closely art-directed. The necessary props and set may be provided, or the photographer may be asked to find or construct them (Fig. 251).

As in any editorial work, there is often considerable room for creative interpretation. Still, this form of photography has the restraint of all design work—communication is the primary objective.

Photojournalism

Magazines and newspapers are the primary outlets for another kind of photography. Good photojournalism stands on its own. It will communicate the meaning and emotion behind an event visually, without depending upon an accompanying story. It often makes an editorial statement while documenting an event. Art directors rarely work with photojournalists, but there is

great creative potential in that association (Fig. 252).

Portrait Photography

Portraits, weddings, and school photography may be shot on location or out of the photographer's studio. Portraiture can be done in a quick, cliché fashion or creatively, telling the personalities behind the faces. Along with the stock shots of the bride and groom and family, the wedding photographer can capture candid moments, wistful glances that show the human side to the formal event.

The famous portrait photographer Yousuf Karsch captured the strength and authority behind British Prime Minister Winston Churchill by removing Churchill's cigar from his mouth and quickly snapping the photo, catching a momentary hostile reaction. As Karsch says in his book of portraits, "So he stands in my portrait in what has always seemed to me the image of England in those years, defiant and unconquerable." Portraits can say a great deal, depending upon the persistence and sensitivity of the photogra-

251. *Amy E. Arntson (Art Director) and Kirby Bock (Photographer). Black/White version of* Graphic Design Basics *cover.*

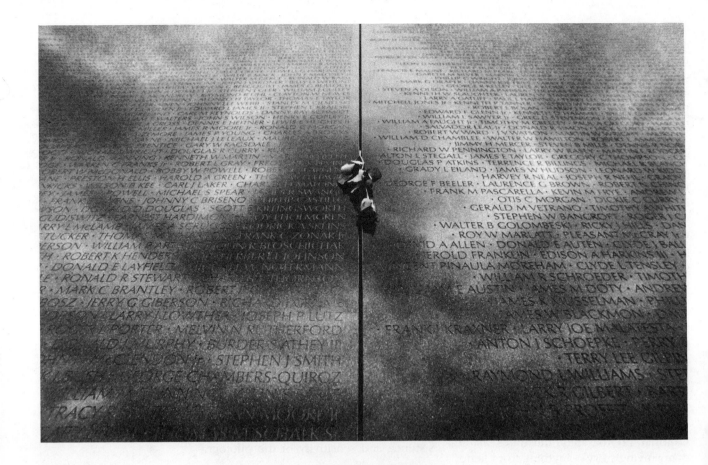

pher, as this photo of a Vietnam veteran demonstrates (Fig. 253).

FINDING PHOTOGRAPHS AND PHOTOGRAPHERS

Stock photograph agencies sell photographs to anyone from advertising agencies to magazines. They have thousands of images on permanent file, which are constantly updated. Any type of photograph is available, with agencies specializing in everything from architecture to current events to the history of civilization. The Bettmann Archives, Black Star Publishing Company, and The Free Lance Photographers Guild are three of hundreds of such services providing images for use in editorial work, advertising, and television. Check your college or university library for books listing such picture sources and describing their specialities. Professional photoresearchers are available to help you secure the necessary photography.

The American Showcase is a full-color reference book used by advertising agencies, public relations firms, and others who want to hire free-lance photographers. Each portfolio page of images is accompanied by the name and address of the photographer who shot them. (You can order the book from American Showcase Inc., 724 Fifth Avenue, New York, NY.)

The Creative Black Book lists all the services an agency might want to purchase, from photographers to illustrators to layout artists. Again, portfolio pages show the work of these artists. (Order it from Creative Black Book, Inc., 401 Park Avenue South, New York, NY.)

Photographers specialize in a variety of areas, each of which calls for unique expertise. As a designer, know what you need to communicate and work with a photographer who knows how to deliver it. Insist upon high standards. Become familiar with the best quality work being done and attempt to match it. Photography is a powerful tool for communication.

EXERCISES

1. Find samples of all the types of photography described in this chapter.
2. Check out a book of photographs by one of the photographers mentioned in this chapter and study it. Ask yourself what is being communicated and how. Analyze pictures in terms of how basic design elements enhance the particular communication.
3. Begin a clippings file of photographs of people, objects, places, and so on. Continue to add to it throughout your career as a student designer. It will serve you well as a design and illustration source.

PROJECT
A Photographic Illustration

Illustrate the cover of a record, tape, or compact disc you enjoy, using a photograph. First find several photographs that are appropriate. You may research and obtain copies, shoot them yourself, or direct a friend in shooting them. Choose one photo for excellence in print quality, design, and communication.

Combine the photograph with the title of the recording and the name of the recording artists. Prepare your comp at actual size. Enlarge, reduce, and crop your photo as desired.

Objectives

Learn how to obtain photographs.

Evaluate the quality of a photograph and its potential in a design.

Practice using a photograph as the main element in a design.

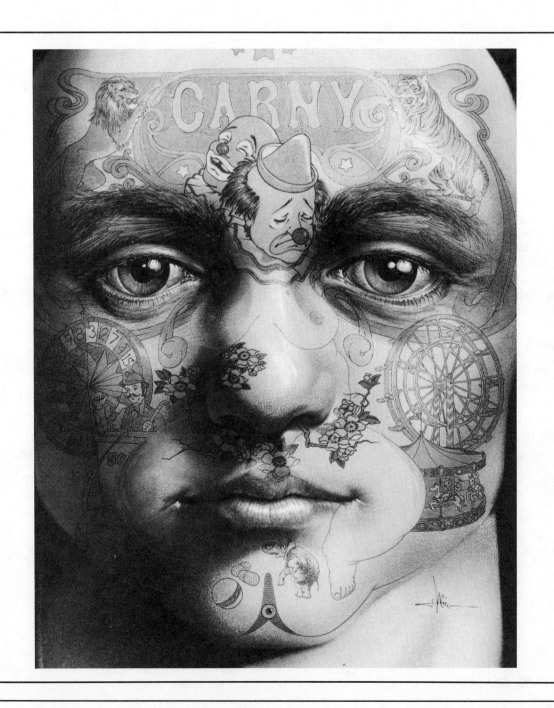

12

ILLUSTRATION

Illustration is a specialized area of art that uses nonphotographic images, usually representational, to make a visual statement. Illustration is created for commercial reproduction. Otherwise, many drawings and paintings done as illustrations look and function as fine art and are exhibited and collected as such. Many painters have worked as illustrators at some point in their careers. Edward Hopper earned his living as an illustrator for the first half of his career. Pablo Picasso and William Blake illustrated books (Fig. 254).

Some designers never actually do an illustration themselves; instead, they purchase free-lance illustration. Some studios hire illustrators who do nothing but illustration, working with other designers who are in charge of typography, photography, layout, and art direction.

There are artists who feel that editorial illustration is the highest and most creative form of design. Nevertheless, however much an illustration may resemble

a painting, the restrictions an illustrator works under are like those in other areas of graphic design. The illustrator works under the guidance of an art director, must

254. *Edward Hopper. L'Année Terrible: On the Rooftops. 1906 or 1909. Watercolor and ink on paper. 21 3/4" × 14 14 3/4" (55.2 37.5 cm). Collection of the Whitney Museum of American Art. Josephine N. Hopper Bequest.*

be concerned about how the work will be reproduced, has to meet a deadline, and is responsible for satisfying a client and a defined purpose.

WHY ILLUSTRATION?

Illustration may be chosen instead of photography for several reasons. It can show something about the subject that cannot be photographed, such as detailed information about how photosynthesis works. It can demonstrate certain things more clearly than a photograph, by enhancing details. For example, it can enlarge tiny engine parts that are difficult to see, and label their functioning. Illustration can also eliminate misleading and unnecessary details that confuse an image, focusing the eye on important characteristics.

Although photography is capable of creating surreal, strongly emotive images, illustration is still the more flexible. It is capable of turning out images of pure fantasy. The hand-drawn quality of illustration is considered by many to have a warmer, more personal quality than photography. Finally, sometimes an illustrator is allowed where a photographer and camera are prohibited, as in the courtroom (Fig. 255).

TYPES OF ILLUSTRATION

Throughout this book you have seen many examples of illustration. It has a variety of looks, depending upon the medium, the style of the illustrator, and the purpose of the illustration. The artwork can be drawn, painted, and assembled with mixed media collage as in Figure 256 or 257. It may be computer-generated, as in Figure 258. The illustrator may use a revived art deco style, a new wave look, a personal style, or a highly informational, descriptive rendering technique. In recent years illustrators have become freer to explore a variety of personal directions. Some have become identified with an emotive style much like the painting movement called neoexpressionism. Other illustrators continue to "draw" inspiration from older movements such as surrealism, art deco, and cubism.

If the field of illustration is varied in imagery, it also is varied in intent. The purpose for an illustration may be to present a

255. *David Kimpton. Court Sketching. Canadian Broadcasting Corporation, Toronto, Canada.*

product, tell a story, or demonstrate a process. It is usually categorized according to its intent into three main areas: advertising, editorial, and special subjects.

Advertising Illustration

Advertising illustration is intended to sell a product or a service—almost anything

that can be offered to a consumer. Commonplace objects must be shown with style and often enhanced with dramatic highlights and surface textures (Fig. 259).

The British-born illustrator Richard Leech describes his work in this fashion: "First, I make a detailed pencil drawing on vellum, building it up bit by bit. Then I have the finished drawing photographed

above left: 256. *Roy R. Behrens. Proposed magazine cover illustration (unpublished). 1985. Xerographic collage, designer's tapes, with pen and ink, 9″ × 12 1/4″ (22.8 × 31 cm). Collection of the artist.*

above right: 257. *Roy R. Behrens. Fugato (Italian for "like a fugue"). Insignia for personal letterhead. 1985. Xerographic collage, 15/16″ × 1 1/16 ″ (2.4 × 2.7 cm). Courtesy the artist.*

below left: 258. *A. Lantieri. Lounger. Created on an Artronics Studio Computer. Copyright Artronics, Inc.*

right: 259. *Richard Leech. Corvette. Air brush illustration. Courtesy the artist.*

THE ANATOMY OF
THE NEW CORVETTE

A. LANTIERI 84

and printed same size on photographic paper, dry mount that print on board, and paint on that surface, using an airbrush for most of it. I estimate the drawing represents about one-third of the total time." Illustrations of this complexity can take Leech six six-day weeks to complete. By contrast, Figure 260 is a computer-generated fashion image that is created with a tremendous economy of time.

Fashion illustration is a specialized area of advertising. A strictly literal drawing will lack the appeal of a drawing that presents the garment in a romantic, stylized manner. As a result, fashion illustration does not always simply convey information about the garment. It often attempts to persuade the viewer with the mood of the illustration. An important and interesting drape or texture of the garment as well as the model's height, pose, and curves are often emphasized for effect. Fashion photography (Chapter 10) shows a similar concern. A fashion illustrator draws from either a live model or a photograph of a model wearing clothes furnished by the client.

Record jacket covers, movie posters, and travel advertisements provide a large market for the imaginative, expressive quality of illustration. They often look and feel like pure editorial illustration.

Editorial Illustration

Editorial illustration is the closest the designer comes to the satisfying indulgence of the painter. In an editorial illustration, the designer/artist may concentrate upon the communication of emotion through an expressive treatment of line and shape and placement. There is usually freedom in editorial illustration to experiment with media and to obscure details in favor of mood.

Editorial illustrations accompany stories and articles in magazines, newspapers, and books. The illustrator must have an idea of the content of the story or article to ensure that the feeling of the illustration as well as the subjects depicted in it are compatible with the text.

Magazines and Newspapers

Magazines depend upon illustration to set a tone and pique a reader's interest (Fig. 261). A single full-page image will often be expected to carry all the visual information for the accompanying story. It is important that the layout artist integrate the illustration into the overall layout. Treatment of the headline and text should reinforce the art through repeated shapes, angles, and careful placement.

Sometimes small spot illustrations are dropped into a page of text to enliven its visual presence. They are often black and white, executed in pen and ink.

Another area that uses a great deal of black and white art is newspaper illustration. Many different kinds of illustration can be found in newspapers, as you search through the sections. Fashion, sports, editorial, product, and technical illustration of charts and graphs are all there. The newspaper will often use color only on the front pages of the sections, or only on special feature articles. Newsprint is a difficult medium to draw for, because it does not reproduce details and nuances in tonal quality well.

Books

The primary use for book illustration today is in cover art and illustration for children's books. Cover art often functions as a form of advertisement; a cover display may convince a consumer to pick up a book and consider buying it. The art should convey information and feeling appropriate to the story and to the age group for which the book is written.

Children's book illustration is a rich field for illustrators because such books are illustrated throughout, unlike most adult novels. Artwork for young children must tell much of the story, with little reliance upon the text. It is responsible for generating excitement and advancing the plot. One of the many excellent children's illus-

trators from the turn of the century is Arthur Rackham (Fig. 262).

Special Subjects

Medical illustration communicates medical knowledge. Absolute accuracy is necessary in these drawings, so the artist must be meticulous. The artist must be better than a camera, able to simplify and clarify and select only what must be shown for complete communication. Training in anatomy and a knowledge of medicine is necessary. Advances in photography and computer technology have made it possible for the camera to photograph and manipulate images in a manner never possible before. This technique is causing a decrease in the demand for hand-drawn illustration requiring meticulous detail.

Architectural illustration is also increasingly done on the computer. Details such as trees, and textures of bricks, tile, or

below left: 261. *Kunio Hagio. Magazine illustration. Reproduced by Special permission of Playboy Magazine. Copyright 1976 by Playboy.*

below right: 262. *Arthur Rackham. A children's illustration from the turn of the century, called "The Golden Age of Illustration."*

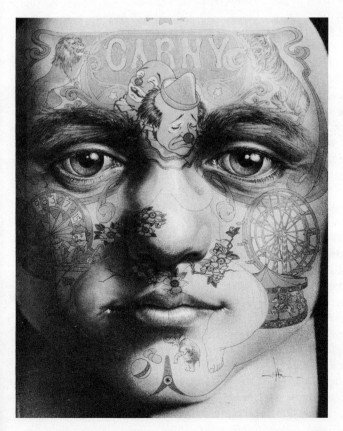

cement can be kept in a computerized clip file and dropped into position on keyboard command.

Scientific illustration is used to show details of surface textures and forms that are difficult or impossible to photograph. Geology and botany are two fields that call upon illustrators.

Every area of illustration that is primarily informational or reportorial is coming to depend upon the speed and flexibility of the computer. Computer-generated images are still illustrations, but they are executed using a new and powerful tool that is capable of showing us things never seen before. Chapter 13 will give you more information on computer graphics.

GETTING IDEAS

The illustrator goes through the same planning and visualizing procedures described in Chapter 1. The first step is getting to know the assignment. This research might call for reading an accompanying text or understanding how a product functions.

Now comes the idea stage. What do you do if you cannot think of any ideas? What if you have only one idea and cannot get beyond it? Try looking at illustrations by other artists. There are many annuals available in hardback and softback that show the most current illustrations. If there are some techniques and treatments that you especially enjoy, try using that approach on your subject. Classics from the history of illustration can also provide food for visual thought. Great artists from Dürer to Goya to Magritte have provided inspiration for illustrators. Try looking through books of photography, both "fine art" photography and simple descriptive photography of subjects related to your project.

As you begin your thumbnail sketches, think about the subject you are working with. Imagine it from every angle, high and low as well as cropped in tight and at a distance. Imagine it shown in different kinds of spatial treatment. Sketch these ideas. Try them in different media. Consider whether your treatment is best suited to working from memory and imagination, from life, or from photographs. Usually as you progress to the rough sketch stage, memory no longer provides enough detail to draw upon. You may find you need additional still life materials or photographs.

Reference Materials

Drawing from life means you will need an object, landscape, or human model posed before you. Drawing from life is most practical when you are using a still life setup or a landscape. Models can get tired, and they can also get expensive. There is however, an immediacy and vitality to life models that may give your illustrations a different quality than you achieve from working with photographs.

Drawing from a photograph is convenient for many reasons. The camera has already converted the subject into a two-dimensional language for you. Cropping is easily visualized by dropping a few pieces of paper around the photo edges. The subject never gets tired.

Reference materials can add authenticity to your work. An excellent source of photographs is the public library. Most major libraries keep picture collections. Once you have the source photo, it is important to adapt it to your needs. It is a good idea for all designers and illustrators to begin a clip file of their own with images of many different subjects. Old magazines are a great source. You may be able to organize magazines by categories instead of cutting out the photographs. *Life* magazine, *People,* and *Newsweek* would fit into a "people" category, whereas the *Smithsonian, National Geographic,* and *Audubon* could fit into a nature category.

When you are working with photographs, respect the photographer as an artist. Do not duplicate a photograph exactly unless it has been shot specifically for you or by you. Copyright infringement law for the use of photographs has gotten increasingly tight in recent years. Your

source photograph must be substantially altered before it will be legal for you to reproduce it in another form as your own artwork.

"Clip art" denotes copyright-free images that can be used as is or altered to suit your needs. Books of clip art are available from many publishing sources (Fig. 263).

There can be disadvantages to working with clip art or relying too closely upon photos. The pre-existing image makes many decisions for you about composition, lighting, and size. The photograph can also give you only one kind of spatial representation. These limitations can be overcome if you remember to use the clip art or photo as a source, not as an answer. It is your interpretation that answers the illustration problems.

Resizing Aids

There are several techniques to transfer the resource image you have selected to your illustration board. Drawing freehand or with a grid for assistance is only one of them. Photographs can be projected from a slide projector, providing excellent details for tracing. An opaque enlarger can be used to reduce or enlarge images onto paper or board. A light table is useful if you do not need to enlarge or reduce your image. Some copy machines will enlarge and reduce, and a stat camera can too, although it is a relatively costly alternative.

Remember that reference sources should not be taken literally, but creatively. Find an interpretation that suits your personality and the job.

CONTEMPORARY VISION

The invention of offset lithography brought an explosion of illustration in the late 1800s. Coming into the twentieth century as a vital force, with new advances in printing technology, illustration has been able to draw inspiration from the fine arts. Painters in the early twentieth century were following an investigation begun by Cézanne. Their art began to reflect the relativity of space, time, point of view, and emotional coloring. Discoveries in science, psychology, and technology supported their depiction of reality as changeable. It could shift, alter, and be processed

263. *Copyright-free clip art is available from a variety of sources for reference and reproduction.*

a.

b.

c.

264a, 264b, 264c.
Michael Vanderbyl. Three self-promotional posters in conjunction with the publication of Seven Graphic Designers *by Takenobu Igarashi. Printed in Japan by Mitsumura Printing Company.*

in the human brain in a variety of ways. The artist could interact and help to shape it.

Much of the art of the twentieth century deals with picture plane space—the construction of a flat pattern on the flat surface of the paper or canvas. There is less illusion to this work; it does not attempt to deny the flat surface it exists upon (Figs. 264a, 264b, 264c). Constructivism and the de Stijl movement worked with picture plane space. Cubism presented reality from multiple points of view. An object might be portrayed simultaneously from the top, the front, and the sides. There is a similarity here to Egyptian art, but a different purpose. This picture plane space is a strong influence in contemporary illustration. Designers and illustrators have always been aware of the flat surface because they have also worked with typography, which encourages flat patterning.

The fauves and the German expressionists in the early twentieth century also emphasized the flat patterning of the surface with bright, flat colors and with images that were personal and highly emotional. This expressive quality appears currently in editorial illustration in various

forms. The emotionally charged image in Figure 265 matches the topic of violence with a violent treatment of line and surface. It becomes what it represents. This union is what illustration is about.

An interest in other forms of spatial representation began to appear in the mid-twentieth century. The painter Paul Sarkisian and other trompe l'oeil artists revived an interest in life-size images inside a space that looks only inches deep (Fig. 266). A French term meaning "fool the eye," trompe l'oeil works extremely well as an illusion of spatial reality. An envelope might really be lying at the bottom edge of that piece of paper. This narrow spatial illusion is an effective technique for an illustrator because the viewer's attention is arrested by that believable unbelievable object trapped on the printed page.

Trompe l'oeil takes advantage of a fascination for the retinal image and for rendering ability. Our culture will probably never lose its admiration for this sort of "reality." Mainstream illustration has always been pictorial in nature. One of the current pictorial movements in illustration is pop art. Pop art is an example of graphic design and illustration that influenced a painting movement. The cartoon-like figures and enlarged dot screens came out of design to influence painting and went back to appear in illustration. Figure 267 was created from a new medium, colored adhesive film.

There are more artists than ever before in history. We have the benefit of a mass communications network to keep us informed on what is happening now in art. We have a documented history of previous art and design movements, and our influences are more numerous than ever. Artists and illustrators are combining many materials and styles. There is a greater variety in illustrative styles and techniques today.

We are a complex society. There is a need for visual artists who will attempt to reconcile all our complexities into a contemporary vision of reality.

EXERCISES

1. Experiment with some of the mixed media shown in this chapter. Concentrate on line quality, texture, and the emotional quality of color. Create sev-

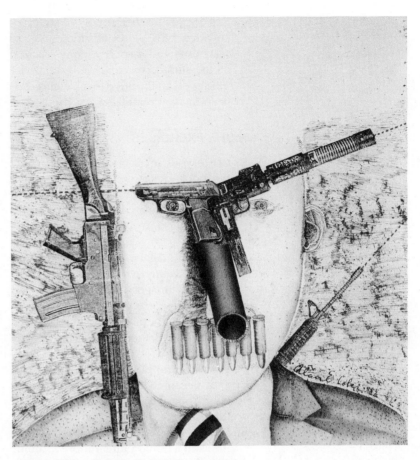

above: 265. *Alan E. Cober. Illustration for the Dallas* Times Herald. *Courtesy the artist.*

below left: 266. *Paul Sarkisian. Untitled. 1976. Acrylic on paper, 28″ × 36″ (71 × 91.4 cm). Courtesy, Nancy Hoffman Gallery, New York. An example of trompe l'oeil.*

below right: 267. *Herb Allison and David Schiedt. One Shining Moment. Pantone film, 12″ × 12″ (30.5 × 30.5 cm). Collection of The Graphics Studio. An example of pop art style.*

eral images, either totally abstract or abstract with pictorial elements. Use your eyes and a spontaneous reaction to the surface to explore visual possibilities on an intuitive level. Figure 268 is an image created by this method.

MORE EXERCISES

1. Go to your local bookstore and study the book jacket covers. Notice which first attracted your attention. Are there any series of related books? What makes their covers into a related series of visuals?

2. Select a magazine with many illustrations. Analyze the use of typography with imagery. Select one or two instances where you feel the typography and general layout enhance the illustration. Bring them to class for discussion.

3. Find an example of an illustration created because a photograph could not have done the job. Bring it to class for discussion.

4. Find an example of a product illustration and a fashion illustration. Examine how they differ from photographs.

PROJECT
Editorial Illustration

Select a book you are familiar with from those listed below (or another with your instructor's approval). Illustrate the story in full color for a front cover design. Both your drawing style and the images you select should reflect the content of the text. Integrate the title of the book and the name of the author into the layout. Plan for their placement as you do thumbnails of your illustration. If you use pressure graphics on your finished artwork, apply them to a clear acetate overlay placed over the entire cover. Your cover design should be 8″ x 10″ (20 x 25 cm), with an approximately 2″ (5 cm) white "matte" around the image area.

Search for photographic sources to use. As you do your thumbnails and roughs, experiment with different points of view. Use the same image cropped in tightly and as a long view. Try a flat patterning and a deep space and a trompe l'oeil approach. Go over these ideas with your instructor before executing the comprehensive for your cover design. Use any combination of media you find appropriate to your

268. *Thom Gravelle. Mixed-media image. Letraset inks, pressure graphics, colored pencil, designer tapes. Courtesy the artist.*

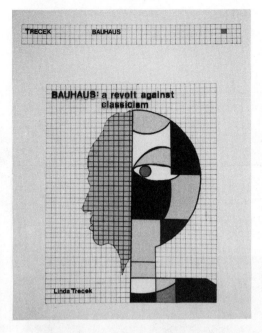

imagery. Experiment. Figures 269 and 270 are student projects based on a similar assignment.

Books

The Hunchback of Notre-Dame by Victor Hugo
Under Milk Wood by Dylan Thomas
Moby-Dick by Herman Melville
The Cocktail Party by T. S. Eliot

Objectives

Experiment with different points of view, different spatial renderings, and different media to find an appropriate illustration for the text.

Practice integrating type with image.

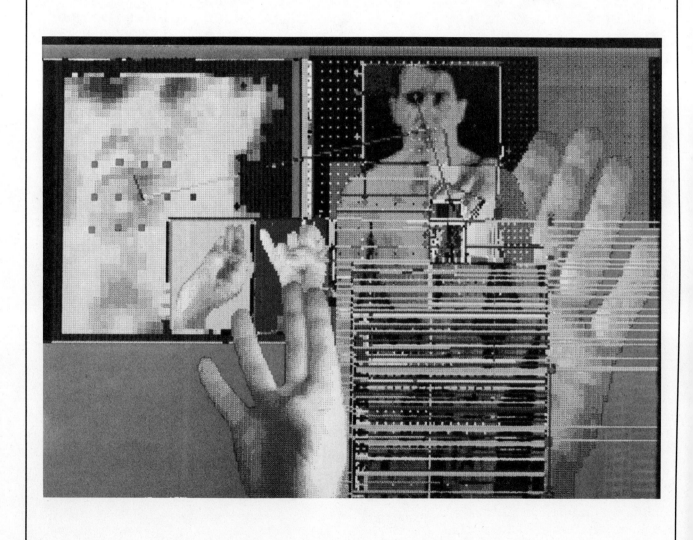

13

COMPUTER GRAPHICS

A NEW MEDIUM

Computers have often been viewed as a cold, dehumanizing force in the world. It is especially interesting, then, to explore the connection between computers and such a warm, humanizing field as art. Visions of technology as a force for evil, grinding mere flesh in its relentless onward movement, abound in post-World War I literature and film. Fritz Lang's 1926 film *Metropolis* showed a world in which demoralized workers toil beneath the earth to support a gleaming city above. The evil of technology is personified in a robot modeled after a heroine named Maria (Fig. 271). The robot is both strongly attractive and coldly threatening, evoking mixed reactions as computer technology does.

The computer's ability to store information and provide access to numerous sources has generated some fear of inva-

271. *Fritz Lang. Maria the Robot from the movie* Metropolis. *1926. Courtesy Wisconsin State Historical Society.*

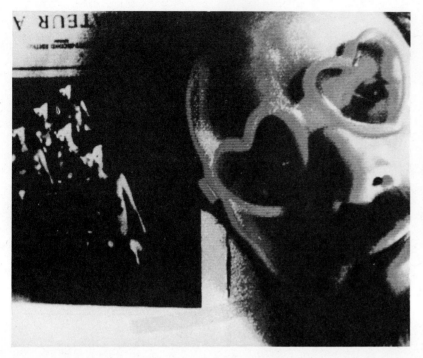

sion of privacy; but such data bases and information networks can also be a powerful tool for communication. It is up to us to use it well. Because graphic design is all about communication, the computer is especially suited to this field.

The computer is as important to the work that is created on it as acrylic or oil on canvas is to the painter. In Marshall McLuhan's famous words, "the medium is the message." The tool we create in turn affects the statement that we make with it. New ways of thinking and doing are born in response to a new medium.

It is also true, however, that acrylic and oil on canvas can say many different things depending upon the intent of the artist. If all artists are subject to the influences of their media, all media are equally subject to the artist. If artists are influenced by new tools, they can also use them to define a new sense of the world (Fig. 272). This computer-generated image makes use of a digitizing camera and plays with a repetition of design elements. The angle of the man repeats the angle of the group

of women. His heart-shaped glasses echo their masks.

When photography was invented, artists feared that "painting is now dead." Many viewed the new medium with suspicion and fear. Computers are the most significant technological advance in art since the invention of photography. They are in turn being viewed with suspicion and fear. True, computers can do things that even photography cannot; they can simulate and manipulate images; but they are unlikely to replace photography, just as photography did not replace painting. The computer will open up new markets and new avenues for artistic expression.

Computer graphics is growing rapidly in many different directions. It is extending our senses by showing us things we have never seen before. It appears well suited to any area where communication and exchange of information is important. Its ultimate "message" need not be dehumanization but human interaction (Fig. 273).

WHAT IS COMPUTER GRAPHICS?

The computer's ability to draw or to display visual information on a video terminal is called computer graphics. Interactive computer graphics allows two-way communication between the artist and

273. *This humorous plug person mimics traditional imaging procedures. Courtesy of Digital Effects, Inc.*

274. *Don Davis.* Voyager 2 at Saturn Minus 3 Hours. *Painting over computer-generated image. Painted for NASA and JPL.*

the computer, as the graphic display constantly reflects the latest command from the artist.

The use of computers to draw pictures is not new. The earliest computers could show a simple visual display of a bouncing ball and calculate its path. The military applications are obvious. Funding for the development of computers and computer graphics in the United States originally came from the defense department.

Although its early development was tied to defense and aerospace, today computer graphics has a wide variety of applications, from engineering, medicine, and business graphics to animation and fine art. The computer can show us things we have never seen before, like simulations of Saturn's rings (Fig. 274). These images were computer-generated and then rendered by an airbrush. Computers can model the DNA molecule with full rotation and manipulation of its parts. They can show us the concentration of chlorophyll in a land mass or internal views of a living brain (Fig. 275). The computer can create images of

compelling beauty that expand our vision and our other senses.

For the designer, the computer can simulate a model of a new automobile, an architectural rendering with varying roof coverings and structural supports. It can show an architect's plan for an exterior from any angle on site, or generate interior designs for client approval (Figs. 276,

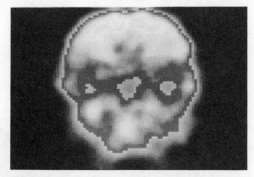

275. *A CAT scan cross section of the brain. Different densities appear in different colors. Courtesy of Digital Effects, Inc.*

What Is Computer Graphics?   **179**

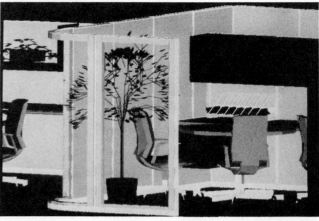

above left: 276.
*Architectural screen shot.
Copyright Intergraph.*
above right: 277.
*Architectural layout/
screen shot. Copyright
Intergraph.*
below left: 278. *Jeff
Gordon (UW–Whitewater
student designer and
animator). Animated self-
portrait. Created on an
Artronics 2000 with
a digitizing camera.
Courtesy the artist.*
below right: 279. *Detail
of cycle animation from
Figure 278. A form
of animation caused by
colors cycling through
the color palette.*

277). It can be used to develop animated logos and advertisements for television (Figs. 278, 279). It can generate special effects and animation for film, and still art and slide shows for illustration and business graphics (Figs. 280, 281, 282). In this chapter, we will cover a brief history of computer graphics, discuss some of the hardware and software available, and look at images with specific application to graphic design.

DEVELOPMENT OF COMPUTER GRAPHICS

In the beginning theorists believed there would be a limited market for computers —perhaps 50 companies in the United States. Application ideas grew quickly, however, from inventory control to airline reservation scheduling. Continual advances in electronics made it possible radically to reduce the size and cost of computers while increasing their speed and efficiency.

Ivan Sutherland's *Sketchpad,* developed in 1962 at M.I.T., was the first interactive computer graphics display. A light pen touched to the video screen could draw a line stretched from the previous point. Later, Sutherland and his graduate students at the University of Utah went on to make some of the major pioneering discoveries in the field of computer graphics image generation.

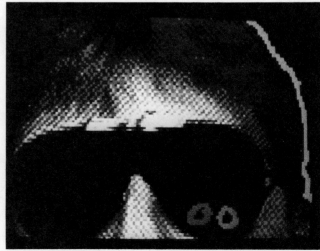

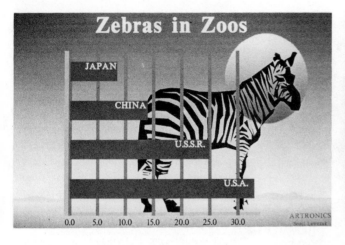

Zebras in Zoos

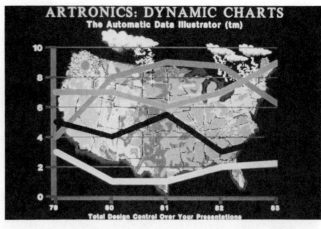

ARTRONICS: DYNAMIC CHARTS
The Automatic Data Illustrator (tm)

Total Design Control Over Your Presentations

They helped develop five steps that create a computer image of a simulated object. First the data defining the object must be input into the computer in the form of a mathematical description. Second, the three-dimensional description must be transformed into a two-dimensional perspective image. Third, a determination of all visible lines or surfaces must be made, and lines or surfaces that should not be seen by the viewer must be eliminated. This step is called hidden line elimination. Fourth, an illumination model must determine the color or shade of each surface. Fifth, the appropriate red, green, and blue intensities must be selected to represent the color specified by the shading model.

Today's software programs and input devices make these procedures seem simple and automatic. Most users are unaware of the program they are manipulating. The artist is free to explore ideas with an instant gratification lacking in other tools. Variations in color scheme can be instantly examined. Adjustments in composition can be tried without losing the original image. A series of visual options can be presented to the client quickly and efficiently. Changes or deletions can be achieved with a minimum of artistic trouble (Fig. 283).

The development of animation has added another dimension to computer art. Thanks to pioneers in computer programming, the artist is free to manipulate the

above left: 280. Zebras in Zoos. Copyright Artronics, Inc.

above right: 281. Weather Map. *Computer graphics are used in television studios and major newspapers to create such maps. Many newspapers output the image to a high-resolution film recorder to generate slides.* Copyright Artronics, Inc.

below left: 282. *Computer graphics and live action are combined in this image. Courtesy of Digital Effects, Inc.*

below right: 283. *Artist at work on the Interact 32 computer. Copyright Intergraph.*

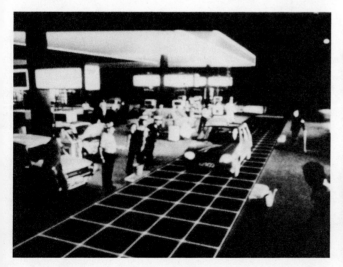

Development of Computer Graphics

"user friendly" program without understanding what makes it work. Sophisticated computer animation can be achieved by TWEEN programs that fill in the steps between key frames while a TWEEP program fills in colors. The movie *Tron* pioneered many animation techniques (Fig. 284).

RASTER AND VECTOR GRAPHICS

Raster scan graphics is the most common computer display. It creates the display the same way a home television does. However, the beam's brightness and color as it moves across the screen is determined not by synchronizing with a studio camera, but by following instructions from the computer itself.

Each spot on the screen, called a pixel, represents a location in the computer's memory. On early black and white displays, the value stored at a pixel only determined whether a spot should be on or off. In color displays, the process is more complex. The computer must check its memory by circuitry to read all the information stored at each pixel. If you are using a RGB (red, blue, green) monitor, the computer graphics circuitry puts out three separate signals controlling the amount of red, blue, and green at each pixel. Most professional systems used in graphic design can generate 16,000,000 colors (Figs. 285, 286).

The resolution of a screen controls its clarity and sharpness. You have probably noticed the jagged edges on computer video games. Because each spot on the screen is a pixel corresponding to a spot in memory, the number of individual pixels will determine the resolution of your image. The more pixels, the higher the resolution and the smoother your image. For print graphics, a high resolution is mandatory. For slides for corporate shows or logos and title screens for television, a resolution of 525 × 525 is smooth enough.

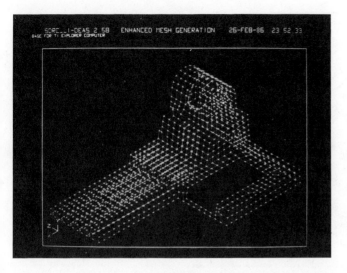

bottom left (p. 182): 285. *Todd Hubler (UW–Whitewater student designer). Self-portrait. Created with 256 values of blue. The computer can be an excellent tool for studying color effects. Courtesy the artist.*

bottom right (p. 182): 286. *Detail of Figure 285, showing individual pixels.*

left: 287. *An engineering analysis on a Texas Instruments Explorer terminal. Courtesy Calma Company.*

Vector graphics works differently from home television. It does not scan points. Instead it creates an image by magnetically dragging the electron beam over the screen, drawing lines. In mathematics a vector is a line with a specific direction and length. In math and in vector graphics, these vectors or lines are drawn from coordinate point to coordinate point on an x,y axis or an x,y,z axis (Fig. 287).

With vector graphics, images of very fine resolution can be drawn (Figs. 288, 289). The lines are continuous rather than formed out of dots or pixels. The images look like fine line drawings and are suitable for drafting and engineering purposes. Raster scan images look more like photographs. Although both raster scan and vector graphics are constantly being improved, raster scan will probably continue to offer more flexibility to the graphic designer and illustrator.

SYSTEMS

Many raster scan systems are on the market for both the professional and the novice. Professional "paint" systems capable of 16,000,000 colors and television quality resolution remain expensive. When animation, higher print quality resolution, or three-dimensional graphics are added, the price goes up considerably. Dicomed, Artronics, Aurora Systems, Dig-

below left: 288. *Graphic output from a SUPERTAB (TM) stress analysis on the Texas Instruments terminal. Courtesy Calma Company.*

below right: 289. *Mold-filling analysis. This computer graphic created on the Texas Instruments Explorer terminal demonstrates computer applications in the plastics industry. Courtesy Calma Company.*

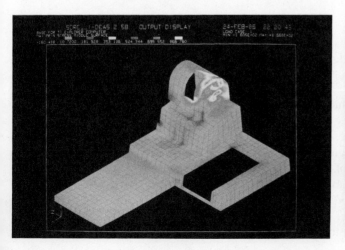

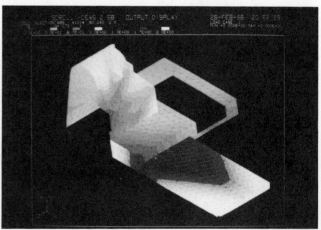

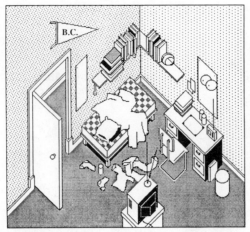

290. *Created on a Macintosh system with output on a laser printer.* From Wheels of the Mind. *Courtesy Apple Computer.*

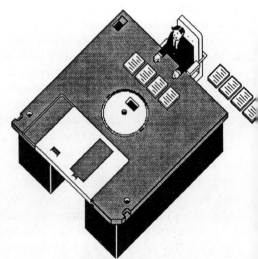

291. *Created on a Macintosh system. From* Wheels of the Mind. *Courtesy Apple Computer.*

ital Equipment Corporation, Quantel, and Via Video are a few of the professional graphics "paint" systems.

Personal computer graphics systems offer less resolution and fewer colors. The Mindset, the Amiga, and the Apple Macintosh are targeted at a beginning level graphics market. This level of microcomputers is increasingly affordable and versatile (Figs. 290, 291). If you are choosing one for yourself, compare resolution, number of colors, available software, compatibility with other systems, communications capabilities and available input devices.

Hardware

The hardware is the physical components that make up a computer graphics system. This hardware is driven by software programs that tell it what to do. The computer graphic artist needs only a general knowledge of the construction of the machine in order to use it.

The central processing unit (CPU) is the main part of the system that holds the memory. Most systems you use will be driven by disk drives. Located in the CPU, these disk drives record and retrieve information, which is stored on magnetic floppy or hard disks. Information is then stored outside the system on these disks.

The visual display terminal (VDT) shows the image as you create it. Some systems come with two terminals: one for the graphic image, and the other for information processing.

Input Devices

There are various input devices. A keyboard is used for inputting commands, writing programs, and word processing, and similar applications. It has a standard set of alphanumeric keys similar to a typewriter, and function keys that can be assigned any input function.

A graphics tablet is a flat surface with an electronic grid of fine wires implanted beneath its surface. Some models operate differently, but the principle remains the same. A stylus or digitizing pen can communicate with the computer by drawing on the surface of the graphics tablet. Most artists find it easy to use because it feels similar to a drawing surface and a pen.

Other hardware input devices, such as touch screens, joysticks, and the mouse, work in similar ways. They use different kinds of electronics to sense position, but all relay coordinates to the computer. A digitizing camera is probably the most user-friendly way to instruct the computer about what image to create.

All these input devices call for a special program in order to send signals back to the computer. The program translates the user's movements of the input device into the display on the screen. Usually a "menu" on the screen will help prompt the user through the available options. These programs are generally referred to as "user-friendly," because the user has only to manipulate a precreated menu and does not need to write a program or understand programming language.

Output Devices

"Soft copy" is the term describing the image that appears on the video screen. It is called "soft" because you cannot touch it or hold it in your hand, and it disappears when the screen is turned off. "Hard copy," however, describes something that can be held, touched, and kept. Paper and photographs are the common forms of hard copy. The ink-jet printer is a standard form of graphics output (Figs. 292, 293).

below near: 292. *Don Miller. Anomaly Series #3. 1987. Ink-jet print from Amiga. 7″ × 9 1/2″ (17.8 × 24.1 cm). Courtesy the artist.*

below far: 293. *Don Miller. Anomaly Series #1. 1987. Ink-jet print from Amiga. 7″ × 9 1/2″ (17.8 × 24.1 cm). Courtesy the artist.*

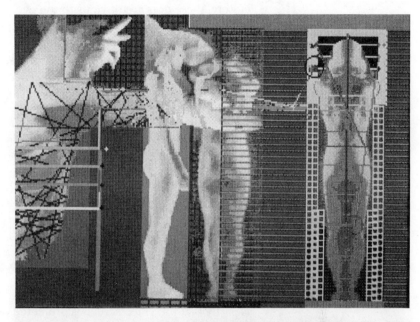

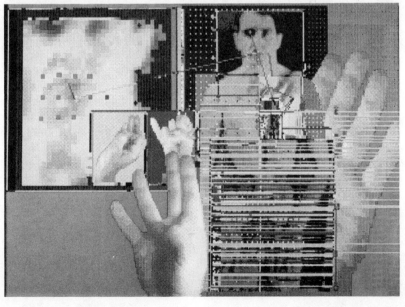

The daisy-wheel printer, also called a "letter-quality" printer, has a single element in the shape of a ball with types for all the characters engraved on it. This ball changes character by repositioning itself so the right part will strike the ribbon.

Dot-matrix printers use only one type element made of a line of pins that strike a ribbon. Characters are formed by different patterns of dots laid down as the head moves back and forth across the paper. When the characters are examined closely, these dots are obvious to the eye. Higher quality printers have a finer matrix of dots. Dot-matrix printers can produce any kind of image as well as alphanumeric characters. Thermal, electrostatic, and laser printers are nonimpact methods of output that currently do not offer high quality color output.

Future printers and plotters will offer better speed, color, image quality, and economy. Hard copy output has lagged behind the rest of computer technology. It has often been a disappointment to the artist wishing to duplicate the complex, intensely colored screen image.

Photography is able to yield a more satisfactory color output than printers. Unfortunately, it also often falls short of the vibrancy of the screen image. The problem is partly that the video screen is projected light, whereas a print is viewed in reflected light. It is also due to the difference in size between the monitor and the print or slide, and to the difference in viewing conditions. The computer screen is interactive; the photographic copy is not. Moreover, to some extent the RGB video process creating the video color is difficult to duplicate in photography. The curvature and reflectiveness of the video screen also cause problems if you try to photograph the screen directly.

To compensate for some of these problems, you can connect a special image recorder camera to the computer. A camera is mounted in a light-tight box with a tiny, high resolution video screen at the end of it, on which the image on your monitor is recreated. The camera takes three exposures, for the red, green, and blue parts of the image. Each pixel has three colors that must be photographed in exact registration for a high quality photographic output. Only a special image recorder camera can do it.

You may use a variety of films in your camera, for prints or slides. Of course, slides can be made into prints of any size. Cibachrome prints are the most resistant to fading and reproduce colors brilliantly. In general, high intensity hues will reproduce better from your video screen than low intensity tones.

Output is an interesting area in computer graphics. It is possible that we place too much emphasis on hard copy output, because we are used to being able to hold a piece of art in our hands. The video image (soft copy) may seem cold and alien only because we are not yet accustomed to it. Certainly it can simplify production. Various forms of design work can be downloaded directly from the video screen to computerized color separator (laser scanners) and prepared for press. Images can be sent between computers for the various proofing and editing stages. A proofreader or editor with a compatible computer can make changes or comments on the screen. These forms of communication between different systems are constantly being improved. Total page makeup can be completed on the monitor. All of these improvements may make the hard copy stage in the field of graphic design less important than it traditionally has been. In the future, the first hard copy may be the final printed piece.

Software

Software is the name for prepackaged programs that instruct the computer how to operate. Software programs translate the movement of digitizing pen and tablet as well as signals from the digitizing camera. These movements are translated into video screen images and into instructions that activate the output device.

Packaged software programs are especially useful to artists who want to use the computer as a tool to create images, without becoming involved in programming. Some programs can be used in several compatible machines, whereas others are written only for a specific computer. The majority of computer graphics jobs in studios, agencies, newspapers, and corporate settings will only require you to learn the software for one particular system.

Packaged software programs only let the artist and designer manipulate images within defined parameters. If you have the interest and the time to learn programming, greater flexibility and creativity will be your reward.

GRAPHIC DESIGN IMAGES

The computer images you are probably most familiar with are on television. When a station is in need of a title or an animated logo, it is more efficient to create one by computer than by traditional illustration. Clip art images and photo files can be stored, recalled, and manipulated into new images by computer. Television studios that prefer the particular soft quality of airbrush may use computers to generate the rough copy, and execute the final copy in a traditional medium. It is still faster and more efficient than working without computer assistance (Fig. 294). Television advertising is another expanding market for computer illustration.

The uses for computer graphics are varied and growing. It can expand our senses and allow us to picture things we have never seen before. It can enhance communication, exploration, and processing of information. It is a medium that may shape the form of our inquiry into it. Nevertheless, it is only one tool. As you have learned, the artist, not the tool, is the creator. An inquisitive, open mind and a love for visual expression are the greatest tools of all.

EXERCISES

1. Look for printed samples of computer-generated advertisements. Why was a computer used in these designs?

294. Nigel Schuster. Current Affairs. *Courtesy Canadian Broadcasting Corporation, Toronto, Canada. A computer was used to comp this illustration, which was then rendered using more conventional tools.*

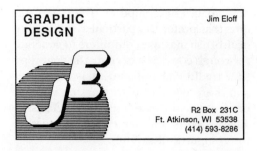

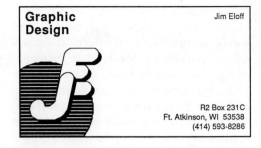

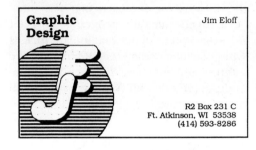

295. *Jim Eloff (UW– Whitewater student designer).*

2. Watch for various forms of computer graphics on television. See how many different types you can find. Keep notes and bring them to class for discussion.

PROJECT
A New Symbol

If your class has access to a microcomputer lab, spend a few hours acquainting yourself with the graphics software. Then design a personal symbol or logo using a computer to generate a variety of polished rough designs. Refer to Chapter 5 for samples of computer-generated advertisements. Use your computer-generated roughs to select a symbol or logo to execute by hand for finished, camera-ready artwork. Figure 295 shows a student's personal logo roughs generated on a Macintosh computer.

HOW TO USE TOOLS AND EQUIPMENT

THE DESIGNER'S TOOLS

Every design, in order to succeed, requires clean execution. Master the tools of the trade. Execution is not the only factor in a successful design, but without it all else fails.

This first section will present the standard tools that designers have used for years. The second section will discuss technical equipment that can make our jobs easier. Master the basic skills and standard tools of the designer before developing a dependency on equipment. Expensive equipment may not always be available.

Papers and Boards

Tracing paper is an invaluable tool because of its transparency. It is convenient for tracing details accurately. It is also excellent for working through rough and thumbnail stages, because a sketch can be traced and reworked without having to redraw from the start. Tracing paper comes in rolls as well as pads. The rolls are useful for preparing overlays with instructions for the printer (Fig. 296).

Layout paper and the several grades of marker paper are less transparent than tracing paper, but they allow tracing on a better paper surface.

Illustration board is used for finished layouts, inking, pasteups, and of course, illustration. There are many surfaces, divided into two categories: hot press and cold press. A hot press surface is smoother and suited for fine detail work such as pasteup, inking, and airbrush. A cold press surface has a slight texture or tooth. When large areas are to be covered with a water-based medium, illustration board is preferable to thinner material. Illustration board is actually drawing paper laminated to a backing board. The rag content of the face paper and the type and thickness of the backing board determine the quality and price.

Mat board is a single-thickness board colored on one side with a variety of surface textures. It is used for mounting or matting work. For your graphic design presentations, use only white, off-white, or gray board. Occasionally black will be appropriate, depending on the value distribution in the artwork. Do not use colored mats; they interact with the colors of the art, distorting its effect and making it hard to imagine the original piece reproduced in magazine, brochure, or poster form without a mat.

296. *Papers and boards.*

Preprinted grid paper with a light blue grid can be used for planning tight designs. It is available on a firmer surface for paste-ups. Many companies have their own grid paper printed to match their publication needs.

Colored paper is excellent for a quick way to visualize and execute a comprehensive. "Fadeless" paper is a brand name for a type of paper that will not discolor quickly. It comes in thin, easy to cut sheets. Avoid construction paper at all costs. It fades quickly and does not cut cleanly. The Color Aid papers have a beautiful coated surface in over 200 brilliant and subtle hues. If you prepare a comprehensive with them, it will have a pure silkscreen look that your offset printer will be hard put to match. PANTONE offers a line of papers that match the printer's ink colors, helping you plan a design that will look much the same after it comes off the press.

Text and cover papers are available from paper companies to enable a designer to prepare a comprehensive on the actual stock the publication will be printed on.

Acetate comes in many thicknesses, with 0.003″ and 0.005″ the most commonly used. It is available in clear, matte (frosted), and prefixed surfaces. The only media that will not crawl or peel on clear acetate are acetate inks and paints. Prepared acetate is a form of clear acetate that will take any medium. Matte acetate also will accept any medium; it is commonly used for color separation overlays.

Acetate film with a transparent color printed on it is available for preparing comprehensives. It comes with an adhesive coating on the back. The ruby and amber colors are also used for mechanicals.

Measuring, Drawing, and Cutting Tools

A *T-square* is a vital tool. They are available in lengths from 18″ (46 cm) to 48″ (122 cm). The steel T-square is the most expensive, but definitely that best investment for graphic design work. You may use it for cutting as well as ruling. The 24″ (60 cm) or 30″ (75 cm) length is the most popular for studio work.

Triangles, usually made of transparent material, are available in a variety of sizes. They are placed along the upper edge of the T-square to create a 90-degree angle. They are used for drawing vertical lines and for checking the alignment of vertical elements (Fig. 297).

Rulers come in a variety of lengths and materials. The stainless steel 24″ (60 cm) is suitable for most needs. Some brands include pica, agate, and point measurements. Of special use to typographers are

297. *Triangle and T-square.*

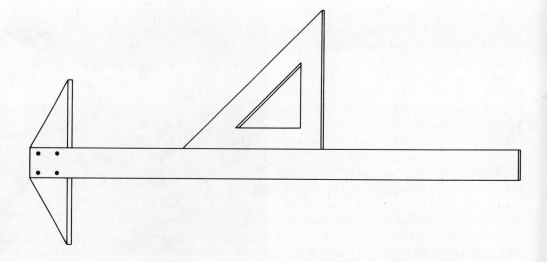

How to Use Tools and Equipment

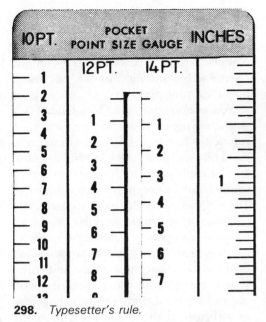

298. *Typesetter's rule.*

rules that also give an immediate visualization of leading measurements in points (Fig. 298).

Templates such as circle and ellipse guides are useful. A packet of French curves will cover a wide variety of needs for irregular curved shapes (Fig. 299).

299. *French curves.*

The *X-acto knife,* a thin-handled tool, is indispensable for many studio needs. It can be fitted with various types of blade. The #11, the most common, can be used for precise, tiny cutting. The #16 has a flatter point and is preferred by some for curve cutting. A flexible swivel X-acto can cut detailed, irregular curves.

The *mat knife* is a heavy-duty knife for cutting mats and other thick materials. It is not to be confused with an X-acto. It is not as flexible, and replacement of blades is more time-consuming (Fig. 300).

Drawing Instruments

A *compass* with interchangeable pen and pencil points will allow you to execute medium-sized circles. The regular 6″ (15 cm) size should suit your needs. A circle template or a special small compass can be used for smaller sizes. For circles larger than 11″ (28 cm) in radius, a beam compass is recommended. Most drawing instrument sets come with several of these items. Also handy are the small blades that can be purchased to insert into compasses for cutting precise circles.

The *divider* is used for dividing distances into equal parts, and for transferring exact measurements without relying on the less precise ruler (Fig. 301).

The *ruling pen* is not used as often now that technical pens have become so reliable. It still has several advantages, however. The ruling pen can give you varying thicknesses of line width, just by an adjustment of the nibs. It also can lay down lines in color, and it can be cleaned quickly by swishing in water (Fig. 302).

Never fill the ruling pen by dipping. Use an ink dropper or loaded brush to deposit ink into the well. Fill the pen with no more than 3/8″ (1 cm) of ink; more will cause the medium to flow too quickly. Use it immediately upon filling, or the liquid will dry and refuse to flow.

When ruling, hold the pen so that both nibs touch the surface of the paper, and tip the pen forward slightly in the direction of the stroke. The nibs of the pen must be

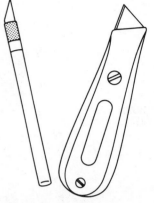

above: 300. *X-acto knife and mat knife.*

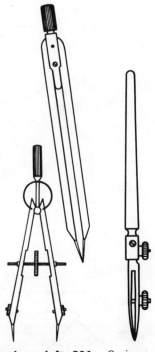

above left: 301. *Spring box compass and dividers.*

above right: 302. *Ruling pen.*

The Designer's Tools

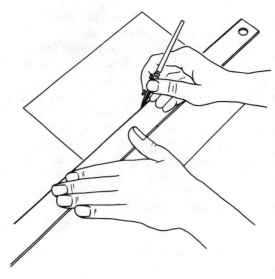

303. *Use of a ruling pen.*

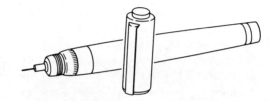

304. *Technical pen.*

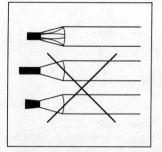

305. *A chisel-point pencil should be perfect.*

parallel to the line being ruled (Fig. 303).

Technical pens hold waterproof drawing ink in cartridges. The ink feeds down a thin tube. Sets are available with varying point sizes. An internal wire ensures against ink clogging. Special compasses and compass attachments are available for technical pens. This pen requires constant use and care to work properly. Carefully read the instructions for handling and cleaning (Fig. 304).

If you choose to comp with a *chisel point pencil*, trim the excess wood from the sides by hand. Be careful not to cut away any of the lead itself, and not to nick it. Expose at least 1/4″ of lead, and then trim the tip into a flat shape. Draw several lines on scrap paper until the pencil is smooth and flat. The sides of the lead should be perfectly parallel, like a chisel (Fig. 305).

Inks, Paints, and Brushes

India ink in a waterproof form is suitable for a variety of general drawing purposes.

Certain brands, such as Higgins Black Magic, work better for heavy coverage over large areas. For your technical pen, the manufacturer will recommend a thin ink. Do not substitute just any ink, because it may clog your pen.

Non-waterproof ink is intended for wash drawings. It should not be used when retouch white may be involved, because the white will pick up the ink and discolor. Do not apply ink over designer's colors or retouch colors except in limited amounts. The ink can cause the paint to flake off.

Gouache, the most popular designer's color, is an opaque watercolor. Some of the brand names for gouache are Winsor & Newton, Grumbacher, Pelikan, and Shiva. When thinned with water, designer's colors can be used with brush, ruling pen, or airbrush. If the color hardens in the tube, water can be injected with a medical syringe to soften it again.

Poster colors are an inexpensive alternative to designer's color. They are also an opaque water-based paint. Transparent watercolor is most often utilized in fine art and illustration, where it is valued for its wash effects. It is not suited to opaque coverage.

Watercolor brushes come in sizes from #000 (useful in spotting photographic prints) to #14. The best quality is red sable, with sabeline a less expensive alternative. Oxhair, camelhair, and white bristle are for less demanding, less exact work. The most commonly used sizes range from #1 to #6. Paint should never be allowed to dry in brushes. Ink cannot be washed out if it is allowed to dry. After a brush is used it should be thoroughly rinsed in warm water and the hairs repointed. Always store brushes tip up or flat; never permit them to rest on their hairs (Fig. 306).

Adhesives

Rubber cement is the most commonly used adhesive in the graphic design studio. It can be dissolved with rubber cement thinner, permitting repositioning of elements. It is not permanent, and it is not intended for fine art, because it can eventually stain work. It is good for flat materials but will not hold on packaging, warped photographs, and so on. Dried rubber cement can be removed by rubbing with the finger, by accumulating a ball of dried rubber cement and rubbing it over the surface, or by applying a rubber cement pickup, available in art supply stores.

The most permanent form of rubber cement application is a double coating. Both surfaces are covered with rubber cement and allowed almost to dry before adhering. Careful positioning is necessary, because the surfaces will bond when touched together. A slip sheet is often used to aid positioning. A sheet of paper is placed over the base surface so that it covers all but a thin line of rubber cement along the top edge. The material to be mounted is placed upon the slip sheet and adhered along the top. The slip sheet is then gradually withdrawn as the two surfaces are allowed to contact and are smoothed together with the hand.

For smaller pieces that require accurate positioning, such as the elements of a mechanical pasteup, a combination of dry

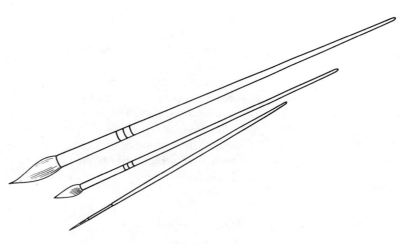

306. *An assortment of water media brushes.*

and wet rubber cement works well. The piece to be mounted is coated with rubber cement and allowed to dry. When you are ready to position it, coat the mounting surface and position the piece while the cement is still wet. It will take a few minutes for the bond to become firm, allowing adjustment.

Coating only one surface with rubber cement and adhering while still wet forms the most temporary and weakest bond.

Wax is the other common form of adhesive in graphic design work (Fig. 307). A small hand-operated or larger electric

307. *An electric waxer.*

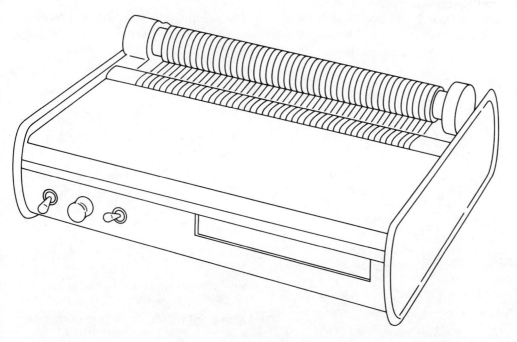

waxer will coat the back of paper with a thin film of warm wax that is pressure-sensitive. During pasteup it is best to run the entire sheet of typeset material through the waxer before cutting it into sections, because small pieces can get stuck in the waxer. The advantage of wax is that it can be repositioned easily without solvent. If a residue of wax remains on the board after a piece has been removed, it can be removed with rubber cement thinner.

Tapes

Drafting tape is used for masking straight edges before paint or ink is applied. It can be removed without damaging the surface of illustration board. It is also available in white. Masking tape is similar to drafting tape, but it has a stronger adhesive. It is suitable for adhering overlays and for taping your surface to the drawing table. Rubber cement thinner will help remove most tapes, should too strong a bond damage your working surface. A little rubber cement thinner on a brush can be gradually "painted" onto the back of the tape, while you ease it up from the surface.

Clear transparent tape should not be used for hinging overlays, because it can tear with use. It can occasionally be used on a mechanical to repair damage if time

and cost effectiveness do not allow a more thorough repair job. A new low-adhesive variety is useful as a mask for preparing artwork.

A variety of black and colored tapes are available with a mild adhesive backing. They are useful for borders, charts, and anywhere inked rules are not appropriate.

Furniture

A *drawing board* or drawing table and adequate lighting are the final tools necessary to complete your studio. The drawing table or board must have a metal edge for T-square accuracy. It should be covered with a protective surface that can be discarded when damaged by cuts. The table is adjustable in height and angle, whereas the board can be propped with a block of wood or books to the desired angle (Figs. 308, 309).

A *lamp* with a long adjustable arm that can be positioned over your artwork is also necessary. A good color balance can be achieved with a combination of light sources, such as daylight and fluorescent, or fluorescent and incandescent.

THE DESIGNER'S EQUIPMENT

The previous section discussed tools that are extensions of the designer's hands.

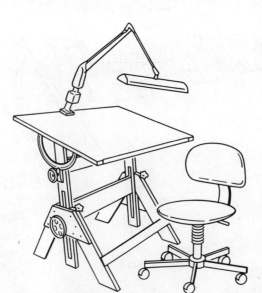

left: 308. *A small drawing table with light.*

above right: 309. *A large drawing table provides a better working surface.*

The equipment discussed in this section is more technical and expensive. It is more closely connected to production than to earlier design stages. It is available in some art departments and studios and not in others. Although it is important to understand this equipment, a student should be able to function creatively and precisely without it.

Enlargement and Reduction Cameras

The *"Lucy"* is the simplest camera available to the designer. Cameras with this generic name project an enlarged or reduced image onto a surface for tracing. The Lucy is useful for checking the look of your design at different sizes. A few cranks of the handle, and you can check your logo at twice its sketched size, or at half size. It is a valuable aid in sizing and resizing elements and for sketching in imagery from photography that would otherwise take considerable time to render. Tracing is a time-saving device. It is a different skill than drawing and illustrating. An artist should choose tracing if the job is most efficiently completed by that method, but drawing if the job calls for an expressive, emotive quality. Every designer should cultivate both drawing skills and design skills.

310. *Total Camera II from Visual Graphics Corporation (VGC) operates in daylight, providing the full range of reproduction services.*

The *stat camera* is a more elaborate and expensive piece of equipment that will also enlarge and reduce artwork. The stat camera, however, works with photographic paper and chemicals. It will shoot straight black and white line art, makes reversals, and converts photos into halftone dot screens (Fig. 310). It is useful for making position stats for layouts and for preparing pasteup elements. Stats cost more than making an enlargement by hand, but they are quicker. A process camera is often used when more complex manipulations and finer screened images are required (Figs. 311, 312). Sometimes

far left: 311. *The nuArc VVE1418 vertical camera features electronic exposure control with eight memory channels for storing exposure information.*

near left: 312. *The NuArc SSTE2024SB horizontal camera is wall-mounted. The lights and copy board are in a separate room from the easel back and processing equipment. This setup creates great physical stability and make it possible to process and shoot simultaneously.*

313. *Exposing a negative on the Chromacheck color proofing system. Courtesy DuPont.*

Color key materials and color proofing systems are used in preparing tight comprehensives. They will display type and art in selected color overlays created from black and white originals (Fig. 313). They can be especially helpful in package design. In many cases, however, it is possible to create a good comprehensive with only cut paper.

Equipment for Setting Display Type

Hand-constructed letterforms are important to the beginning designer. Drawing the letter leads to an understanding of structure in both the positive and negative areas and to an appreciation for the beauty and variety in letterforms. Hand-constructed type often shows a better understanding of the design relationships in letter spacing than machine-set type. It is used for custom design of trademarks such as logos and symbols, book and movie titles, and so on.

Dry transfer lettering is used for display type when one-of-a-kind hand-constructed lettering is not necessary. The letters of the alphabet come printed on a transparent sheet. Placing the sheet placed on the artwork and gently rubbing causes a letter to release from the sheet and transfer to the working surface (Fig. 314). In case of

the fine tuning and precise relationship between elements is lost when a designer turns from hand execution to machine execution. The experienced designer will factor in the three considerations of speed, cost, and quality before deciding how to proceed. The joy of being a student designer is that quality and learning usually take precedence.

314. *Using dry transfer lettering.*

How to Use Tools and Equipment

error, the letter can be removed by touching with masking tape. There are hundreds of type styles available, some of them in a limited range of colors for comprehensive presentations. It is easy to optically control the placement and spacing of dry transfer letters, but it takes practice to apply them evenly without cracking.

Photodisplay lettering is a method of setting display type photographically. The many brands of photodisplay systems on the market all have a variety of type fonts and sizes. The VariType Headliner is a popular brand name. On the majority of these systems, the type font comes on a disc or strip, which is inserted in the machine. Each letterform is positioned so that a light flash will expose it onto photosensitive material. Most machines set type in a single line on a strip of paper or film, which must be developed in chemicals. The strips are then trimmed and pasted up (Fig. 315). This method is good for pasteup but not for comprehensives. Display type can also be set on the typesetting equipment dis-

cussed in the next section, which also handles body copy.

Typesetting Equipment

The other forms of typesetting are used for the text type of the body of an article, advertisement, book, or brochure. A designer may be only specifying style and format, not setting the type. Because computers are becoming part of everyday life, however, it is a good idea to know how to type at a keyboard. There are jobs where each designer has a computer terminal.

The first method of typesetting was hand lettering. Books were rare and restricted to the elite and the monastic community. Gutenberg invented a hand-set method of movable type around 1450. With each new typesetting invention, the printed word has become more accessible.

Hot type, a form of machine-set type, was invented in the late nineteenth century. The Linotype and Monotype machines set text-size type by keyboard control (Fig. 316). Type matrices fall into position as the keyboard is operated. The matrices are then set in molten metal, creating a line of relief letterforms on one edge. The matrix

315. *The phototypositor 3200 sets a variety of type styles and headline sizes. Copy output is a long strip of durable paper.*

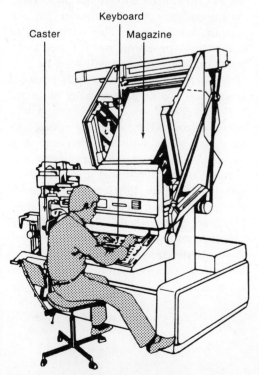

Caster   Keyboard   Magazine

316. *An early Linotype machine.*

317. *The Linotype™ Graphic System with Linotronic ® 300 laser imagesetter. Capable of high-quality line art and halftones up to a 300-line screen, and of crisp, clear type.*

is removed, and the type is assembled in a long format called a galley for printing on a letterpress press. After use all metal is remelted.

Cold type is a photographic method of setting text-size type, also called phototypesetting. Introduced in 1950, it has taken over the typesetting industry, replacing hot type, as it is faster, more efficient, and more versatile. All the cold type systems store type characters on a disc or drum; as each character is selected a lens projects it onto photographic material. Because the type is photographic, not metal, it can be overlapped for a variety of effects. The output from this kind of system is a sheet of paper, which is pasted up and converted photographically into a metal plate for printing on an offset or gravure press.

Computers drive the phototypesetting systems on the market today. Not only can they fit a great variety of type sizes and styles into selected formats, but they can output the copy many times in different fonts and formats without repeated input. Some systems permit the operator to lay out a complete page of type, indi-

cating photographs and reversals. Pasteup is eliminated, as a one-page paper proof is ready for camera, or a film proof is ready for platemaking (Fig. 317). These layout systems are useful for high volume layout where the format can be easily systematized, such as books or college catalogs.

We saw in Chapter 13 how computers are being used to create effective graphics. For now, professional computer typesetting equipment and computer graphics systems are separate. The integration of computer typesetting and creative computer graphics imaging will soon be possible. Desktop publishing with personal computers is a rapidly growing industry.

However sophisticated, the system does not design: The designer does. Although pasteup skills may become antiquated, good design skills never will. Stay abreast of technological developments, but develop those timeless skills. Graphic design has a constant potential for change, learning, and growth. Growth without direction and quality control is not enough —not for the designer, for the client, or for society. We always will need good, intelligent design.

How to Use Tools and Equipment

GLOSSARY

Abstraction A simplification of existing shapes.

Acetate overlay A clear plastic overlay that permits the positioning of units on a pasteup that cannot be put together on a single sheet.

Additive primaries Red, blue, and green, which combine to produce white light.

Aerial perspective The creation of a sense of depth and distance through softening edges and decreasing value contrast.

Aliasing The visual effect that occurs on a computer's visual display screen whenever the detail in the image exceeds the resolution available. It looks like "stair stepping."

Analogous colors Hues that lie next to one another on the color wheel.

Applied art and design Disciplines that use the principles and elements of design to create functional pieces for commercial use.

Ascender The section of a lowercase letter that extends above the x-height.

Asymmetrical balance The distribution of shapes of different visual weights over a picture plane to create an overall impression of balance.

Balance The distribution of the visual weight of design elements.

Body type Type smaller than 14 point, generally used for the main body of text. Also called text type.

Boldface A heavy version of a typeface.

CAD/CAM Computer-aided design/computer-aided manufacturing.

Camera-ready art Artwork that has been assembled and prepared for reproduction on a process camera.

Centered type Lines of type of varying length that have been centered over one another.

Central processing unit (CPU) The part of a computer system that contains the circuits that control and execute all data.

Character count The number of characters in a piece of copy. This number is used in copyfitting calculations.

Closure When the eye completes a line or curve in order to form a familiar shape.

Cold type Copy prepared by photographic keyboard typesetting.

Color The way an object absorbs or reflects light.

Color wheel The part of color theory that demonstrates color relationships on a circle.

Combination mark A trademark that combines symbol and logo.

Complementary hues Colors that are opposite one another on the color wheel.

Comprehensive (comp) A highly finished layout for presentation.

Computer graphics The branch of computer science that deals with creating and modifying pictorial data.

Continuation When the eye is carried smoothly into the line or curve of an adjoining object.

Continuous-tone art Black and white art, such as illustrations or photographs, with a range of values. Must be reproduced with a halftone screen.

Copyfitting The process of determining the amount of space it will take to set copy in a specific type size and style.

Counters The white shapes inside a letterform.

Crop To eliminate the unwanted sections of image area.

Cropmarks Short fine lines drawn on the image to indicate a cropped area, or at the corners of a pasteup to indicate where printed sheet will be trimmed. When used to indicate trim size, they can be called trim marks.

Direct advertising Any form of advertising issued directly to the prospect through any means that does not involve the traditional mass media.

Direct mail Advertising in which the advertiser acts as publisher.

Direct marketing Sale of goods or services direct to the consumer without intermediaries. Can include door-to-door sales.

Disk An off-system data storage device for computers, consisting of one or more flat circular plates coated with magnetized material.

Display type Any type over 14 point.

Dropout Copy that is reversed out of a halftone or a tint screen background.

Duotone A two-color halftone reproduction made from one-color, continuous-tone artwork.

Egyptian A slab-serif type category.

Font A complete set of type of one size and one variation on a typeface.

Figure-ground The relationship between the figure and the background of an image.

Focal point The area of a design toward which the viewer's eye is primarily drawn.

Gestalt A unified configuration having properties that cannot be derived from simple addition of its parts.

Gripper edge The leading edge of paper as it feeds into a press. Usually it calls for an unprinted margin of about 3/8" (1 cm).

Gutter The inner section of a page caught in the center binding.

Halftone The reproduction of continuous-tone art, such as a photograph, through a screen that converts it into dots of various sizes.

Hard copy A printed copy of an image produced on a computer screen.

Hardware The physical components of a computer graphics system, including all mechanical, magnetic, and electronic parts.

Horizontal balance The visual balancing of the left and right sides of a composition.

Hot type Typesetting in which the type is cast in molten metal.

Hue The name of a given color. Hue is one of the three properties of color.

Intensity The saturation or brightness of a color. Intensity is decreased by the addition of a gray or a complement.

Justify To align lines of type that are equal in length so both edges of the column are straight.

Kerning Selectively altering the spaces between letter combinations for a better fit.

Keylining Drawing an outline on a finished pasteup to indicate the exact position for art that will be stripped in by the printer. Used when hairline registration is important.

Layout The hand-rendered plan for a piece to be printed.

Leading The amount of space placed vertically between lines of type.

Line art Black and white copy with no variations in value. Suitable for reproduction without a halftone screen.

Logo A trademark of unique type or lettering, spelling out the name of a company or product.

Lowercase The small letters of an alphabet.

Masking film A red film used to block out selected areas of a pasteup where screened images will be positioned on the negative.

Menu-driven A computer graphics system that operates when a user selects options from those displayed on the monitor.

Mechanical A camera-ready pasteup, which contains all copy pasted in position for printing.

Modern A type category that has great variation between thick and thin strokes and thin, unbracketed serifs.

Monochromatic color The use of a single hue in varying values.

Nonobjective shapes Shapes that are pure design elements, not related to any pictorial source.

Non-photo blue pencil A light blue pencil whose lines will not reproduce when photographed by a process camera.

Old style type A type category characterized by mild contrast between thicks and thins, and by bracketed serifs.

Pasteup An assemblage of the elements of a layout, prepared for reproduction.

Phosphor A material coating the inside of a picture tube. When an electron beam hits this coating, the phosphor emits light in proportion to the voltage of the beam.

Pica A typographic measurement of 1/6" (0.4 cm).

Pictogram A symbol that is used to cross language barriers for international signage.

Picture plane The flat surface of a two-dimensional design, possessing height and width, but no depth.

Pixel An individual picture element. It is the smallest element of a computer image that can be separately addressed.

Preseparated art Art that has been separated onto acetate overlays by the pasteup artist before being sent to the printer.

Point A typographic measurement of 1/72 inch, or 1/12 pica.

Primary colors The three basic pigment colors of light—red, blue, and green—from which all other colors can be made are called "additive" primaries because when added together they produce white light. "Subtractive" primaries are the magenta, cyan, and yellow of process printing.

Process camera A large graphic arts camera used to make film negatives and positives for platemaking.

Proximity Visually grouping by similarity in spatial location.

Ragged right (or left) An unjustified column of type in which lines of varying length are aligned on either the right or left side.

Raster graphics A type of computer graphics in which an electron beam moves back and forth across the video display monitor, activating individual display units called pixels.

Registration Fitting two or more printing images on the same paper in exact alignment.

Resolution The ability of a computer graphics system to make distinguishable the individual parts of an image.

Reversal A change to opposite tonal values, as when black type is altered to white.

Reversible figure/ground A relationship in which it is likely that figure and ground can be focused on equally.

Rough A layout plan that comes after preliminary thumbnails, and is usually executed in half or full size.

Runaround Type that is fitted around a piece of artwork.

Sans serif Letterforms without serifs. (See Serif.)

Saturation The intensity or brightness of a color. Saturation is decreased by the addition of gray or a complementary color.

Scan line On a raster scan computer monitor, one traversal of an electron beam across the picture.

Secondary colors Hues obtained by mixing two primary colors.

Serif The stroke that projects off the main stroke of a letter at the bottom or the top.

Shade A darker value of a hue, created by adding black.

Shading film Commercially available textured screens of line art on a transfer sheet.

Shape A figure that has visually definable edges.

Similarity grouping The visual grouping of images with similar shape, size, and color.

Software Computer programs.

Spec Short for "specifying." To write type specifications (line length, size, style, leading) on copy.

Stable figure/ground The unambiguous relationship of object to background.

Stress The distribution of weight through the thinnest part of a letterform.

Subtractive primaries Magenta, cyan, and yellow—the colors left after subtracting one additive primary from white light.

Surprint Line art superimposed over a screened area of the same color.

Symbol A type of trademark to identify a company or product. It is abstract or pictorial but does not include letterforms.

Symmetrical balance The formal placement of design elements to create a mirror image on either side. A less common form of symmetrical balance also creates the mirror image vertically.

Tertiary colors Hues obtained by mixing a primary color with a secondary color.

Thumbnail A first stage, miniature plan for a layout.

Tint A light value of a hue, created by adding white.

Tint screen A flat, unmodulated light value made of evenly dispersed dots, usually achieved by stripping a piece of halftone film into the area on the negative that the artist has masked out.

Tone A hue that has been decreased in intensity by the addition of black or a complement.

Trademark Any unique name or symbol used by a corporation or manufacturer to identify a product and to distinguish it from other products.

Transitional type A category of type that blends old style and modern, with emphasis on thick and thin contrast and gracefully bracketed serifs.

Type family The complete range of sizes and variations of a typeface.

Typeface Style of lettering. Each family of typefaces may contain variations on that typeface, like "italic."

Typesetting The composition of type by any method.

Unjustified type Lines of type set with equal word spacing and uneven length.

Uppercase The capital letters.

Value The lightness or darkness of a color or a tone of gray.

Variety The variations on a visual theme causing contrast in a design.

Vector graphics A type of computer graphics in which graphic data are represented by lines drawn from coordinate point to coordinate point.

Vertical balance The visual balancing of the upper and lower portions of a composition.

Visual texture The visual creation of an implied tactile texture.

Weight The lightness or heaviness of a visual image.

Windows Solid black or red areas of the pasteup that will convert into clear areas on the negative for a screen to be stripped onto.

Word spacing The varying space between words, often adjusted to create a justified line of copy.

x-height The height of the body of a lowercase letter like an *a*, with no ascenders or descenders.

BIBLIOGRAPHY

BASIC DESIGN (Chapter 1)

ALBERS, JOSEF, *Interaction of Color.* New Haven, Conn.: Yale University Press, 1972.

BAUMGARTNER, VICTOR, *Graphic Games.* Englewood Cliffs, N.J.: Prentice-Hall, 1983.

BEHRENS, ROY, *Design in the Visual Arts.* Englewood Cliffs, N.J.: Prentice-Hall, 1984.

BEVLIN, MARJORIE, *Design Through Discovery.* New York: Holt, Rinehart and Winston, 1985.

HARLAN, CALVIN, *Vision and Invention: A Course in Art Fundaments.* Englewood Cliffs, N.J.: Prentice-Hall, 1970.

ITTEN, JOHANNES, *The Art of Color.* New York: Van Nostrand Reinhold, 1974.

KEPES, GYORGY, *Language of Vision.* Chicago: Paul Theobald, 1969.

LAUER, DAVID, *Design Basics.* Holt, Rinehart and Winston, 1979.

McKIM, ROBERT H., *Experiences in Visual Thinking.* Monterey, Cal.: Brooks, Cole, 1980.

GRAPHIC DESIGN HISTORY AND PRACTICE (Chapter 2)

BAYER, HERBERT, et al., eds., *Bauhaus 1919– 1928.* New York: Museum of Modern Art, 1938.

BERRYMAN, GREGG, Notes on Graphic Design and Visual Communication. Los Altos, Calif.: William Kaufmann, 1979.

BOCKUS, WILLIAM H., *Advertising Graphics.* New York: Macmillan, 1970.

BOOTH-CLIBBORN, EDWARD, *The Language of Graphics.* New York: Harry Abrams, 1980.

CIRKER, HAYWARD, and BLANCHE CIRKER, *Golden Age of the Poster.* New York: Dover, 1971.

CRAIG, JAMES, *Graphic Design Career Guide.* New York: Watson-Guptill Publications, 1983.

GLASER, MILTON, *Milton Glaser: Graphic Design.* Woodstock, N.Y.: The Overlook Press, 1983.

HOFFMAN, ARMIN, *Graphic Design Manual.* New York: Van Nostrand Reinhold, 1965.

HURLBURT, ALLEN, *Layout: The Design of the Printed Page.* New York: Watson-Guptill Publications, 1977.

MOTHERWELL, ROBERT, *Dada Painters and Poets.* New York: Wittenborn, Schultz, 1951.

MULLER-BROCKMANN, JOSEF, *The Graphic Artist and His Design Problems.* New York: Hastings House, 1961.

MULLER-BROCKMANN, JOSEF, *A History of Visual Communication.* New York: Hastings House, 1971.

NELSON, ROY PAUL, *Publication Design.* Dubuque, Iowa: William C. Brown, 1983.

RAND, PAUL, *A Designer's Art.* New Haven, Conn.: Yale University Press, 1985.

RAND, PAUL, *Thoughts on Design.* New York: Van Nostrand, Reinhold, 1971.

SCHEIDIG, WALTER, *Crafts of the Weimar Bauhaus 1919–1924.* New York: Reinhold Publishing, 1967.

SMITH, ROBERT CHARLES, *Basic Graphic Design.* Englewood Cliffs, N.J.: Prentice-Hall, 1986.

SNYDER, PECKOLICK, *Herb Lubalin.* New York: American Showcase, 1985.

VISUAL PERCEPTION (Chapters 3–5)

ARNHEIM, RUDOLF, *Art and Visual Perception.* Berkeley: University of California Press, 1974.

BEHRENS, ROY, *Art and Camouflage.* Cedar Falls, Iowa: North American Review, 1981.

BLOOMER, CAROLYN M., *Principles of Visual Perception.* New York: Van Nostrand Reinhold, 1976.

GOMBRICH, E. H., *Art and Illusion: A Study in the Psychology of Pictorial Representation.* New York: Pantheon Books, 1960.

GOMBRICH, E. H., JULIAN HOCHBERG, and MAX BLACK, *Art, Perception, and Reality.* Baltimore, Md.: Johns Hopkins University Press, 1972.

GOODMAN, NELSON, *Languages of Art.* Indianapolis: Bobbs-Merrill, 1968.

GREGORY, R. L., *Eye and Brain.* New York: McGraw-Hill, 1966.

GREGORY, R. L. *The Intelligent Eye.* New York: McGraw-Hill, 1970.

ZAKIA, RICHARD, *Perception and Photography.* Rochester, N.Y.: Light Impressions Corporation, 1979.

TYPOGRAPHY (Chapter 6)

CARTER, ROB, et al., *Typographic Design: Form and Communication.* New York: Van Nostrand Reinhold, 1985.

CRAIG, JAMES, *Designing with Type.* New York: Watson-Guptill Publications, 1980.

DAIR, CARL, *Design with Type.* Toronto: University of Toronto Press, 1982.

DÜRER, ALBRECHT, *On the Just Shaping of Letters.* Mineola, N.Y.: Dover, 1965.

MASSIN, *Letter and Image.* New York: Van Nostrand Reinhold, 1970.

MCLEAN, RUARI, *Jan Tschichold: Typographer.* Boston: David R. Godine, 1975.

RUDER, EMIL, *Typography.* New York: Hastings House, 1981.

TSCHICHOLD, JAN, *Asymmetric Typography.* New York: Van Nostrand Reinhold, 1980.

PRODUCTION TECHNIQUES (Chapters 7–9)

CAMPBELL, ALASTAIR, *The Graphic Designer's Handbook.* Philadelphia: Running Press, 1983.

CRAIG, JAMES, *Production for the Graphic Designer.* New York: Watson-Guptill Publications, 1974.

GATES, DAVID, *Graphic Design Studio Procedures.* Monsey, N.Y.: Lloyd-Simore Publishing, 1982.

Graphic Artists Guild Handbook: Pricing and Ethical Guidelines. New York: Graphic Artists Guild, 1984.

Pocket Pal. New York: International Paper Company, 1986.

SANDERS, NORMAN, *Graphic Designer's Production Handbook.* New York: Hastings House, 1982.

ADVERTISING, PHOTOGRAPHY, ILLUSTRATION, COMPUTER GRAPHICS (Chapters 10–13)

CASSANDRE, A. M., *A. M. Cassandre.* St. Gall, Switzerland: Zollikoffer & Company, 1948.

DEKEN, JOSEPH, *Computer Images: State of the Art.* New York: Stewart, Tabori & Chang, 1983.

DOUGLAS, TORIN, *The Complete Guide to Advertising.* New York: Chartwell Books, Inc., 1984.

Dover Pictorial Archives. Mineola, N.Y.: Dover, 1979.

GREENBERG, D., et al., *The Computer Image.* Reading, Mass.: Addison-Wesley, 1982.

HOWELL-KOEHLER, NANCY, *Vietnam, The Battle Comes Home: Photos by Gordon Baer.* Dobbs Ferry, N.Y.: Morgan & Morgan, 1984.

KERLOW, ISSACE V., and JUDSON ROSEBUSH, *Computer Graphics for Artists and Designers.* New York: Van Nostrand Reinhold, 1986.

PITZ, HENRY, *200 Years of American Illustration.* New York: Random House, 1977.

VAIZEY, MARINA, *The Artist as Photographer.* New York: Holt, Rinehart and Winston, 1982.

WHELAN, RICHARD, *Double Take.* New York: Clarkson N. Potter, 1981.

WILSON, STEPHEN, *Using Computers to Create Art.* Englewood Cliffs, N.J.: Prentice-Hall, 1986.

PERIODICALS AND ANNUALS

AIGA Graphic Design, USA. New York: Watson-Guptill Publications, annual, 1980–present.

AV Video. Torrance, Calif.: Montage Publishing, Inc.

Ballast. Roy Behrens, ed. Cincinnati, Ohio: Cincinnati Art Academy.

Communication Arts. Palo Alto, Calif.: Coyne & Blanchard, Inc.

Fine Print. San Francisco, California.

Graphis. Zurich, Switzerland: Walter Herdig.

How. New York: RC Publications.

Print. Washington, D.C.: RC Publications.

Print Casebooks. Washington, D.C.: RC Publications, six annual volumes, 1975–present.

Step-by-Step Graphics. Peoria, Ill.: Dynamic Graphics Educational Foundation (DGEF).

U & LC. New York: International Typeface Corporation.

MATERIALS LIST

24″ T-square (stainless is preferable)
assorted French curves
45/90 degree triangle
pica rule
5″ ruling pen
technical pen
technical pen ink
"Graphic White" retouch paint
X-acto #1 knife/blade assortment
India ink
watercolor brushes #1 and #3
tempera paints or designer's gouache
scissors
tracing paper roll
pencils (4H, 2B, 4B, and light blue)
erasers, pink pearl and kneaded
rubber cement
masking tape
sketchbook (minimum size of 8 1/2″ x 11″)
graph paper
proportion scale
circle template
fadeless art paper
pen cleaner for technical pens
compass with ruling pen attachment and extension bar
crow quill pen
standard penholder and assorted points
drawing board

INDEX